Beyond the River Chebar

Beyond the River Chebar

Studies in Kingship and Eschatology in the Book of Ezekiel

DANIEL I. BLOCK

CASCADE *Books* • Eugene, Oregon

BEYOND THE RIVER CHEBAR
Studies in Kingship and Eschatology in the Book of Ezekiel

Cascade Books
An Imprint of Wipf and Stock Publishers
199 W. 8th Ave., Suite 3
Eugene, OR 97401

www.wipfandstock.com

ISBN 13: 978-1-4982-1658-6

Cataloguing-in-Publication data:

Block, Daniel I.

    Beyond the river Chebar : studies in kingship and eschatology in the book of Ezekiel / Daniel I. Block.

    xviii + 238 pp. ; 23 cm. Includes bibliographical references and indexes.

    ISBN 13: 978-1-4982-1658-6

    1. Bible. O.T. Ezekiel—Criticism, interpretation, etc. 2. Bible. O.T. Ezekiel-Theology. 3. I. Title.

BS1545.52 B57 2013

Manufactured in the U.S.A.

Contents

Illustrations

Preface

My FASCINATION WITH EZEKIEL began in 1978, when it dawned on me that Ezekiel was the only prophet to fulfill his ministry entirely in a foreign land. I began to ask how his environment might have colored his ministry and the book that preserves his work. I discovered that links and influences are everywhere: in his geographic references, the *akkadianisms* and *aramaisms* in his vocabulary, his iconographic images, and his conceptual framework. This is just one of many reasons why the book is both so fascinating and such a riddle. As Christian interpreters of the Hebrew Bible we must always ask at least three questions: (1) *What does the text* say? [the text-critical question]; (2) *What did the text mean to the original audience?* [the hermeneutical question]; (3) *What does the text mean to me?* [the theological and practical question]. However, there is a fourth that is especially important when reading Ezekiel: (4) *Why does the text say it like that?* [the generic and cultural question]. Without reference to the world in which Ezekiel lived many features in the book remain enigmatic and unclear, if not confusing and meaningless.

At first the riddle of Ezekiel was a personal and private matter. A telephone call from R. K. Harrison in Toronto in 1982 changed all that. When he asked if I would be interested in producing a commentary on this book for the New International Commentary on the Old Testament series (Eerdmans), I thought foolishly that it might take me four or five years. Little did I realize what a challenge and delight this project would be. After living with this prophetic priest for fifteen years I sometimes felt like I knew the man personally; at other times he left me totally bewildered by his utterances, if not angry over his portrayal of God.

All that is known of Ezekiel derives from his book. He was a son of Buzi (1:3), taken captive to Babylon in 597 BCE, along with King Jehoiachin and 10,000 others, including political and military leaders and skilled craftsmen (2 Kgs 24:14–16). As noted above, Ezekiel was the only

Israelite prophet to carry out his ministry entirely outside Israel's homeland. He received his call five years after he was deported to Babylon by Nebuchadnezzar in 597 BCE. This tragedy, foreseen by the Prophet Isaiah more than one hundred years earlier (2 Kgs 20:16–18), represented the culmination of a series of historical events. After the horrendous apostasies of Manasseh, the godly king Josiah (640–609 BCE) attempted sweeping religious reforms (2 Kgs 23:1–25), but it was too little and too late. The doom of the nation had already been determined. According to the Hebrew historians, Josiah's successors were all wicked. His son, Jehoahaz, ruled only three years before the Egyptians deposed him and replaced him with his brother Jehoiakim (609–598 BCE). Babylon replaced Egypt as the dominant political force in the ancient Near East after the battle of Carchemish in 605 BCE. Under Nebuchadnezzar the Babylonian army marched as far south as Jerusalem, claiming Judah as his vassal. At this time Daniel and his three friends were taken to Babylon apparently as hostages, but from the divine perspective to prepare the way for the arrival of masses of Judeans in 597. Because Jehoiakim rebelled against Babylon in that same year, Nebuchadnezzar removed him from the throne and replaced him with his son Jehoiachin, but he too resisted the Babylonians, and Nebuchadnezzar deported him and all the upper classes (including Ezekiel) to Babylon and put his uncle Zedekiah on the throne. Remarkably, Zedekiah also resisted Nebuchadnezzar's authority. Finally, in 587 BCE Nebuchadnezzar's armies besieged Jerusalem, and the city fell in 586 BCE.

Ezekiel lived in his own house near the River Chebar, an irrigation canal that channeled the Euphrates River into surrounding arid areas. He was married and ministered from his own home (3:24; 8:1; 33:30–33). His wife died suddenly (24:18), but he was not allowed to mourn his loss. But we know Ezekiel primarily as a prophet who received oracles from God and passed them on to the people (cf. 2:5; 33:33). However, his obvious priestly interests give good reason to interpret him primarily as a priest who also functioned as a prophet. YHWH's call to him came in his thirteenth year (1:1), the age priests normally were inducted into office (Num 4:30). In Jerusalem, he would have inherited the priestly office and prepared for it by traditional means. However, in exile the call came dramatically and directly from God. In a vision he was called into divine service and ushered into the presence of God. In autobiographical notes Ezekiel described his reactions to events with priestly sensitivities, especially to issues involving cleanness and uncleanness (4:14). Some of the actions God assigned to him were appropriate only for a priest: "bearing the iniquity" of the people (4:4–6) and not mourning the death of his wife (24:15–27; cf. Lev 21:4–5). This is especially true of temple visions in which YHWH himself took Ezekiel into the temple and guided him throughout the building (chs. 8–11; 40–43). In both visions Ezekiel's legitimate presence in the temple is contrasted with the illegitimate presence of others (8:7–18; 44:1–14). In his preaching and teaching Ezekiel fulfilled the role of a priest charged with the responsibility of teaching the Torah in Israel (Lev 10:11; Deut 33:10a). Ezekiel delivered oracles received from God, permeated by Mosaic theology and forms. Priestly ministry is associated with sacrifices and other tabernacle/temple rituals (cf. Deut 33:10b). But removed from Jerusalem, Ezekiel could not carry out temple duties. The primary priestly function left was teaching. Ezekiel presents a model of the priest as teacher of the Torah.

This is not to deny him prophetic status or prophetic functions. Normally priests engaged in prophetic ministry through the Urim and Thummim (Num 27:21). However, denied official priestly vestments, Ezekiel could not use these objects. As a prophetic priest he received messages directly and verbally from God. Like his contemporary, Jeremiah, Ezekiel initially resisted God's call. This accounts for the nature of the opening vision, the intent of which was to overwhelm him and break his resistance (1:1–28a); for YHWH's warning to him not to be rebellious (2:8); for Ezekiel's deep emotional disturbance at his call (3:15); for the harshness of YHWH's warning not to fail as a watchman (3:16–21); and for the severe restrictions of his call (3:22–27). Once he accepted the call, he proclaimed God's messages fearlessly. Because he displayed many bizarre actions, some have characterized Ezekiel as neurotic, paranoid, psychotic, or schizophrenic. However, his unusual behavior derives from his utter obedience to God. Ezekiel was gripped by the Spirit of God, had a profoundly theological perspective on contemporary historical events, and exhibited an unflinching determination to deliver the messages just as God gave them.

This book is a sequel to *By the River Chebar: Historical, Literary, and Theological Studies in the Book of Ezekiel*. Like the studies in that volume, those presented here reflect my longstanding interest in Ezekiel, the man and his book. This collection is arranged as follows: a general essay on Zion theology; three studies related to Ezekiel's perception of kingship and the Messiah; three essays on the Gog oracle (Ezek 38–39); and two on Ezekiel's concluding vision (Ezek 40–48).

Acknowledgments

FOR MORE THAN TWENTY-FIVE years now I have been immersed in the study of the book of Ezekiel. My findings regarding this enigmatic prophet have been publicized in my two-volume commentary on the book (NICOT, Eerdmans), and in the more than two dozen studies I have presented at professional meetings or published in separate journals and monographs. With the encouragement of Robin Parry and the administrators of Wipf & Stock Publishing, we have collected eighteen of these papers and prepared them for publication in two volumes. Although I am responsible for these essays, both volumes are the fruit of a community of friends and scholars who have inspired, nurtured, pushed, and corrected me.

Of course, in acknowledging those who have aided and inspired me along the way pride of place must go to the prophet himself, as well as to those who collected, organized, and edited the prophetic priest's work to produce the biblical book of Ezekiel. The adventure represented by this volume and its companion volume began more than a quarter century ago, when my eyes were opened to the rich resources from the ancient Near East that could be used to interpret the oracles from the River Chebar. Because the essays in this volume were produced over a span of twenty-five years the quality may be uneven, and the references in earlier essays dated. Our commitment to publishers has been to reproduce these essays virtually as they were originally published (with allowance for correction of known errors and stylistic consistency), so we have generally not updated the bibliography. My work, *The Gods of the Nations*, represents a notable exception. All references are to the most recent reprinting of the second edition (Wipf & Stock, 2013). However I should note that apart from the Appendix, the pagination of the 2000 Baker/Apollos is retained.

Throughout my pilgrimage the voice of Ezekiel has been ringing in my ears, but there have been many who have aided him by supporting me in my research on this remarkable book. I am especially indebted to colleagues and friends from the Ezekiel Section of the Society of Biblical Literature, who have accompanied me on this quest. We often disagree in our methods and our conclusions, but these have not prevented us from carrying on our conversations with respect and civility. My own work on Ezekiel has been especially influenced and framed by two scholarly giants from the Jewish world. No one has inspired me more nor had a greater affect on my work than Moshe Greenberg, the author of countless articles on issues related to Ezekiel and two magnificent volumes on the book in the Anchor Bible series.[1] Although Professor Greenberg would undoubtedly disagree with many of my conclusions, after decades of atomizing approaches to biblical interpretation his appeal for a "holistic interpretation" was both refreshing and encouraging. The other significant influence has been Jacob Milgrom. Given the "priestly" nature of Ezekiel's ministry and the "priestly" character of much of his book, Milgrom's massive commentaries on Leviticus proved invaluable for interpreting this book. Most recently, it was a special joy to learn that he also found my work useful as he sought to complete Greenberg's project.[2] Between these two Ezekiel scholars I have had the pleasure of getting to know many others, including those whose essays and commentaries on the book have greatly enhanced my understanding and challenged me to think more deeply on interpretive cruces: Leslie Allen, Iain M. Duguid, Christopher J. H. Wright, Katheryn Pfisterer Darr, Margaret S. Odell, Steven Shawn Tuell, and Paul Joyce.

I also acknowledge the influence of students who have walked with me as I have walked with Ezekiel. In addition to undergraduates and graduate students in this country and in Canada, I have had the inestimable privilege of sharing my discoveries from the book in international educational settings in Moscow, Copenhagen, Athens, Singapore, Hong Kong, and Medellin, Colombia. Not only have students' interest all over the world inspired me, but in each context they have offered keen insights to which my North American eyes are blinded.

---

1. Moshe Greenberg, *Ezekiel 1–20: A New Translation with Introduction and Commentary* (Anchor Bible 22; New York: Doubleday, 1983); Greenberg, *Ezekiel 21–37: A New Translation with Introduction and Commentary* (Anchor Bible 22A; New York: Doubleday, 1997). I expressed my indebtedness to Professor Greenberg in a short paper, "In Praise of Moshe: A Tribute to Moshe Greenberg," at a memorial session in his honor at the annual meeting of the Society of Biblical Literature in Atlanta, GA, 2010. See the Appendix, "In Praise of Moshe: A Tribute to Moshe Greenberg," in *By the River Chebar*, 253–58.

2. See Jacob Milgrom and Daniel Block in conversation, *Ezekiel's Hope: A Commentary on Ezekiel 38–48* (Eugene, OR: Wipf & Stock, 2012).

I must acknowledge the specific help of faculty colleagues and student assistants who have read and encouraged me along the way. Some of these are acknowledged in footnotes to the essays included here. Many assistants have performed mundane tasks for me, scouring databases and libraries for secondary materials that might aid in our interpretation, or proofreading drafts for factual errors and stylistic infelicities. Specifically, for this project I must acknowledge the assistance of Jordan Brown, who had the difficult task of retrieving all the essays in this volume and creating editable documents, and Carmen Imes, who provided invaluable counsel in planning this volume, proofreading and editing, and assembling the bibliography. And special thanks must be expressed to Daniel Lanz, my assistant, and Ellen, my wife, for their assistance in the tedious task of indexing this volume. I am also grateful for the editorial assistance provided by the editors at Wipf and Stock, without whose work this project would never have seen the light of day.

Since most of the essays in this volume have been published elsewhere, I must express my deep gratitude to editors of journals and publishers of books for their grace and willingness to let us reprint what they had made available earlier. In keeping with our promise, we have acknowledged the original place of publication on a separate page below, as well as at the beginning of each reprinted article. The versions presented here retain the essence of each original publication. Naturally, to produce a coherent volume and to follow the stylistic standards of Cascade Books, we have had to modify these essays stylistically—some more than others. Where needed, we have corrected errors of substance or form in the original, and in a few minor details my mind has changed. But readers should find no dissonance between the present forms of these essays and the original publications. Special thanks are due to Robin Parry and Christian Amondson, for their enthusiasm for this project and the efficiency with which they have handled all the business and editorial matters. From the first overture from Robin prior to the annual meeting of the Society of Biblical Literature in Atlanta, they have encouraged us and offered all the help we needed to produce it to their specifications. Thanks also to Patrick Harrison for his editing and wonderful typesetting work in preparing this volume for publication.

I am grateful to the administrators and my faculty colleagues at Wheaton College, for the unwavering institutional support and encouragement they offer, not only by creating a wonderful teaching environment, but also for providing the resources for our research. I am deeply grateful to

Bud and Betty Knoedler, who have given so generously to underwrite my professorial chair. It is a special grace to know them not only as supporters of Wheaton College, but also as personal friends. Ellen and I are grateful for their daily prayers on our behalf. I eagerly also acknowledge Ellen, to whom I dedicated the first volume of my NICOT commentary (Eerdmans). She is indeed מַחְמַד עֵינַי, "the delight of my eyes,"[3] who has stood by me as a gracious friend and counselor for more than four decades. Without her love and wisdom, the work represented here would either never have been finished, or it would have taken a different turn.

Finally, we must give praise to God. Unlike others who serve gods of wood and stone, that have eyes but don't see, ears but don't hear, and mouths but don't speak, we have a God who speaks. In ancient times he spoke through the mouths of his servants the prophets, including Ezekiel, but he has spoken more recently and even more clearly in the person of Jesus Christ his Son (Heb 1:1–2). Although many have difficulty finding divine grace in the book of Ezekiel, the God Ezekiel serves is embodied in Jesus Christ, full of grace and truth (John 1:16–17). To him be all the praise and glory.

---

3. See Ezek 24:16.

Credits

I HEREBY GRATEFULLY ACKNOWLEDGE permission to republish articles that have appeared elsewhere:

Chapter 2: "Transformation of Royal Ideology in Ezekiel" was originally published in *Transforming Visions: Transformations of Text, Tradition, and Theology in Ezekiel*, edited by M. Lyons and W. Tooman, 208–46. Princeton Theological Monograph Series 127; Eugene, OR: Pickwick, 2010.

Chapter 3: "The Tender Cedar Sprig: Ezekiel on Johoiachin" was originally published in *Hebrew Bible and Ancient Israel* 1 (2012) 173–202.

Chapter 4: "Bringing Back David: Ezekiel's Messianic Hope" was originally published in *The Lord's Anointed: Interpretation of Old Testament Messianic Texts*, edited by P. E. Satterthwaite, R. S. Hess, and G. J. Wenham, 167–88. Grand Rapids: Baker, 1995.

Chapter 5: "Gog and Magog in Ezekiel's Eschatological Vision" was originally published in *"The Reader Must Understand": Eschatology in Bible and Theology*, edited by K. Brower and M. Elliott, 85–116. Leicester, UK: InterVarsity, 1997.

Chapter 6: "Gog in Prophetic Tradition: A New Look at Ezekiel 38:17" was originally published in *Vetus Testamentum* 42 (1988) 154–72.

Chapter 7: "Gog and the Pouring Out of the Spirit: Reflections on Ezekiel 39:21–29" was originally published in *Vetus Testamentum* 37 (1987) 257–70.

Abbreviations

AHW   *Akkadisches Handwörterbuch.* Edited by W. von Soden. 3 vols. Wiesbaden: Harrassowitz, 1965–81.

ANET   *The Ancient Near East in Pictures Relating to the Old Testament.* 3rd ed. Edited by J. B. Pritchard. Princeton: Princeton University Press, 1954.

ARAB   D. D. Luckenbill. *Ancient Records of Assyria and Babylonia.* 2 vols. New York: Greenwood, 1968. Reprint of 1927 edition.

AV   Authorized Version

BCE   Before the Common Era, traditionally referred to as B.C.

BDB   F. Brown, S. R. Driver, and C. A. Briggs, *A Hebrew Lexicon of the Old Testament.* Oxford: Clarendon, 1907.

BHS   *Biblia Hebraica Stuttgartensia*

BM   British Museum

CAD   *The Assyrian Dictionary of the Oriental Institute of the University of Chicago.* Edited by A. L. Oppenheim, et al. Chicago: The Oriental Institute, 1956–.

CE   Common Era, traditionally referred to as A.D.

COS   *The Context of Scripture.* Edited by W. W. Hallo. 3 vols. Leiden: Brill, 1997–2002.

CTA   *Corpus des tablettes en cunéiformes alphabétiques découvertes à Ras Shamra-Ugarit de 1929 à 1939.* Edited by A. Herdner. Mission de Ras Shamra 10. Paris: Geuthner, 1963.

DCH   *Dictionary of Classical Hebrew.* Edited by D. J. A. Clines. Sheffield, UK: Phoenix, 1993–.

EA	El-Amarna tablets. According to the edition of J. A. Knudtzon. *Die El-Amarna-Tafeln mit Einleitung un Erläuterungen.* Leipzig: Hinrichs, 1908–15. Reprint, Aalen: Otto Zeller, 1964. Supplemented in A. F. Rainey, *El-Amarna Tablets 359–379.* 2nd ed. AOAT 8. Neukirchen-Vluyn: Neukirchener, 1978.
HALOT	Ludwig Koehler, Walter Baumgartner, and J. J. Stamm. *The Hebrew and Aramaic Lexicon of the Old Testament.* Translated and edited under the supervision of M. E. J. Richardson. 4 vols. Leiden: Brill, 1994–99.
IBD	*The Illustrated Bible Dictionary.* 3 vols. Edited by J. D. Douglas. Leicester, UK: InterVarsity, 1980.
IBHS	Bruce K. Waltke and M. O'Connor. *An Introduction to Biblical Hebrew Syntax.* Winona Lake, IN: Eisenbrauns, 1990.
JB	Jerusalem Bible
KAI	H. Donner and W. Röllig, *Kanaanäische und Aramäische Inscriften.* 3 vols. Wiesbaden: Harrassowitz, 1966–69.
LXX	The Septuagint (more precisely the Greek Old Testament).
MT	Masoretic Text
NASB	New American Standard Bible
NEB	New English Bible
NIV	New International Version
NJPSV	New Jewish Publication Society Version (Tanakh)
NRSV	New Revised Standard Version
NT	New Testament
OT	Old Testament
REB	Revised English Bible
SBL	Society of Biblical Literature
Syr.	Syriac Version
UT	*Ugaritic Textbook.* C. H. Gordon. Analecta orientalia 38. Rome: Pontifical Biblical Institute, 1965.
Tg.	Targums (Aramaic Versions)
Vg.	Vulgate (Latin Version)

Zion Theology in
the Book of Ezekiel[1]

The Problem

IN ORDER TO DEAL with the issue of Zion theology in the book of Ezekiel, we need first to summarize what we mean by Zion theology. Scholars generally recognize several basic tenets of this strain of Israelite religious thought: (1) In the worship of YHWH at the national temple in Jerusalem, the deity's enthronement is a central feature. (2) Located on the "peak of Zaphon" (יַרְכְּתֵי צָפוֹן, Ps 48:3[2]), Zion is the center of the universe. (3) The election of Zion by YHWH is closely tied to the election of David. (4) From Zion YHWH's reign of peace and justice extends to the entire world.[2]

For students of Zion theology, Ezekiel is problematic for several reasons. First, and most obvious, as Zimmerli has noted,[3] along with the absence of many other theologically significant expressions,[4] the name

1. A version of this paper was presented to the Society of Biblical Literature in Philadelphia, PA, November 20, 1995.

2. See the summaries by Levenson, "Zion Traditions," 1098–99; Albertz, *History of Israelite Religion*, 1:135–37. For fuller discussion see Ollenburger, *City of the Great King*; Levenson, *Sinai and Zion*.

3. See the discussion by Zimmerli, *Ezekiel 1*, 22–23.

4. The absence of words for "praise" or "petition" contributes to the somber tone of the book, but note also the absence of theological expressions like "grace" (חנן),

"Zion" is missing in the book of Ezekiel.[5] As is well-known, the significance of the name "Zion" grew considerably in the half-millennium from the founding of the Israelite monarchy under David to the exile of Judah in the sixth century. We can identify at least four phases in the evolution of the usage of the name. (1) Originally Zion appears to have referred to the Jebusite fortress on the ridge between the Tyropoeon Valley and the Wadi Kidron. When David captured the "stronghold of Zion" he changed its name to the City of David.[6] (2) With the construction of the temple, the meaning of "Zion" was extended both spatially and theologically to identify the Temple Mount.[7] (3) By a process of metonymy, the name Zion came to refer to Jerusalem itself, the city where the temple was located.[8] (4) By further metonymy, like the name Jerusalem, in later prophecy Zion came to denote the people of Israel.[9] Ezekiel's avoidance of Zion in the first and last senses is understandable. On the one hand, he shows no interest in the early history of the monarchy. On the other, as a designation for the people of Israel, "Zion" is rare elsewhere, and there is no need for an alternative to the conventional "Israel." However, given Ezekiel's special interest in the temple,[10] the Temple Mount,[11] and the city of Jerusalem, his avoidance of the name in these contexts is striking.

Second, the kingship of YHWH, whose enthronement features prominently in Zion theology, receives little attention in Ezekiel's ministry. YHWH is explicitly referred to as מֶלֶךְ only once, in 20:33, but the context has nothing to do with enthronement celebrations. On the contrary, the emphasis is on YHWH's active and wrathful gathering of Israel that he may judge them in the wilderness. In the first temple vision (chs. 1–11) the כְּבוֹד יְהוָה ("glory of YHWH") is seen abandoning its abode inside the temple, and taking its place on the portable throne carried by the cherubim. The link with traditional enthronement notions is vague at

---

"trust" (בטח), "to be firm" (אמן), "salvation" (ישע), "redeem" (גאל, פדה), the verb "to bless" (ברך) and "blessed" (אשרי) and "curse" (ארר); and references to "love" (אהב), "covenant faithfulness" (חסד), and "fear" (ירא) toward God by his people.

5. So are other expressions often associated with Zion theology, the most striking of which is יְהוָה צְבָאוֹת, "YHWH of hosts." On the place of this expression in Zion theology see most recently Mettinger, "YHWH Zebaoth," 720–24.

6. The change in designation is referred to in 2 Sam 5:7, 9.

7. E.g., Ps 48:1–3 [1–2]; 78:68–69; 87:2; 132:13–16.

8. Cf. the interchanging of "Jerusalem" and "[Fair] Zion" in Lam 2:6–8.

9. Isa 51:16; Zech 2:7 [11].

10. See especially chapters 8–11 and 40–48.

11. Note the reference to the "high mountain" in 40:2.

best. Ezekiel 43:6–9 is more suggestive. After observing in visionary form the כְּבוֹד יְהוָה entering the temple, here Ezekiel hears YHWH declare the temple to be the place of his throne and the place of the soles of his feet, where he will dwell among the descendants of Israel forever. However, in context, his occupation of the throne is not the occasion for celebration, but of warning. Never will the house of Israel, inclusive of its kings, defile his holy name again.

Third, while Ezekiel perceives Jerusalem as the center of the international universe, her position here has little resemblance to the role of Zion in Zion theology. In 5:5 YHWH affirms that he has set Jerusalem in the midst of the nations (בְּתוֹךְ הַגּוֹיִם). To YHWH Jerusalem was not just another city among many; rather with him in the past she had enjoyed "most favored nation" status. Minimally this must mean that the world is invited to watch how YHWH cares for his people. However, instead of serving as a paradigm of divine grace she had publicly set a new standard of evil. If Ezekiel hereby intends an allusion to Zion theology, his intention is well-veiled.

In 38:12 he describes the regathered nation of Israel living securely "on top of the world." The meaning of טַבּוּר הָאָרֶץ in 38:12 continues to engage scholars. The common rendering "navel of the earth," which derives from LXX's ὀμφαλόν, is perpetuated in the Vulgate's *umbilici terrae*, as well as in pseudepigraphic,[12] and rabbinic writings,[13] and is reflected in several renowned medieval maps.[14] But many modern interpreters have abandoned the literal "navel" explanation, preferring to see here a figure of speech for "the center of the earth." By this understanding the land of Israel/Zion is viewed as a sort of cosmic midpoint.[15] This accords better with later Hebrew;[16] and with our prophet, who had earlier declared that YHWH had placed Jerusalem in the middle of the nations (5:5). The expression טַבּוּר הָאָרֶץ occurs elsewhere only in Judg 9:37. There it describes

12. Jubilees 8:19 reads, "Mount Sinai [was] in the midst of the desert and Mount Zion [was] in the midst of the navel of the earth." Cf. also 1 Enoch 26:1. Josephus (*Wars* 3.3.5) notes that some called Jerusalem the navel of the country.

13. *B. Yoma* 54b, "The world was created from Zion"; *Midrash Tanḥûma Qedoshim*, 10, "As the navel is situated in the center of a person, so is the land of Israel—in the center of the world." See also *Sanhedrin* 37a.

14. See particularly the map from the thirteenth-century Latin manuscript of the book of Psalms and the sixteenth-century "clover leaf" map, reproduced and discussed by Beitzel, *Moody Atlas*, 201–3.

15. Cf. NRSV, NJPS, REB, NASB, NIV, JB.

16. Jastrow, *Dictionary of the Targumim*, 529.

Mount Gerizim overlooking Shechem, which some contend was con-sidered by the Canaanites as the navel, viz., center of the land of Canaan.[17] Some also draw support for this understanding from extra Israelite attestation to the notion of a navel or center of the earth.[18]

However this interpretation suffers from several major weaknesses, and should probably be abandoned.[19] (a) The etymology of טַבּוּר is un-certain. Admittedly, it is used of the umbilical cord in Mishnaic Hebrew and later Aramaic, but the Old Testament itself provides no support for this interpretation.[20] Furthermore, Biblical Hebrew possesses a word for "navel" or "umbilical cord," that Ezekiel himself has used שֹׁר in 16:4.[21] (b) Ezekiel 5:5 refers, not to a cosmic center, but to Jerusalem's position in the context of her neighbors. (c) The context of Judg 9:37, specifically the previous verse, suggests a more mundane denotation, "elevated ground."[22] (d) There is no obvious need for a reference to either the navel or the center of the earth in the present context. In fact, its juxtaposition with "unwalled villages" points to some safe and secure location. This require-ment is fully met if טַבּוּר הָאָרֶץ is interpreted as an elevated plateau without external fortifications, as in Judg 9:37. Fifth, this interpretation finds early support in the Targum, which translates the word as תֶּקְפָּא, "stronghold."[23] In any case, Ezekiel here speaks of Israel as a nation regathered in the land, not the city of Jerusalem where the worship of YHWH is centered. Any allusion to Zion theology in this text is more in the mind of the reader than in the text itself.

17. Anderson, "Place of Shechem," 10–11.

18. (1) A circular sixth-century-BCE map of the world from Babylon locates this city in the center surrounded by neighbors, some positioned irrespective of their actual location (cf. Beitzel, *Moody Atlas*, 197–98; Unger, *Babylon*, 20–24). (2) In Greece, Homer saw the navel in the geographic midpoint of the sea (*Odyssey* 1.50). (3) Major Greek oracle sanctuaries such as those at Didyma, Miletus, and Delphi were viewed as the navel of the earth. (4) According to Aristides the Eleusinian mystery cults reserved this honor for Athens. (5) Islam ascribes this status to Mecca. For dis-cussion and bibliography see Terrien, "Omphalos Myth," 315–38; cf. Zimmerli, *Ezekiel* 2, 311.

19. So also Talmon, "הַר *har*," 437–38.

20. Ahroni ("Gog Prophecy," 12–13) accepts the omphalic interpretation here, but sees the presence of the phrase as an argument for the late date of the Gog prophecy.

21. See also Song 7:3[2]; Prov 3:8.

22. So also Thomas, "Mount Tabor," 230.

23. Kimchi explains this translation geographically, as a reference to the territory of Israel being elevated higher than the rest of the countries. See Levey, *Ezekiel*, 107.

Fourth, while Zion theology ties the election of Zion as the seat of YHWH's throne closely with the election of David,[24] Ezekiel never links these motifs. In the judgment oracles of chapters 4–24 both temple and dynasty come under the fury of divine wrath, but always in different contexts. The Davidic house is entirely out of the picture in the vision of the departure of the כְּבוֹד־יְהוָה, "glory of YHWH" from the temple (chs. 8–11). Correspondingly, in judgment pronouncements directed against the Davidic house, the temple is out of the picture.[25] Similarly, while Ezekiel's salvation oracles do indeed envision the restoration of the Davidic dynasty and YHWH's re-occupation of the throne (43:6–9), election terminology is avoided in both instances. In 34:23–24 the prophet conjoins notions of Davidic shepherdship (= kingship) with peace, security, and prosperity, but without any reference to the temple. Ezekiel 37:21–28 looks more promising, inasmuch as references to the establishment of David as shepherd king over Israel and YHWH's dwelling among his people in his sanctuary (מִקְדָּשׁ) occur in the same context.

However, the language of this passage is scarcely typical of Zion theology. Furthermore, references to the Israelites living on the land that YHWH gave to Jacob, and the promise of YHWH's residence among his people as an extension of the covenant formula, also link this passage with the Abrahamic and Israelite (Mosaic) covenants respectively. While the references to the נָשִׂיא provide a link with the David of 34:23–24 and 37:25 in the final temple vision, he is not presented as a royal figure after the order of the Davidic dynasty, but as the hands on patron of the cult.

Fifth, although Ezekiel's restoration oracles include visions of final peace,[26] this peace bears no direct links with Zion theology. To be sure, Ezekiel knows of YHWH's victory over the nations (34:27–28; cf. 38–39), of his "covenant of peace" (בְּרִית שָׁלוֹם),[27] even of the destruction of the enemies' weapons,[28] but in each case the style and tone of the description bear little resemblance to other Zion theology texts. Specifically, as Kathe Darr has observed,[29] Ezekiel's vision of the future is narrowly parochial. He does indeed recognize the universal implications of YHWH's future actions. YHWH will magnify himself, sanctify himself (38:23), and set his

24. Pss 78:70–72; 132:11–12, 17–18.
25. Ezek 12:1–16; 17:1–24; 19:1–14.
26. Ezek 34:25–32; 37:26; 38:8.
27. Ezek 37:26; cf. Isa 2:2–4; Mic 4:1–4.
28. Ezek 38:9–10; cf. Pss 46:10–11[9–10]; 76:4[3]; Isa 2:4; Mic 4:4.
29. Darr, "Wall around Paradise," 271–78.

glory among the nations as they experience his acts of judgment (39:21)—and they will know that he is YHWH (38:23). But this is a far cry from the extension of his reign of peace and justice to the ends of the earth. He comes the closest in the coda to his riddle on the Davidic dynasty in 17:22–24, where YHWH plucks a יֹנֶקֶת, "sprig, shoot," from the topmost crown of the cedar and plants it on "a high and lofty mountain," and "the high mountain of Israel," where it takes root and grows into a gigantic tree that offers shade and a place for nests for birds of every kind. Then all the trees of the field (foreign nations?) will recognize him as YHWH. One may recognize here resemblances to other passages celebrating the exaltation of Zion, but the motif is veiled almost beyond recognition.

Sixth, while Ezekiel's vision of the reconstituted nation focuses on a city to the south of a very high mountain (40:2), the heart of the city is taken up with the temple. However, Ezekiel avoids naming this city either by its historical designation (Jerusalem) or by its theological name (Zion). On the contrary, he separates the residence of YHWH, the temple, from the city, which he names יְהוָה שָׁמָּה, "YHWH *Shammah* (YHWH is There)" (48:35). This city bears no resemblance whatsoever to the Jerusalem of Zion theology. It is not located in Judah, the tribe of David. In fact, it is not associated with David at all. Special lands are indeed set aside for the נָשִׂיא, presumably a Davidide, though this identity is withheld, but the city is in the midst of Levitical and priestly property; it is not a royal estate. On the contrary, the city belongs to the people; all the gates are named after the twelve tribes of Israel. In this allocation not only is the king out of the picture; in treating "each [tribe] like his brother," the allotments of land demonstrate a new egalitarian ideal designed to prevent the social injustices of the past. Even the design and function of the city reflects Ezekiel's fundamental social premise that all citizens have equal rights to the worship of YHWH. And despite the prophet's exclusivist vision, aliens are welcome here. But they must come on YHWH's terms. If they identify with the faith of his people they are entitled to all the rights and privileges extended to the physical heirs of the traditions. However important Zion theology may have been for the prophet, again the paradigmatic features have been totally suppressed.

THE EXPLANATION

This cumulative set of problems raises the question, "What has happened to traditional Zion theology in the preaching of Ezekiel?" It is inconceivable that he was ignorant of the Zion traditions. Contra Rainer Albertz, it is equally unlikely that Ezekiel is hereby starting a branch of the reform priesthood fundamentally opposed either to traditional Zion theology, or later Deuteronomist images of the royal state cult.[30] One misunderstands Ezekiel if one finds in this book a sweeping repudiation of the Davidic monarchy and/or a total repudiation of royal involvement in the cult. To be sure, the cult of deceased kings is denounced, and future royal encroachments into the sacred sphere of the temple are precluded (43:7–9). However, the נָשִׂיא of chapters 40–48, undoubtedly a royal figure, retains an important cultic function: as patron of the cult he supervises the temple activities and provides the offerings for the sacrifices.

But why have the paradigmatic traditions of Zion theology been so overwhelmingly suppressed in this book? The most likely answer is to be found in the theological crisis to which the exilic prophet Ezekiel speaks. Ezekiel ministered in a context where Israelite confidence in YHWH was founded upon an official orthodoxy, that rested on four immutable propositions, four pillars of divine promise: the irrevocability of YHWH's covenant with Israel; YHWH's ownership of the land of Canaan, which he had granted to Israel as an eternal possession; YHWH's eternal covenant with David; and YHWH's residence in Jerusalem, the place he had chosen for his name to dwell (Fig. 1). The last two of these relate to what scholars conventionally refer to as Zion theology.

As I see it, Ezekiel's overriding rhetorical purpose is to transform his audience's perception of their relationship with YHWH, exposing delusions of innocence, and offering a divine understanding of reality. His pursuit of this goal divides into two discreet parts, separated by the announcement of the messenger from Jerusalem, "The city has fallen!" (33:21). Prior to the fall of Jerusalem Ezekiel's prophecies consist of negative pronouncements of judgment upon his people for their infidelity to the covenant. Contrary to prevailing opinion among his people, the people of Judah have no reason to hope in YHWH's rescue. This message is communicated in chapters 4–24 by systematically attacking the pillars on which official orthodoxy constructed its notions of eternal security. If Judah will be destroyed—and she will—it will not happen because YHWH has reneged on his covenant commitment or repudiated Zion theology. He will abandon his temple and send his people into exile in a foreign land because the people of Israel have been unfaithful to him. This covenantal treachery demanded the rupturing of the deity-nation-land relationships.

30. Albertz, *History of Israelite Religion*, 480–93.

Figure 1: A House of Pride: The Foundations of Israel's Security

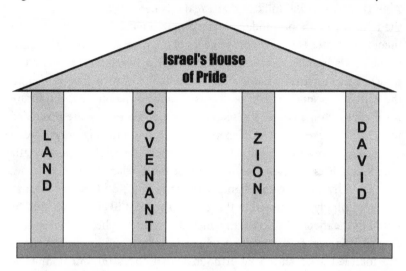

But after 586 BCE the tone and emphasis of Ezekiel's prophesies change. Once the old illusions of spirituality have been destroyed, he can look forward to a new day when the tri-partite association is restored and all three parties experience covenant shalom. In the process Ezekiel affirms that official orthodoxy, including Zion theology, had indeed been founded on truth. YHWH's covenant promises are eternal. The earlier problem had not been the veracity of the divine word, but the illegitimate appropriation of that word by those who failed to keep the terms of the agreement. Accordingly, in his vision of the new day, Ezekiel offers hope by systematically reconstructing the pillars on which the nation's security had been based in the first place. In both, the judgment and the restoration, the word of YHWH is affirmed: not only the immediate prophetic word, whose fulfillment confirms Ezekiel's status as an authorized messenger of YHWH, but especially the ancient word, declared in the promise to the Fathers, the covenant at Sinai, the promise to David, and the election of Jerusalem as his dwelling place.

However, Ezekiel's vision of the future cannot afford simply to reverse the horrors of the divine judgment recently experienced by his people or to reconstruct the old social and theological order. Past wrongs must righted; past abuses forever resolved. To achieve this goal the political wings of the Davidic dynasty needed to be clipped and the relationship of the Davidic house to the cult totally revamped. Ezekiel is not fundamentally opposed to Zion theology or the monarchy, but the misadministration of the past must never return. Accordingly, the revived David functions as the servant and direct under-shepherd of YHWH (34:23–24; 37:21–28). In so doing, the *shalom* that YHWH had envisioned for his people may finally be realized. But this peace will not happen until YHWH resumes his rightful place in the temple and David is reinstalled as king over all Israel.

Transformation of Royal Ideology in Ezekiel[1]

INTRODUCTION

SCHOLARS HAVE LONG RECOGNIZED both Ezekiel's dependence upon earlier texts and traditions and his creative adaptation of earlier materials for his own rhetorical context. This is most obvious in his use of the Torah.[2] The purpose of this paper is to explore how Ezekiel adapts and transforms traditional and textual materials in his portrayal of Israel's monarchy. Our investigation will be divided into three parts: (1) Ezekiel's portrayal of the history of Israel's monarchy; (2) Ezekiel's portrayal of the monarchy in his day; (3) Ezekiel's portrayal of the future of the monarchy. Unlike other books in the prophetic corpus,[3] the book of Ezekiel lacks a formal introduction declaring the historical context of his ministry. Nevertheless, based on the information provided by the opening notice of the date of his inaugural vision and call to prophetic office, the prophet was born in 623 BCE, four years after Jeremiah's call to prophetic service

1. This essay was originally published in *Transforming Visions: Transformations of Text, Tradition, and Theology in Ezekiel*, edited by M. Lyons and W. Tooman, 208–46. Princeton Theological Monograph Series 127. Eugene, OR: Pickwick, 2010.

2. See most recently Lyons, *From Law to Prophecy*. Also, Kohn, *New Heart and New Soul*.

3. Isa 1:1; Hos 1:1; Amos 1:1; Mic 1:1; Jer 1:1–3.

(Jer 1:2), and seventeen years into the reign of Josiah (640–609 BCE). Therefore, for the purposes of this paper the accession to the throne of Josiah in 64 BCE (2 Kgs 21:18–25) marks the boundary between the past and present of Israel's monarchy, and the death of Jehoiachin in exile marks the boundary between the present and the future of the monarchy. We shall explore Ezekiel's disposition toward the monarchy in each of these three periods separately.

EZEKIEL'S PORTRAYAL OF THE HISTORY OF ISRAEL'S MONARCHY

From Ezekiel's revisionist histories of Israel in chapters 16 and 23, specifically his focus on Jerusalem and Samaria, the prophet was obviously aware of the separate political histories of the northern kingdom of Israel and the southern kingdom of Judah. Although these were the capital cities of separate nations, Ezekiel knew that their populations were ethnically related, for he refers to them as sisters in these chapters (cf. 16:46 and 23:4).[4] Inasmuch as the prophet explicitly refers to these two nations (שְׁנֵי גוֹיִם) as "two kingdoms" (שְׁתֵּי מַמְלָכוֹת; 37:22), it is also evident that Ezekiel knew that these two nations were ruled by kings.[5] But Ezekiel expresses no awareness of the circumstances that led to the creation of these two monarchies, nor even that there ever was a time when north and south were united under a single monarchy. Nor does he show any interest in the history of the northern kings.

Although hints of the history of Judah's monarchy are vague, from texts like 34:2–10 and 43:7–9 it is clear that Ezekiel had a negative view of the kings of Judah. In the former he accuses the רֹעֵי יִשְׂרָאֵל, "shepherds of Israel," of exploiting their subjects for personal gain instead of caring for them. In 43:7–9 Ezekiel associates kings (מְלָכִים) with divine name-defiling actions involving harlotry (= idolatry), illicit funerary practices, and the encroachment of sacred space with construction projects. It is unclear in both cases whether these charges apply to Ezekiel's royal contemporaries or whether he has longstanding abuses of the office in mind.[6]

4. This should not be pressed too far, since he also identifies Sodom as Jerusalem's sister in 16:46–52.

5. While the originality of מֶלֶךְ in the MT of 37:22 is disputed (Papyrus[967] and LXX read ἄρχων, on which see further below), שְׁתֵּי מַמְלָכוֹת is not. Papyrus[967] and LXX read δύο βασιλείας.

6. According to 2 Kgs 21:4–15 earlier prophets had responded to Manasseh's

Whatever the case, one gets the impression that the exilic prophet has intentionally suppressed much of the memory of Israel's monarchy, as if it were a bad dream. This impression is reinforced in several ways. First, in Ezekiel's creative reconstruction (or should we say deconstruction?) of the history of Israel and Judah (16:1–34; 20:5–28; 23:2–21) he never alludes to the human kings of Israel, let alone hints at their involvement in the crimes for which the nation is charged. When royal language occurs, the king is YHWH.[7] Second, in contrast to Jeremiah, who identifies his royal contemporaries by name 100 times, and earlier kings more than twenty times,[8] Ezekiel never mentions a king of Israel or Judah by name. David's name occurs four times (34:23, 24; 37:24, 25), but in each instance he has in mind a future king. And Jehoiachin's name appears in 1:2, but this verse derives from an editorial hand and actually represents the exception that proves the rule.

Third, instead of identifying Israel's rulers as מְלָכִים, "kings," Ezekiel prefers to refer to them by the archaic expression, נְשִׂיאִים, "princes." He does indeed use the former expression more than thirty times, especially when speaking of foreign kings (see Table 1), and on occasion to refer to his royal contemporaries as kings.[9] The only exception occurs in 43:7–9, where the prophet mentions that in the past, along with the people, their kings have defiled YHWH's holy name with harlotry and abominable funerary practices.

---

crimes by announcing the eventual destruction of the nation because of his crimes. But the history of court-sponsored idolatry goes back much farther than Manasseh's reign to the time of Solomon (1 Kgs 11:1–8).

7. In 20:33 YHWH declares that in the future he will be king (מֶלֶךְ) over Israel. YHWH's kingship is also implied in 16:10–14, where YHWH lavishes on Jerusalem (representing Israel) the treasures and the culinary fare of an ancient monarch, and through his lavish generosity she attains royal status herself (מְלוּכָה, v. 13). Joyce overlooks this text in his otherwise excellent discussion of the kingship of YHWH in Ezekiel: "King and Messiah in Ezekiel," 332–36.

8. His contemporaries included: Josiah (18x), Jehoahaz (1x, as Shallum, 22:11), Jehoiakim (22x), Jehoiachin (10x, also as Coniah and Jeconiah), Zedekiah (49x); earlier kings, David (14x), Solomon (1x), Hezekiah (3x), Manasseh (1x), Amon (2x).

9. Ezek 7:27 (indeterminate //נָשִׂיא); 17:12 (Jerusalem's king, i.e., Zedekiah); 17:16 (Zedekiah, caused to reign).

Table 1: The Usage of מֶלֶךְ and נָשִׂיא in Ezekiel

Status	מֶלֶךְ	נָשִׂיא
Divinity (YHWH)	YHWH will be king 20:33	
King(s) of Judah	Jehoiachin 1:2 indeterminate 7:27 //נָשִׂיא Jerusalem's king 17:12 Zedekiah [caused to reign] 17:16 one king reigning 37:22 [2x] over one kingdom My servant David, shepherd 37:24 plural 43:7 [2x] plural 43:9	indeterminate 7:27 // מֶלֶךְ in Jerusalem (Zedekiah) 12:10 plural (Jehoahaz and Jehoiakim) 19:1 plural delivered to sword 21:17[12] wicked X of Israel (Zedekiah) 21:30[25] former oppressive rulers 22:6 former oppressive rulers 22:25 My servant David, shepherd 34:24 My servant David 37:25 my princes will no 45:8 longer oppress princes, put away violence 45:9
Patron of the Cult		44:3a, 3b; 45:7, 8, 9, 16, 17, 22; 46: 2, 4, 8, 10, 12, 16, 17; 48:21a, 21b, 22a, 22b
Foreign Kings	Babylon 17:12; 19:9; 21:24[19], 26 [21]; 24:2; 26:7 (3x, "king of kings"); 29:18, 19; 30:10, 24, 25a, 25b; 32:11 Egypt 29:2, 3; 30:21, 22; 31:2; 32:2 (pharaoh) Tyre 28:12 Edom 32:29 Of the earth 27:33 Of many peoples 32:10 Of the coastlands 27:35 Generally 28.17	no prince in Egypt 30:13 = pharaoh princes of the sea 26:16
Chieftains		princes of Kedar 27:21 princes of Edom 32:29 //מְלָכִים princes of the earth 39:18 //גִּבּוֹרִים

Opinions on why Ezekiel avoided the term מֶלֶךְ ("king") when speaking of Israel's kings vary. Since outside this book references to the office of נָשִׂיא ("prince") occur most frequently in the narratives concerning Israel's wandering in the desert, where leaders of tribes and clans were supposedly apolitical sacral figures, some suggest that by using this term the prophet was trying to reestablish this role as primary also for the monarch.[10] Others argue that Ezekiel prefers נָשִׂיא over מֶלֶךְ because the latter emphasizes the ruler's role as military leader, while the former speaks of his role as a moral and spiritual leader.[11] It seems more likely that Ezekiel avoids מֶלֶךְ because in his mind the expression carries overtones of independence and arrogance, while נָשִׂיא expresses, more appropriately, the king's status as a vassal of YHWH. This interpretation seems to be supported by his linkage of the latter term with עֶבֶד, "servant, vassal," in 34:23–24 and 37:24–25, his reference to past kings as נְשִׂיאַי, "my princes" in 45:8.[12] Ezekiel's problem is not with the monarchic institution in principle, but with the way those who have sat on the throne of David have exercised their power. Within his theocratic perspective, YHWH is Israel's real king, and the occupants of the throne, the descendants of David, are his vassals. Because they have historically acted contrary to the divine will (Deut 17:14–20), and "done evil in the eyes of YHWH,"[13] they do not deserve the title מֶלֶךְ.

10. Cf. Levenson, *Theology of the Program*, 142. However, not only is Ezekiel's perspective on the pre-monarchic period quite negative (cf. 20:10–26), but the image of the נָשִׂיא in chapters 40–48 also ill suits a wilderness context.

11. Accordingly to Cooke on 37:24–25 (*Ezekiel*, 403), the Davidic king was to "hate pastoral charge, to watch over the morals and religion of his people." Cf. Vawter and Hoppe (*A New Heart*, 204), who suggest he was "to devote himself entirely to the study of the Law (Deut 17:18–20)." This view is represented most recently by Crane, *Israel's Restoration*, 122–23: "Overall, we find one theology that has a resurrected and restored United Kingdom requiring a king, even a Davidic 'military' king, and then another theology where this Davidic נָשִׂיא would lead the people in spiritual pursuits, and not military activities." For an evaluation of Crane's view see further below.

12. Though the last kings are obviously also recognized as vassals of earthly foreign rulers: Zedekiah was a vassal of Nebuchadnezzar (12:10; 17:16 [he was "made king" (הִמְלִיךְ) by Nebuchadnezzar]; 21:30[25]); Jehoiakim was a vassal of the king of Egypt (19:4–9). According to Tuell (*Law of the Temple*) the נָשִׂיא in chapters 40–48 was a vassal of the king of Persia. However, 17:16 suggests that the distinction should not be overstated. If נָשִׂיא actually bears a stronger nuance of vassalage, it might have been more natural for Ezekiel to speak of Zedekiah as "installed, set up" as prince by the Babylonian overlord. Cf. 1 Kgs 11:34, where YHWH says, כִּי נָשִׂיא אֲשִׁתֶנּוּ כֹּל יְמֵי חַיָּיו, "for I will make him prince all the days of his life." Duguid (*Ezekiel and the Leaders*, 57) rightly asserts that here נָשִׂיא obviously denotes a king.

13. Ezekiel never uses the expression, though his colleague Jeremiah does (52:2), and the deuteronomistic historian uses it at least eighteen times (1 Kgs 15:26, 34;

EZEKIEL'S PORTRAYAL OF THE MONARCHY IN HIS DAY

Our understanding of Ezekiel's disposition toward the history of Israel's monarchy in general and his adaptation of Israel's traditions is admittedly grounded largely on negative evidence—in this case absence of evidence is significant. As we explore his use of ancient texts and traditions to portray the last kings of Judah we witness an increasing transparency on this issue.

Josiah

The only possible allusions to Josiah surface in chapters 17 and 18. In the coda to the prophet's riddles concerning the eagle, the top sprig of a cedar tree from Lebanon, and the spreading vine, in 17:22–24 he uses a special expression to highlight the freshness of the sprig: רַךְ, "tender." It is widely recognized that "the tender (sprig) from the topmost of its young twigs (מֵרֹאשׁ יֹנְקוֹתָיו רַךְ) is a harbinger of the messianic figure who will be presented in greater detail in later salvation oracles. However, Ezekiel's choice of this word also points backward. While the books of Kings in their present form cannot have been composed at the time of this oracle, Josiah's reputation as a ruler of piety and devotion to YHWH must have been well-known.[14] The word רַךְ provides a remarkable link with 2 Kgs 22:19 (= 2 Chr 34:27), where the prophet Huldah speaks of the tenderness (רַךְ) of King Josiah's heart, as demonstrated in his contrition before YHWH and his response to the hearing of the curses in the Torah. Although Antti Laato missed this connection, this lexical link may buttress his thesis that Josiah provided the prophets with the model for the messianic king.[15]

While the case is somewhat weaker, this lexical connection may have influenced the arrangement of chapters 17–19, in which we find an oracle presenting a tri-generational succession of cases (18:5–17) sandwiched between two metaphorical oracles concerning the dynasty. Although a wider application was probably intended in the original rhetorical

---

22:53; 2 Kgs 8:18, 27; 13:2; 14:24; 15:9, 18, 24, 28; 17:2; 21:2, 20; 23:32, 37; 24:9, 19; cf. 2 Chr 21:6; 22:4; 33:2, 22; 36:5, 9, 12).

14. Second Chronicles 35:26–27 suggests these may even have been available in some written form.

15. Laato, *Josiah and David Redivivus*. Josiah is the only person in the Hebrew Bible who is recognized as being totally devoted to YHWH according to the paradigm of Deut 6:4–5. Second Kings 23:25 notes that there was no king in Israel who turned to YHWH "with all his heart/mind (לְבָבוֹ), with all his being (נַפְשׁוֹ) and with all his resources (מְאֹדוֹ), according to the entire Torah of Moses."

context,[16] according to this interpretation, Ezekiel has in mind the reigns of three of the last kings of Judah: Josiah (vv. 5–9), Jehoiakim (vv. 10–13), and Jehoiachin (vv. 14–20) respectively.[17] According to Laato:

> [T]he aim of Ezek 18 in its present context was to argue for Jekoniah's (or his family's) legitimate inheritance of the Davidic throne (as suggested in Ezek 17:22–24) in spite of the curse uttered in Jer 22:24–30. Jekoniah is responsible only for what he himself has done not for what his father has done. If he returns to YHWH and does not follow his father's evil acts he will prosper.[18]

Through this arrangement of oracles the editor urges the reader not to ascribe injustice to YHWH for the way he has treated the members of the royal house.

Jehoahaz

Two major oracles in Ezekiel focus on the fates of the last kings of Judah, viz., chapters 17 and 19. Both are highly poetic in style, cast in the form of extended metaphors. Only the latter involves Jehoahaz. While the preamble to chapter 19 identifies this text as a dirge, in reality it exhibits the features both of a riddle (חִידָה, cf. 17:2) and parody.[19] Ezekiel has taken the form of a qînâ and infused it with alien content. This is not only a funeral song, but also a riddle that deals enigmatically with a living reality—the fate of the Davidic dynasty.

The preamble to the dirge announces that this oracle concerns the princes of Israel (נְשִׂיאֵי יִשְׂרָאֵל) generally. The dirge itself concerns a pride of lions, specifically a mother lioness and two of her cubs. But whom do these lions represent? More precisely, what is the lioness?[20] One's first impulse is to identify the lioness as Hamutal, the wife of Josiah and mother of Jehoahaz and Zedekiah (2 Kgs 23:31; 24:18). However, this interpretation is excluded by the portrayal of her second cub in verses 5–9, which

16. On which see Darr, "Proverb Performance," 197–221; Darr, "Ezekiel," 1257–62.

17. In addition to Laato (*Josiah and David Redivivus*, 162–64), see Zimmerli, *Ezekiel 1*, 72.

18. Laato, *Josiah and David Redivivus*, 358.

19. Yee, "Anatomy of Biblical Parody," 565, defines a parody as "the literary imitation of an established form or style."

20. Note the form of the question and its answer with which the dirge opens: מָה אִמְּךָ לְבִיָּא, "What is your mother? A lioness!"

most identify as Jehoiakim, who is identified elsewhere as the son of Zebidah, the daughter of Pedaiah of Rumah (2 Kgs 23:36). Perhaps the lioness functions symbolically for Judah or the Davidic dynasty[21] but then Ezekiel should have used the masculine, לָבִיא. The switch to the feminine, לְבִיָּא, suggests the referent must be feminine, probably Jerusalem, which, like other geographic names, is consistently identified as feminine in the book.[22] If this is correct, Ezekiel minimizes their genealogical participation in the dynasty of David and highlights their geographical location.

> Of the first cub the dirge says:
> She raised up one of her cubs; he became a young lion.
> He learned to capture prey; he devoured humans.
> The nations heard about him; in their pit he was caught.
> They dragged him off with hooks to the land of Egypt. (19:3–4)

Since Jehoahaz was the only king of Judah taken to Egypt (2 Kgs 23:34), scholars generally agree the first lion represents the immediate successor to Josiah. Although Jehoahaz reigned only for three months, it was long enough for the deuteronomistic historian to characterize him as one "who did the evil in the sight of YHWH" (i.e., defected from YHWH to other gods) just as his predecessors had done (2 Kgs 23:31b).[23]

If Ezekiel's portrayal of this cub as a violent creature is natural, his metaphorical description of human rulers is traditional. The predatory habits of lions serve as a common figure for the violence of humans in the Hebrew Bible. The psalmists portray their enemies as ravaging lions,[24] and the prophets apply the metaphor to invading armies.[25] The vocabulary of Ezekiel's portrait of this lion suggests he may have adapted Nahum's description of the invading Assyrians (Nah 2:12–13[11–12]):

> Where now is the den of lions (אֲרָיוֹת),
> the feeding place of the young lions (כְּפִרִים);
> Where the great feline (אַרְיֵה), the lion (לָבִיא) stalked
> and the lion cub (גּוּר אַרְיֵה) with nothing to fear?
> The lion (אַרְיֵה) tore (טָרַף) victims for its cubs (גְּרוֹתָיו),
> And strangled the prey for his lionesses (לְבִאֹתָיו);
> He filled his lairs with kill (טֶרֶף),

21. This was our interpretation in *Ezekiel 1–24*, 604.

22. So also Odell, *Ezekiel*, 237–39.

23. Jeremiah has a short note on Jehoahaz (Shallum, Jer 22:10–12), but he adds nothing to the picture.

24. Ps 7:2[1]; 10:9; 17:12; 22:13, 21[12, 20]. Cf. also Prov 28:15 and 1 Pet 5:8.

25. Isa 5:29; Hos 5:14.

His dens with mangled flesh (טְרֵפָה).

But Ezekiel's lion is not satisfied with ordinary prey; he develops a particular appetite for human flesh.[26] His notoriety spreads quickly to the surrounding nations, who combine forces to capture him and drag him off with hooks to Egypt. While our text is silent on why this upstart lion was taken to Egypt, the geographic reference offers the first concrete clue to the human behind the symbol.[27]

Jehoiakim

Though some argue that Ezek 18:10–13 applies to Jehoiakim, the only clear reference in Ezekiel to this king, the son of Josiah by a second wife, Zebidah (2 Kgs 23:36), occurs in the second part of this dirge (Ezek 19:5–9):

> When she realized her wait was in vain, and her hope had vanished,
> She took another one of her cubs, and appointed him a young lion.
> He strutted about among the lions, and he became a young lion.
> He learned to capture prey, and he devoured humans.
> He consorted with his widows, and laid waste their cities.
> The land and all its inhabitants were appalled,
>   at the sound of his roaring.
> The nations from the surrounding provinces
>   took up arms against him.
> They spread out their net against him; in their pit he was captured.
> With hooks they put him in a neck-stock,
>   and brought him to the king of Babylon.

26. For biblical references to humans being devoured by lions, see 1 Kgs 13:24–28; 20:35–36; 2 Kgs 17:25–26. The motif is common in ancient Near Eastern art. See the sandstone relief from Musawarat es-Sofra from early Ptolemaic Egypt (Keel, *Symbolism of the Biblical World*, 75, fig. 101), and the unfinished basalt carving from Nebuchadnezzar II's Babylon (fig. 102). See also the remarkable carved ivory plaque from the ninth-century-BCE palace of Ashurnasirpal II, which depicts a lion killing a Nubian. Barnett, *Ancient Ivories*, pl. 49, fig. d; Amiet, *Art of the Ancient Near East*, fig. 111; *IBD* 2:723. For further discussion of the ancient Near Eastern background to the imagery, see Block, *Ezekiel 1–24*, 600–1; Lang, *Kein Aufstand*, 97–98.

27. Cf. Jeremiah's vague reference to Shallum being taken captive and dying in the land of his captors.

Although the second lion has been identified with Jehoiachin, Jehoiakim, and Zedekiah,[28] on balance, Jehoiakim seems the strongest candidate.[29] But even then Ezekiel plays loose and free with the historical record, especially with the origins and the end of his reign. Whereas 2 Kgs 23:34–35 credits his elevation to kingship to Pharaoh Neco, Ezekiel has the lioness taking the initiative. Whereas the historian recounts in summary terms the transfer of his vassaldom to Nebuchadnezzar, his rebellion, his death and his succession by Jehoiachin, Ezekiel portrays him captured by a hunter and taken to the king of Babylon, to stifle his roar on the mountains of Israel. But the picture of the lion devouring human prey, laying waste the landscape, and terrifying the inhabitants with his roaring accords with the image of Jehoiakim's oppressive rule as painted by Jeremiah (Jer 22:13–23). When Ezekiel describes the exploitative and self-serving character of past rulers in 34:2b–6 the freshest illustration in his mind will have been Jehoiakim. The same applies to his allusion to earlier kings (נְשִׂיאִים) in 45:8–9. Within Ezekiel's lifetime, Jehoiakim in particular embodied this tyrannical style. Instead of promoting the health of the people, the hearts of Israel's kings were lifted high over their brothers (אָחִים, Deut 17:20), and they exploited them ruthlessly for selfish ends. But this dirge also presents a curious irony. Because Israel's rulers are heartless and ruthless, intent on exploiting their subjects and tearing them up like lions tear up their prey, first the Egyptians and then the Babylonians are portrayed as deliverers, rescuing the people from their oppressors and ending their tyrannical reigns. Ezekiel paints a similar picture in 34:10, where YHWH declares that he will rescue his flock from the jaws of their shepherds, so they will no longer be prey for them. With the phrase וְהִצַּלְתִּי צֹאנִי מִפִּיהֶם, literally, "I will rescue my flock from their mouth," the prophet turns on its head the normal pastoral image of the shepherd rescuing his sheep from wild animals, and fulfilled by the ideal shepherd, David himself:

> Your servant used to keep sheep for his father; and whenever a
> lion or a bear came, and took a lamb from the flock, I went after
> it and struck it down, rescuing the lamb from its mouth; and if
> it turned against me, I would catch it by the jaw, strike it down,
> and kill it. Your servant has struck down both lions and bears,
> and this uncircumcised Philistine shall be like one of them, for

28. For discussion of the merits of each candidate see Block, *Ezekiel 1–24*, 604–6; Begg, "Identity of the Princes," 358–65.

29. Two recent commentators have gone separate ways on this issue: Darr ("Ezekiel," 1270) follows my approach; Odell (*Ezekiel*, 235–36), prefers Zedekiah.

he has defied the armies of the living God. (1 Sam 17:34–36,
NRSV)

Amos paints a similar picture:

Thus says YHWH: As the shepherd rescues from the mouth of
the lion two legs, or a piece of an ear, so shall the people of Israel
who live in Samaria be rescued, with the corner of a couch and
part of a bed. (Amos 3:12)

Remarkably, these are the only texts in the entire Hebrew Scriptures where
we encounter the idiom, הִצִּיל מִפִּי, "to rescue from a mouth." Ezekiel hereby casts Israel's kings in an anti-Davidic mold. Not only have they not
rescued the people from "every wild beast" (כָּל־חַיַּת הַשָּׂדֶה, v. 5); they have
morphed into ravenous lions themselves.

Having explored the referents for the principals in the dirge we may
now consider the traditional and textual roots of Ezekiel's leonine metaphor. Although the lion was a common symbol for royalty in the ancient
Near East,[30] the inspiration for Ezekiel's development of the figure in this
dirge apparently derives from Jacob's blessing of Judah in Gen 49:8–9:

Judah, your brothers will praise you;
your hand will be on the neck of your enemies;
your father's sons will bow down to you.
You are a lion's cub (גּוּר אַרְיֵה), O Judah;
you have gone up (עָלִיתָ) from the kill (מִטֶּרֶף), my son.
Like a lion (אַרְיֵה) he crouches (רָבַץ) and lies down.
Like a lioness (לָבִיא), who dares to rouse him?

These leonine terms, all of which are found in our text, show that
the influence of Gen 49:8–9 extends beyond the central motif to the very
words the prophet uses.[31] The echoes of Gen 49:8–9 in Ezek 19:1–9 suggest that as the heirs of Jacob's prophecy the last kings of Judah were utter
failures and their captivity by foreign powers was perfectly justified.
Beyond describing the demise of Jehoahaz and Jehoiakim, this dirge
will go on to signal the end of the dynasty—at least as the Israelites have

---

30. The Medinet Habu relief of Rameses III places the representation of a lion
beside the triumphant king; see Keel, *Symbolism*, 86, fig. 103. For a neo-Assyrian representation see the seal of Ashurbanipal, *IBD* 2:907. Cf. also the Israelite seal inscribed,
לשמע עבד ירבעם, "belonging to Shema' servant of Jeroboam [II]," with a beautifully
carved lion emblem. See *IBD* 1:753.

31. In Rev 22:16 "Lion of the tribe of Judah" serves as a messianic title.

known it. The people may not bank on the dynastic promise of Gen 49:8–9 as grounds for their security in the face of the Babylonian threat.

Jehoiachin

Jehoiachin's name occurs only once in Ezekiel, in the editorial clarification of the context of the prophet's inaugural vision and commission as prophet (1:2). But he is the subject of two prophecies, the first part of the riddle of chapter 17, and the last part of the dirge of chapter 19.

Jehoiachin is described as the topmost sprig of a cedar (17:2–4). No text illustrates Ezekiel's bi-fold perspective on Israel's monarchy as dramatically as his metaphoric riddle in chapter 17. The chapter divides into four parts, which, based on the subject matter, are arranged chiastically as follows:

> A The Riddle of the Cedar Sprig (vv. 2–3)
>   B The Riddle of the Vine (vv. 5–10)
>   B' The Interpretation of the Riddle of the Vine (vv. 11–21)
> A' The Interpretation of the Riddle of the Cedar Sprig (vv. 22–24)

However, based on the function of the parts these segments exhibit a strange AA'BB' pattern, with the interpretation of the second riddle following immediately after the riddle itself, as we would expect, and the interpretation of the first being delayed until the end. Technically, only the first short segment and the first four clauses of verse 22 pertain to Jehoiachin. The remainder of the interpretation concerns a future far beyond him.

Although Ezekiel's main concern in the first scene of this extended and complex metaphor is Jehoiachin, the primary character in the first scene of this riddle is a magnificent eagle (v. 3). Throughout the ancient world the eagle served not only as a positive symbol of strength (Isa 40:31) and royal splendor,[32] but also as a fearful symbol of terror. Esarhaddon's boast, "Like a furious eagle I spread my pinions to destroy my enemies,"[33] illuminates the meaning of Hosea's reference to the Assyrian hordes as "an eagle coming against the house of YHWH" (8:1). Ezekiel's nearer predecessor, Habakkuk, had described the Babylonians as "an eagle swooping

---

32. With Sennacherib's reference to the eagle as "the prince of the birds" (Luckenbill, *Annals of Sennacherib*, 36), compare Pindar's "king of the birds" (*Olympian Odes* 13.21). On the eagle as a royal symbol in the ancient Near East see Lang, *Kein Aufstand*, 33–38.

33. Borger, *Inschriften Asarhaddons*, §44. Cf. also §65.

down to devour" (1:8).[34] But this eagle is different; he is cast as a genuinely benevolent figure, plucking off a sprig of a cedar (that is about to be cut down?), taking it away to Babylon, and planting it there, apparently in very favorable circumstances.

By having the great eagle fly to Lebanon, where he plucked off the top of a cedar, Ezekiel has adapted a stock phrase, "cedars of Lebanon."[35] The association of these cedars with the royal constructions in Jerusalem[36] encourages an association with the dynasty. However, in an act quite uncharacteristic of eagles, the magnificent bird snipped off the "crown"[37] and carried the shoot of fresh growth[38] off to a foreign land, identified enigmatically as a commercial territory and a city of merchants. Ezekiel does not provide a motive for the eagle's actions. However, since in the Hebrew Bible a city is by definition a dwelling or group of buildings surrounded by defensive walls built for the protection of the residents, in contrast to the fields outside where crops and vineyards are planted, the purpose of bringing the sprig to this city of merchants presumably was for safekeeping, as merchants protect their goods in warehouses within the walls of the city. In any case, both the image of the bird and his actions are painted in positive noble strokes.

Unlike the central core of this chapter, which consists of a second metaphor of the vine (vv. 5–10) and then follows this up immediately with an interpretation (vv. 11–21), the opening scene lacks an interpretation,

34. Cf. also Deut 28:49; Jer 4:13; 48:40; 49:22; Lam 4:19; and the reduction of Nebuchadnezzar to the level of the symbol of his pride in Dan 4:30–33.

35. Elsewhere Ezekiel himself will speak of "the cedar in Lebanon" (Ezek 31:3 [cf. vv. 15–16) and "the cedar from Lebanon" (Ezek 27:5; cf. Ezra 3:7).The phrase "cedars of Lebanon" occurs often: Judg 9:15; Isa 2:13; 14:8; Ps 29:5; 104:16; cf. 1 Kgs 5:12[14]; Isa 37:24); "cedars in Lebanon" occurs in Ps 92:13; cf. 1 Kgs 5:13[4:33]; 2 Kgs 14:9; "Lebanon" and "cedars" occur in parallel lines in Jer 2:23; Zech 11:1; and Song 5:15. References to foreigners importing cedar lumber from Lebanon are common: Israel (1 Kgs 5:22–28[8–14]; 2 Chr 2:7–15; Song 3:9); Egypt (*ANET*, 243), Assyria (Isa 37:24), Babylon (*ANET*, 307).

36. One of Solomon's royal buildings was called "the house of the forest of Lebanon" (1 Kgs 7:2).

37. The expression צַמֶּרֶת, "crown," occurs only in Ezekiel. Here and in verse 22 it is paralleled with רֹאשׁ, "peak." In 31:3, 10, 14 the צַמֶּרֶת of the tree is very high, reaching into the clouds (cf. the place name Zemaraim, "twin peaks" in Josh 18:22). The form, derived from צֶמֶר, "wool," may have been suggested by the woolly appearance of clouds around the treetops.

38. The parallel expression רֹאשׁ יְנִיקוֹתָיו (from יָנַק, "to suck") concretizes the image of צַמֶּרֶת by referring to the fresh growth of the evergreen, which is still tender and easily plucked off by a bird (17:22).

leaving the reader to ponder over its significance—until the coda in verses 22–24. While many delete the coda as a post exilic insertion,[39] without it the riddle of verses 3–4 remains unresolved. As will be the case in the interpretation of the riddle concerning the vine, so verses 22–24 declare that behind the actions of the magnificent eagle (Nebuchadnezzar) we are to see the actions of YHWH. Ultimately he is the one who plucks the sprig from the top of the cedar, and sets it (in a secure place), until the time is right to retrieve it and plant it on a high and lofty mountain.

But who does this sprig, this foremost of the fresh young twigs of the cedar (רֹאשׁ יְנִיקוֹתָיו) represent? If the cedar represents the Davidic dynasty, the freshness of the sprig suggests either a youthful king or one whose tenure was cut off shortly after assuming the throne.[40] These qualifications could apply either to Jehoahaz, the twenty-three year old son of Josiah who reigned only three months before he was taken away to Egypt (2 Kgs 23:31–34), or to Jehoiachin, the eighteen year old son of Jehoiakim, who also reigned only three months before he was taken away to Babylon (2 Kgs 24:8–16). However, since the interpretation to the riddle of the vine identifies the magnificent eagle with the king of Babylon and expressly declares that he came to Jerusalem and took its king (and the princes) back to Babylon, the sprig obviously refers to Jehoiachin. The significance of his transplant to Babylon cannot be fully established until we have considered the rest of the coda below. For the moment, we note simply that, contra 2 Kgs 24:9 and 2 Chr 36:9,[41] so far this riddle has nowhere suggested a negative reason for his removal from the cedar and his deportation to Babylon. On the contrary, the reference to "the land of merchants" and the "city of traders" opens the door for a beneficent purpose.[42]

Jehoiachin is also described as the branch of a vine (19:10–13). Without warning the subject of the dirge in chapter 19 changes from a zoological (a pride of lions) to a horticultural metaphor (a vine). However, as in verses 2–9 the primary figure (lioness, vine) is presented as the mother (אִמְּךָ) of the secondary figures (cubs, branches). Displaying strong lexical

39. For a defense of its inclusion, see Block, *Ezekiel 1–24*, 549–50.

40. Compare the characterization of the sprig as רַךְ, "tender" in verse 22 with Prov 4:3–4, "When I was a son with my father, tender (רַךְ), and my mother's favorite, he taught me and said to me, 'Let your heart hold fast my words; keep my commands and live.'"

41. This dim view of Jehoiachin is also shared by Jeremiah (Jer 22:24–30). In chapter 19 Ezekiel's evaluation of Jehoiachin will be quite negative.

42. According to 2 Kgs 25:27–30, Nebuchadnezzar's successor Evil-merodach also had a favorable view of Jehoaichin.

links with chapter 17, verses 10–14 describe an extra-ordinary plant, planted beside abundant waters (מַיִם רַבִּים) and producing fine fruit and thick foliage. It sent out special kinds of branches: מַטּוֹת עֹז, "strong staves," and שִׁבְטֵי מֹשְׁלִים, "scepters of rulers," which represent "the official insignia of a tribal chieftain."[43] Its crown reached high into the clouds and could be seen for miles around, only to be uprooted and dried up and burned.

Whereas vines normally grow near the ground (cf. 17:6), this plant is a monstrosity, sending its profusion of branches up into the sky. If Ezekiel's audience had linked this image with the riddle of chapter 17, they might have interpreted its wild growth as a representation of hubris, which is answered by divine judgment.

Despite the links with 17:1–10, a shift in the symbolic significance of the vine is evident. Whereas the previous plant had represented an individual king, Zedekiah, in this instance, the vine (mother) represents either the tribe/nation of Judah, from which more than one ruler sprouts, or, the city of Jerusalem, since גֶּפֶן is treated as feminine and the vine is portrayed as the "mother" of its branches.[44] But she has abandoned her natural function as a producer of grapes, and assumed the posture of a huge tree, a symbol of arrogance of nations.[45] In the story this self-aggrandizement provokes the wrath of YHWH, who punishes her by uprooting and humiliating her, subjecting her to the east wind (the Babylonians), and transplanting her in a foreign land. By this interpretation this is not only an indictment of Judah's kings, but also of Jerusalem herself, and the nation she represents.

In this part of the dirge the strong branches are best interpreted as a figure for the Davidic dynasty, the succession of royal rulers who have sprouted from the tribe of Judah in Jerusalem, with the מַטּוֹת that serve as שִׁבְטֵי מֹשְׁלִים, "scepters of rulers," representing not one, but two kings. The first, Jehoiachin, was torn off, withered and burned (removed from the throne), and then transplanted with the vine in the desert (deported to Babylon). By this interpretation the two dirges involving lions and the branches of the vine present the last four kings of Judah according to their historical order: Jehoahaz, Jehoiakim, Jehoiachin, Zedekiah.

43. Thus Milgrom, *Numbers*, 143, on Aaron's rod (Num 17:16–26[1–11]). Ezekiel's reference is reminiscent of Jer 48:17, which pairs מַטֵּה־עֹז, "a mighty scepter," with מַקֵּל תִּפְאָרָה, "A magnificent rod." Psalm 110:2 links the same expression with the Davidic dynasty.

44. Thus Odell, *Ezekiel*, 240–41. Compare Israel portrayed as a vine in chapter 15.

45. Cf. the portrayal of Assyria and Egypt as huge cedars in chapter 31.

Zedekiah

Ezekiel is more transparent in his hostility toward Zedekiah than toward any other king. His negative disposition is evident from the opening line of the book. Instead of dating his inaugural vision and commission to prophetic service according to the accession year of the regnant king, which was customary throughout the ancient Near East, he dates them according to his own birth date. And the editor adds insult to injury by synchronizing Ezekiel's thirtieth year, not with the year of Zedekiah's reign, but with the year of the previous king's exile (1:1–3). This attitude toward the king is evident in three oracles that concern him directly.

The Sign-act (12:1–16). This prophecy consists of three parts: YHWH's charge to Ezekiel to perform a strange sign act (vv. 1–6); a summary report of the prophet's actions in response (v. 7); and YHWH's interpretation of the significance of the action (vv. 8–16). Although the interpretation ends with a prediction of the destruction of the nation—apparently in fulfillment of the covenant curses in Leviticus 26 and Deuteronomy 28—the focus is actually on "the prince" (הַנָּשִׂיא, vv. 10–13). The interpretation paints a shocking picture, casting YHWH in the role of a hunter who spreads his net over Zedekiah, captures him, and drags him away to Babylon (v. 13). Although the oracle suggests that the nation's demise is punishment for their rebellion (v. 2) and abominations (תּוֹעֵבוֹת, v. 16), it offers no reasons for the king's fate. Its purpose is simply to demonstrate that the Judeans hope in rescue from the Babylonian threat based on the presence on the throne of a descendant of David (2 Sam 7) is futile.

The Renegade Vine (17:5–21). The picture changes, however, in the metaphoric riddle of the renegade vine in chapter 17, the bulk of which concerns Zedekiah (vv. 5–21). Like the sign-act concerning this man in chapter 12, the present riddle about Zedekiah divides into two parts: the extended metaphor (vv. 5–10) and the interpretation (vv. 11–21). The link between these texts is reinforced by the description of YHWH's direct actions against the king (v. 20), which echo almost verbatim the earlier statement (12:13). However, whereas the interpretation of the sign-act in chapter 12 had been silent on Zedekiah's crimes, the explanation of the riddle charges Zedekiah with despising the oath and breaking the covenant (in which he had declared himself a faithful vassal of Nebuchadnezzar) by seeking the aid of Egypt against the Babylonians (vv. 13–18). But the prophet interprets this political treason as an act of treachery against YHWH (vv. 19–20).

But there is another element in the presentation that deserves comment. The common element in the two parts to the riddle involving the cedar sprig (vv. 3–4) and the rebellious vine (vv. 5–10) is the magnificent eagle, cast in the roles of a horticulturalist. Whereas in the first he had snipped off a tender cedar sprig and taken it away (to preserve it), here he takes a seed and plants it in extremely favorable conditions, so that it sprouts and grows into a large vine, sending its branches out in all directions.

With this riddle Ezekiel seizes upon traditional images and deliberately adapts and distorts them for rhetorical effect. According to Ps 80:9–20[8–19], YHWH took a vine (Israel) from Egypt and with his right hand planted it in its own place (cf. Jer 2:21). Isaiah had added to the image by highlighting YHWH's special care for the vine, and describing how the plant had responded, producing only rotten grapes, illustrative of Israel's covenantal infidelity (Isa 5). Hosea associated the bad fruit explicitly with idolatry (Hos 10:1). In Jer 12:10 YHWH complains that many shepherds (rulers) have turned his vineyard into a wasteland. Earlier, in Ezek 15:1–7, the exilic prophet had taken the image a step farther, declaring that the vine was inherently worthless, fit only for fuel for fire.

In view of Ezekiel's previous denunciations of Judah's apostasy, and especially in light of his use of the metaphor of the vine in chapter 15, on first hearing, the reader is tempted to interpret the vine in chapter 17 as the nation of Israel, which was planted by YHWH (the eagle) in a fertile land,[46] but which turned from him, its source of life, to other gods (the second eagle). But the interpretation of the riddle takes the metaphor in a shocking new direction. The vinedresser is not YHWH but Nebuchadnezzar, and the vine is not the nation primarily, but the nobility of Jerusalem, if not the royal family and Zedekiah himself. Verses 12–14 allude to an earlier event when Nebuchadnezzar had apparently brought the king and his associates to Babylon and entered into a covenant relationship with them. Like the actions of the eagle involving the cedar sprig, this is portrayed as a positive development for the good of the king and his nation with him. However, the foolish vine abandoned its normal nature and function and sought its security elsewhere.[47] Because Zedekiah contemptuously violated the oath and broke his covenant as a vassal of Nebuchadnezzar

46. Simian-Yofre ("Ez 17,1–10 como enigma y parábola," 27–43) maintains this parable is open to several interpretations, and that the two provided in verses 17:11–12 and 22–24 do not exhaust its meaning.

47. Cf. Lang, *Kein Aufstand*, 39.

by seeking the aid of Egypt (the second eagle), he is sentenced to death in Babylon (vv. 13–16).

But in verses 18–21 Ezekiel adds a new twist. Because Nebuchadnezzar had appeared as YHWH's agent, treachery against him was treachery against YHWH, and for this the king had become the target of divine fury and his nation would be destroyed. Zedekiah represented the antithesis of the future David, who will be introduced as "my vassal" (עַבְדִּי, 34:23–24; 37:24, 25). With this announcement of the doom of the dynasty Ezekiel robs the people of one of the pillars on which they based their security— the presence of a descendant of David on the throne of Judah.

The Doomed Branch (19:14). Through the sign-act in 12:1–16 Ezekiel had predicted the doom of Zedekiah, and through the riddle of 17:15–21 he had justified his doom. The dirge for the dynasty in chapter 19 resumes the metaphor of the vine and ends with a brief reference to this last king of Judah:

> Fire has gone forth from the bough of its shoots.
> It consumed its fruit.
> No strong branch, no ruler's scepter, remained in it. (19:14)

This declaration lays no specific charge against Zedekiah; apparently his only problem was that he was a part of a dynasty characterized by arrogance (v. 11).

With the burning up of the vine, Ezekiel's riddle comes to a close. With Gen 49:8–12 as his point of departure, the prophet has retraced the events of Judah's final decades in four episodes, each of which revolves around the respective occupants of the Davidic throne. In the process he has declared the futility of any hopes based upon YHWH's covenant with the Davidic house. The promises of God to the ancestors are no guarantee of divine blessing for their descendants. Nor is the promise to the house of David of an eternal dynasty (2 Sam 7) an unconditional guarantee of their rule in Jerusalem.

The Wicked Prince (21:29–32[24–27]). If the sign-act of chapter 12 and the dirge of chapter 19 have been silent on the cause of YHWH's hostility to Zedekiah specifically, things change dramatically in a paraenetic appendix to an oracle announcing the imminent arrival of Nebuchadnezzar and his armies in 21:29–32[24–27]. After an impassioned announcement of doom against the people of Judah for their crimes in verse 29[24], Ezekiel's tone reaches a fever pitch in verses 30–32[25–27]:

O you! O vile one! O criminal! O prince of Israel, whose day has
arrived in time for your final punishment. Thus has the Lord
YHWH declared: Remove the turban! And take off the tiara!
Let nothing remain the same! Exalt the low and bring down the
high! Topsy-turvy! Topsy-turvy! Topsy-turvy! That's what I will
make it—a disaster without equal—until he comes to whom the
judgment belongs, and to whom I will give it.

Forgetting completely YHWH's manipulation of Nebuchadnezzar's
divinatory actions (vv. 21–22[16–17]), the prophet launches into a tirade
against Zedekiah, unequalled in this book or any other prophet for its
forthrightness and harshness. He focuses his hearers' attention on the king
with a quadrupled vocative, "You! O vile one! O wicked one! O prince
of Israel!" The prophet does not elaborate on the king's wicked actions,
but he probably has in mind minimally the violation of his vassal oath
(17:11–21), which will lead to his inevitable demise.[48]

Ezekiel's excitement becomes even more evident in verses 31–32[26–
27]. Following the opening citation formula, Ezekiel calls on the king to
relinquish authority by removing the insignia of royalty, to take off his
turban and crown. With זֹאת לֹא־זֹאת, "This not this," viz., "Let nothing
remain the same,"[49] the prophet calls for a ruthless upsetting of Judean
social structures. The cry of "Exalt the low and bring down the high,"
that is, "Let the slaves rule, and the rulers be enslaved!" involves the same
words we had seen in 17:24 with reference to trees. In this call for change
Ezekiel foresees not only the termination of the dynasty but also a revolu-
tion affecting all strata of society.

The prophecy climaxes in verse 32[27] with the three-fold
עַוָּה עַוָּה עַוָּה, which plays on עָוֺן (v. 30[25]), from the same root, "to twist, to
bend." The image presented recalls the cosmic and cataclysmic disintegration envisioned in Isa 24:1–3, the only other occurrence of the word:

Look! YHWH will strip the earth bare, and lay it waste.
He will twist (עִוָּה) its surface, and scatter its inhabitants.

48. Verse 30b[25b] is syntactically difficult. With Hebrew אֲשֶׁר־בָּא יוֹמוֹ, "whose day
is coming," compare Ezekiel's reference to "the day of Egypt" in 30:9. For comparable
references outside Ezekiel, see Block, *Ezekiel 1–24*, 690. Hebrew בְּעֵת עֲוֺן קֵץ, literally
"time of guilt, end!" speaks not only of the moment of Zedekiah's punishment, but also
the termination of his iniquitous behavior.

49. Dijkstra and de Moor, "Problematic Passages," 204, translate "Whatever the
outcome . . ." based on Akkadian, *anniam la anniam* and *annnitam la annitam* (cf.
AHW, 53; *CAD* 2.137) and Ugaritic *'an l'an yšpš / 'an l'an 'il ygdrk* (CTA 6:IV:46–47).
For a different understanding of this text (and different reference), see M. S. Smith,
trans., "The Baal Cycle," 159–60.

> The layman shall be like the priest; the servant like his master.
> The maid like her mistress; the buyer like the seller.
> The lender like the borrower; the creditor like the debtor.
> The earth will be laid totally waste and completely despoiled,
> For YHWH has declared this word.[50]

The anarchy predicted for Jerusalem is not merely the result of social or political incompetence; it is YHWH who turns the world upside down.[51]

The oracle ends with a sinister reinterpretation of an ancient promise concerning Judah's hegemonic position within Israel. Earlier we had observed Ezekiel's exploitation of Gen 49:8–9 and 11–12 in the dirges of 19:2–9 and 10–14 respectively. Except for a reference to the scepter in 19:11, the prophet had skipped over Gen 49:10. He redresses this problem in 21:32[27]. The messianic/christological interpretation of עַד־בֹּא אֲשֶׁר־לֹו הַמִּשְׁפָּט וּנְתַתִּיו, "until he comes to whom the judgment belongs and I will give it to him," has a long history.[52] It imposes on this text a meaning of מִשְׁפָּט, viz., "right, claim," found nowhere else in the book.[53] "Judgment" in the sense of "punishment" suits the context perfectly. The person to whom the task of "judgment" is delivered is none other than Nebuchadnezzar. Rather than delivering a ray of hope, Ezekiel envisions the imminent fall of Jerusalem, an event which no Messiah would prevent.[54] This is not to say that Gen 49:10 is out of the picture. On the contrary, the prophet has turned a sacred text upside down, transforming an ancient promise on which his audience has staked its hopes, and transformed it into a frightening prediction of doom.[55] On Ezekiel's lips, Gen 49:10 is not about tribute and subordination of the world to Judah, but the judgment of Judah by

50. For a comparable extra-biblical description of anarchy see "Admonitions of Ipu-Wer," in *ANET*, 442–43; *COS* 1.42 (p. 96).

51. Compare Esarhaddon's description of nature twisted out of shape because of the fury of Marduk over the moral and cultic crimes of the Babylonians. In heaven and on earth ominous signs concerning the ruin of humankind (*ḫalāq mitḫarti*) appeared (thus *CAD* 10/2.l35; Borger, *Inschriften Asarhaddons*, 14–15; cf. *ARAB* 2, §§642, 649).

52. See my commentary, *Ezekiel 1–24*, 692.

53. So also Wevers, *Ezekiel*, 169. Elsewhere the word means "justice" (18:5, 19, 21, 27; 33:14, 16, 19), "judgment" (23:24), or "custom" (23:24; 42:11). Cf. Lust, "Messianism and Septuagint," 184–86.

54. For other non-messianic interpretations see Pili, "Possibili casi di metatesi," 457–71, who proposes to reverse the letters of שילה, yielding הליש, viz., "Till the lion comes to whom the obedience of the peoples shall belong." Cf. Gen 49:9. Caquot, "parole sur Juda," 5–32 (followed by Lang, *Kein Aufstand*, 119) finds in Shiloh an abbreviation for Solomon.

55. Cf. Fishbane, *Biblical Interpretation*, 502–3.

the principal representative of that world that was to bow before the tribe.[56] With his condemnation of the Davidic house, the people may think Ezekiel has directly contradicted the Davidic tradition and the divine promises.[57] However, until and unless the Israelites cease their rebellion (מָרָה) against YHWH, there is no security in David.[58]

EZEKIEL'S PORTRAYAL OF THE FUTURE OF THE MONARCHY

So much for the past and the present. What about the future? If the point of Ezekiel's judgment is to demolish the pillars on which the people have based their security, the aim of his restoration oracles is to declare that the judgment will not be the last word. Ultimately, because the promises of YHWH are in fact irrevocable, the people cannot be forever divorced from the land; they will not be forever divorced from YHWH; YHWH will not abandon his temple forever; and the Davidic house will not be eliminated forever. After the judgment, in the distant future, the house will be reconstructed, which means that David will be back. Ezekiel's declarations on this subject are found in four texts.

The Cedar Sprig (17:22–24)

As Joyce rightly observes, this is the third of only four hopeful declarations of hope in the first twenty-four chapters.[59] Our earlier discussion of the cedar sprig in Ezekiel's riddle of chapter 17 had focused on verses 3–4, which has the magnificent eagle (Nebuchadnezzar) plucking off one of the topmost twigs (רֹאשׁ יְנִיקוֹתָיו) and taking it to the land of merchants, the city of traders (Babylon). The eagle's purpose in transporting the sprig is not specified, though we suggested this may be interpreted as a benevolent act resulting in the sprig's preservation. The interpretation to this segment of the riddle provided by the coda of verses 23–24 seems to confirm this understanding.

56. Cf. Moran, "Gen 49,10," 424–25.

57. Like the psalmist in Ps 89:39–52[38–51]; cf. 2 Sam 7:1–16; Pss 89:2–5[1–4], 20–38[19–37]; 132:10–12.

58. One of his favorite epithets for the nation is בֵּית מְרִי, "house of rebellion." Ezek 2:5–6; 3:9, 26–27; 12:2–3; 14:6.

59. Joyce, "King and Messiah in Ezekiel," 327. Each of the four messages of hope in chapters 1–24 seems to address one of these pillars: 11:14–21 (land), 16:59–63 (covenant relationship), 17:22–24 (king), and 20:4–44 (divine residence).

Several features of this passage deserve comment. First, as in verses 19–20, behind the great eagle is YHWH himself. Ultimately he is the one who removed the sprig from the cedar. Second, the nature of YHWH's action in setting (נָתַן) the sprig is unclear (v. 22). Apparently this is a short-hand expression for the divine equivalent to the eagle's action in bringing the sprig to the land of merchants and depositing it (שִׂים) it in the city of traders (v. 4), presumably for safekeeping.[60] Whatever the action, it contrasts sharply with the fate of the branch burned in 19:14. Third, skipping over the sprig's exile in the land of merchants, YHWH takes the sprig and plants it on a very high mountain, where it provides a home for every kind of birds.[61] The tree itself is an enigma. On the one hand, it is a stately cedar (אֶרֶז אַדִּיר, v. 23) but on the other hand, it yields fruit for food, and evoking admiration for its magnificence.[62]

Ezekiel's botanical imagery in verses 22–24 is reminiscent of the language of other prophets, who had spoken of the messianic scion who would revive the Davidic line as a חֹטֶר, "shoot," and a נֵצֶר, "branch" (Isa 11:1) or as a צֶמַח, "sprout" (Jer 23:5).[63] However, whereas Isa 11:1 creates an image of a stump that has been cut down (as an act of judgment, though because of the irrepressible life of the roots new shoots emerge from the stump), here the sprig is cut off by YHWH from the top, without any reference to judgment. Apparently this is as an act of benevolence, ensuring the survival of a branch of the tree until the judgment has passed.[64]

The planting of the tree on the high mountain of Israel, and especially its growth into a fruitful and stately tree under which birds of every kind will rest, adapts a well-known extra-biblical and biblical motif of the cosmic tree.[65] Typically this tree is portrayed as a huge plant with its crown reaching into the heavens and its roots going down to the subterranean

60. The verbs שִׂים in verse 4 and נָתַן in verse 22 function as virtual synonyms for שָׁתַל, "to transplant." Cf. the actions with respect to the vine (vv. 7, 8) and the sprig at the end (vv. 22, 23).

61. Hebrew כֹּל צִפּוֹר כָּל־כָּנָף, literally, "every bird, every wing," recalls Gen 7:14.

62. The triad of expressions, עָנָף, "boughs," פֶּרִי, "fruit," and אַדִּיר, "stately, noble," invites comparison with the eagle's intentions for the vine in verse 8, but this is an entirely different type of plant.

63. Cf. also Jer 33:15; Zech 3:8; 6:12.

64. As noted above, Ezekiel's characterization of the sprig as רַךְ, "tender," hints at a Josianic figure. Cf. 2 Kgs 22:19; 23:25.

65. The birds that nest in the tree do not symbolize the nations but come as refugees. Cf. Isa 16:1–5; Amos 9:11–15; Zech 9:9–10. Similarly, Laato, *Josiah*, 163. The nations are represented by all the trees of the field that acknowledge YHWH in the next verse.

streams from which it draws its nourishment.[66] Although discussion of the tree is missing in cuneiform sources, according to S. Parpola, in Assyrian iconography the tree functions as an imperial symbol, representing "the divine order maintained by the king as the representative of the god Aššur, embodied in the winged disk hovering over the tree."[67]

While Ezekiel may have been first introduced to the "cosmic tree" motif in Babylon,[68] the present passage may also have been inspired by Isa 11:1–10, where the elements of a newly sprouted messianic shoot, the mountain of YHWH, and peaceful co-existence with wild animals are all conjoined. This tree is planted on the mountain of Israel, an obvious allusion to Mount Zion (cf. Isa 2:2–4; Mic 4:1–3). Although this mountain will become increasingly significant in later oracles, only here in Ezekiel are the motifs of Davidic line and Zion brought together.[69] In so doing the prophet reminds the exiles that YHWH had not forgotten his covenant with David (2 Sam 7). The dynasty would survive the deportation; it would be revived within the context of its original founding, and its protective influence would be felt all around the world.

The last verse highlights the universal impact of the tree with a complex version of the recognition formula. One might have anticipated that when all the trees, that is, all the dynasties of the earth as representatives of the nations, observe the splendor, productivity, and protection offered by the tree, they would fall down before it in homage and submission. But this oracle is not about Davidic imperialism; it is about the cosmic

66. This tree is not to be associated with the "Tree of Life" in a paradisiac garden. Cf. Wallace, "Tree of Knowledge and Tree of Life," 658. For studies on the tree as a symbol of an ordered world in the face of the threat of death in ancient Near Eastern written and visual sources see Winter, "Lebensbaum," 57–88; Gowan, *When Man Becomes God*, 102–6. Cf. also Frese and Gray "Trees," 27–28; more recently, Walton, *Ancient Near Eastern Thought*, 175–76.

67. Parpola, "Assyrian Tree of Life," 167. Parpola finds confirmation of this conclusion in the observation that the king sometimes takes the place of the tree between the winged genies. In these contexts the king represented the realization of the cosmic order in man. He is "a true image of God, the Perfect Man" (168).

68. In 31:1–18 Ezekiel develops the motif as a symbol of Egypt in much greater detail. In Daniel 4 the world tree represents Nebuchadnezzar.

69. The mountain motif is absent from 34:23–24 and 37:24–25. The present association is reminiscent of Ps 78:68–73 and 132:10–18, both of which juxtapose the election of David and the establishment of his dynasty with the choice of Mount Zion as YHWH's dwelling place. On Zion as a world mountain see Clifford, *Cosmic Mountain*, 131–60.

sovereignty and fidelity of YHWH, which is highlighted by four sensitively constructed parallel lines:

> I bring down the high tree,
> I make high the low tree;
> I dry up the green tree,
> and I make the dry tree flourish (17:14).

These gnomic declarations recall many similar statements in the Hebrew
Bible.[70] For a concrete illustration of bringing down the high, the listeners
need look no farther than Zedekiah, whose fate had been described in
verses 19–21. As for the low being lifted up, this must refer to Jehoiachin.
He may be currently languishing in captivity in Babylon, but his line will
live. His scion will be restored to the throne of Israel, and elevated to the
status of universal king.

To the exiles Ezekiel's words may have seemed like an impossible
dream, but they are guaranteed in the final three lines. YHWH has spoken; he will act. The foundation for this oracle is found in his covenant
with David, communicated four centuries earlier by Nathan the prophet
(2 Sam 7). Not only had YHWH promised him eternal title to the throne
of Israel; David had recognized its cosmic significance with his enigmatic interpretation of Nathan's oracle as "the instruction for humanity"
(תּוֹרַת הָאָדָם, 2 Sam 7:19). YHWH had not forgotten his ancient word. The
dynasty would survive the exile. Indeed its best years were still to come.

Earlier in 11:5–12 Ezekiel had disputed the claims of those who
had escaped the deportation of 597 BCE, arguing that this was a sign of
YHWH's favor toward them. In response Ezekiel declared that Jerusalem
should not be viewed as a pot protecting the people from danger, but as a
trap holding them for the outpouring of divine fury, and the exile should
be interpreted not as a sign of divine rejection, but of election. YHWH had
removed them from Jerusalem to spare them the conflagration to come,
and in Babylon he personally became their "small sanctuary."[71] Our text
suggests that what the remnant of the exiles was to the future of the nation,

---

70. Involving שפל and גבה: Ps 138:6; Isa 5:15; 10:33; Ezek 17:24; 21:31. Involving
שפל and רום: 1 Sam 2:7; 2 Sam 22:28; Ps 18:28[27]; 75:8[7]; 138:6; Isa 2:11–12, 17;
10:33; 57:15; Ezek 21:31.

71. The enigmatic statement, "And I became to them a sanctuary in small measure
(וָאֱהִי לָהֶם לְמִקְדָּשׁ מְעַט) in the lands where they had gone" (v. 16) should probably be
related to 37:27, "My sanctuary shall be over them" (וְהָיָה מִשְׁכָּנִי עֲלֵיהֶם). Greenberg
(*Ezekiel 21–37*, 757–58) rightly sees in the latter a transformation of the tabernacle primarily as a symbol of God's dwelling amidst Israel to a sheltering presence over them.

33

Jehoiachin was to the dynasty. While the enemies wreak their havoc on the people, the land, the temple, and the dynasty, Babylon would provide refuge both for the exiles and for a remnant of the house of David.[72]

My Servant David, the נָשִׂיא ("prince") / the מֶלֶךְ ("king")

Ezekiel 34:22–24 and 37:23–25 contain the most overtly messianic language in the book. There is no need here to retrace my analysis of these texts in an earlier article and in my commentary.[73] Our focus here will be on Ezekiel's use of antecedent traditions to present the future of monarchy.

Ezekiel 34:22–24

Ezekiel's first explicit reference to the Messiah occurs near the end of an extended restoration oracle in which YHWH poses as a benevolent divine shepherd, rescuing his beleaguered human flock from the tyranny of exploitative rulers and bullying members within the flock (34:1–31). For a brief moment, in verses 23–24, the focus shifts to the appointment of David as (under)shepherd of YHWH's flock, followed by a presentation of the covenant of peace that YHWH establishes with his people.[74] These verses are packed with vital information on the new shepherd's status

72. The role of Babylon is analogous to that of Egypt in the narratives of Genesis. In Gen 45:7–11 and 50:20–21 Joseph informs his brothers that his presence in Egypt was part of God's plan to secure the existence of the chosen family while a famine devastated the region.

73. Block, "Bringing Back David," 172–83 (reprinted below, pp. 74–93); Block, *Ezekiel 25–48*, 294–309; 406–24.

74. On these two features as fundamental elements of Jewish messianism in the Second Temple period, see Levey (*The Messiah*, xix), who defines the messianic age as follows:

> The predication of a future Golden Age in which the central figure is a king primarily of Davidic lineage appointed by God. . . . It was believed that during the time of the Messiah the Hebrew people will be vindicated, its wrongs righted, the wicked purged from its midst, and its rightful place in the world secured. The Messiah will pronounce doom upon the enemies of Israel, will mete out reward and punishment in truth and in justice, and will serve as an ideal king ruling the entire world. The Messiah may not always be the active agent in these future events, but his personality must always be present, at least as the symbol of the glorious age which will be ushered in.

within Israel: (1) The ruler will be installed (הֵקִים) by YHWH himself after the exiles have returned to the land that YHWH would give them; (2) The ruler will be shepherd over (עַל) YHWH's people, but unlike the self-serving shepherds of verses 1–10, he will actually tend the flock; (3) The ruler will be singular (רֹעֶה אֶחָד), reversing the division of Israel into northern and southern kingdoms that occurred after the death of Solomon (1 Kgs 11–12); (4) The ruler will be David, the name appearing here for the first time in the book; (5) The ruler will be the servant of YHWH; (6) The ruler will be a נָשִׂיא, "prince," in the midst of his people; (7) The ruler will function within the context of YHWH's covenant with Israel (cf. vv. 24a, 25).

Although chapter 34 as a whole represents an exposition of Jeremiah's oracle in Jer 23:1–6, Ezekiel's portrait of the future ruler makes heavy use of other antecedent texts and traditions.[75] His installation by YHWH after the exiles have returned to their patrimonial homeland recalls Deut 17:14–20. The king is not portrayed as a military figure who leads the Israelites in a battle of conquest. As shepherd he will not tend his people like the self-serving shepherds of verses 1–10, but according to the ideal established for David in 2 Sam 7:7; 1 Chr 17:6; and Ps 78:70–72. Like the rest of the prophets, Ezekiel perceived the nation as one and recognized as legitimate only the Davidic dynasty.[76] In identifying the new ruler as David, Ezekiel follows a longstanding prophetic tradition, rooted ultimately in YHWH's eternal and irrevocable covenant with David (2 Sam 7; Ps 89:3–4, 19–29[2–3, 18–28]).[77] This understanding is reinforced by the epithet, עַבְדִּי, "my servant," which recalls the traditional view of David's willing subordination to YHWH. The expression is used of David twice in 2 Sam 7:5 and 8 and twenty-nine times elsewhere in the Hebrew Bible and mirrors ten-fold self-designation as עַבְדְּךָ, "your servant," 2 Sam 7:19–29. The collapse of the Davidic house with the deportation of Jehoiachin in 597 BCE and the execution of Zedekiah in 586 BCE had raised doubts about YHWH's fidelity to his word. Ezekiel hereby reminds his hearers that in the immediate context YHWH may have suspended the benefits of his covenant with David, but he has not retracted it.

75. Cf. Block, *Ezekiel 25–48*, 275–76.

76. Ezekiel will expand on this notion in 37:15–24, where the term אֶחָד, "one," occurs no fewer than eleven times.

77. Cf. Isa 9:5–6[6–7]; 11:1, 10; Hos 3:5; Amos 9:11; Jer 23:5. Gross, "Israel's Hope," 125–26, follows Hossfeld, *Untersuchungen zu Komposition und Theologie des Ezekielbuches*, 230ff. and 284ff., in deleting the reference to David as a late intrusion, dependent upon Ezek 37:24–25.

Ezekiel's use of the archaic title נָשִׂיא, "prince," contrasts with Hos 3:5 and Jer 3:5, both of which had referred explicitly to "David their king." However, it is consistent with his efforts elsewhere to downplay the roles of Israel's monarchs, and harks back to 1 Kgs 11:34, where it is said of Solomon, "I will make him נָשִׂיא all the days of his life for the sake of David my servant." Far from denying the ruler's true kingship, by referring to him as a נָשִׂיא rather than a מֶלֶךְ Ezekiel deliberately distinguishes him from the recent occupants of the office. Officially the נָשִׂיא may be "the promoted one," but as one in the midst (בְּתוֹךְ) of Israel, his heart will not exalted about his kinsfolk (cf. Deut 17:19–20).

In this arrangement, YHWH is the divine patron of the people; David is his representative and deputy. As David himself had acknowledged in 2 Sam 7:23–27, YHWH's granting his house eternal title to the kingship was not an isolated act, concerned only about the well-being of the king. That he appoints him within the context of his covenant relationship with the people is highlighted by the fact that this entire section (vv. 23–31) is framed by versions of the covenant formula (vv. 24, 30–31). This ruler's role is not to win allegiance to himself but to serve the relationship between people and deity.

Ezekiel's announcement of the appointment of a new David for Israel was intended to instill new hope in the hearts of the exiles. Contrary to appearance, the demise of the Davidic house in 586 BCE did not reflect divine impotence or indifference to previous commitments. These events had not only fulfilled previous prophetic utterances;[78] they also set the stage for a dramatic new act of YHWH when the decadence of the old order would be removed. The prophet hereby challenges his people to look forward to a new day when YHWH's Davidic servant would be reinstated in accordance with his eternal and irrevocable covenant.

Ezekiel 37:22–25

The second reference to the restoration of the Davidic dynasty occurs in the interpretation of a sign act involving two pieces of wood on which are inscribed the names Judah and Joseph. Ezekiel is instructed to unite these two sticks as a symbolic gesture promising the eventual reunification of all the tribes of Israel in one nation (37:16–28).[79] The interpretation proper

78. Cf. 12:1–16; 17; 19.
79. On which see Friebel, *Jeremiah's and Ezekiel's Sign-Acts*, 362–69.

(vv. 21–28) offers an anthology of Ezekielian restoration ideas,[80] bringing his salvation oracles to a fitting conclusion. This verbal explanation divides into two parts (verses 21–24a; 24b–28), each with its own covenant formula (vv. 23, 27). Verses 21–24a are preoccupied with the reunification of the nation under one shepherd; verses 24b–28 with the eternality of YHWH's restorative acts. Accordingly, the specification of one shepherd over all of Israel in verse 24a belongs to the preceding, rather than that which follows, and the identification of David as מֶלֶךְ in verse 24a ties in with the use of the same word in verse 22, but contrasts with Ezekiel's preferred designation for Israel's rulers, נָשִׂיא in verse 25. This division of verses 21–28 results in two panels of approximately equal length.[81]

Although the first panel echoes key elements from 34:22–24,[82] here the distinctive emphasis is on creating "a single nation" (גּוֹי אֶחָד) under "one king" (מֶלֶךְ אֶחָד) from two nations (שְׁנֵי גוֹיִם) and, two kingdoms (שְׁתֵּי מַמְלָכוֹת, v. 22). The textual tradition on the title for this ruler in 37:22, 24 is inconsistent. Where MT identifies this head as a מֶלֶךְ, "king," LXX and Papyrus[967] read ἄρχων, generally assumed to reflect נָשִׂיא, "prince," in the Vorlage.[83]

In view of the strong arguments of J. Lust and A. S. Crane, I can now accept that the *Vorlage* to the Old Greek text may well antedate the Hebrew text underlying MT.[84] However, I remain unconvinced that the *Vorlage* to the Old Greek text read נָשִׂיא rather than מֶלֶךְ.[85] On the one hand, LXX renderings of מֶלֶךְ when used of Israel's kings vary. On the other hand, the explanations for the shift in MT from נָשִׂיא to מֶלֶךְ strike me as unnecessarily

---

80. For summaries see Lust, "Ezekiel 36–40," 526–27.

81. In MT the first panel consists of seventy-two words; the second of sixty-eight.

82. "My servant David," "one shepherd," the covenant formula.

83. Papyrus[967] is dated to the late second or early third century CE, hence pre-hexaplaric. For the publication see Johnson, Gehman, and Kase, eds., *John H. Scheide Biblical Papyri*.

84. See especially Crane, *Israel's Restoration*, 207–64; Lust, "Ezekiel 36–40," 517–33; Lust, "Textual Criticism," 28–31; Lust, "Major Divergences," 83–92.

85. See Schunck, "Attribute des eschatologischen Messias," 651, n. 3; Rofé, "Qumranic Paraphrases," 173, attributes LXX to a theological revision in the *Vorlage*. See further below.

speculative.[86] But even if MT reflects a change from נָשִׂיא to מֶלֶךְ,[87] those

86. Whereas Lust earlier attributed the changes in arrangement and the reading in this case in MT to Pharisaic reactions against apocalyptic views ("Ezekiel 36–40," 532), he later admitted its "highly hypothetical" nature ("Textual Criticism," 30). More recently Crane has argued that MT was produced as a Hasmonean "military call to arms" under a Davidic leader and "a call to purity or spiritual renewal." See *Israel's Restoration*, 253–63. However, the former interpretation overplays the militaristic nature of מֶלֶךְ and underestimates the militaristic overtones of נָשִׂיא.

On the one hand, it is true that one of the roles of the מֶלֶךְ was to lead the nation in battle against foreign enemies (1 Sam 8:20), but this was only one of his roles. Along with vanquishing enemies, in the ancient Near East kings were expected to dispense justice internally, providing care and security for his subjects, and ensure the proper operation of the national cult. Indeed, Deut 17:14–20 expressly prohibits a militaristic stance: the primary task of the מֶלֶךְ was to read the Torah for himself, and his primary role is to embody covenant righteousness by walking in the ways of YHWH and not allowing his heart to be lifted up above his countrymen. Cf. Block, "Burden of Leadership," 259–78. Furthermore, while other prophets charged Israelite kings with pursuing overly militaristic policies, this is not a pronounced theme in Ezekiel. Admittedly in chapter 17 he accuses Zedekiah of despising his oath of vassalage to Nebuchadnezzar by seeking an alliance with Egypt and sending envoys there that Pharaoh might aid him in his resistance to the Babylonian overlord. However, Ezekiel presents the king as relatively passive in this military context. Whereas centuries earlier the people had demanded a king who would go out before them and fight their battles (1 Sam 8:20), here Zedekiah is portrayed as hiring outsiders to fight his battles. And even if this oracle paints him as a military leader, this is an isolated text.

On the other hand, this interpretation underplays the potentially militaristic overtones of נָשִׂיא. In the book of Numbers, which reflects the traditional use of the word, נְשִׂיאִים were tribal and clan leaders whose responsibilities were primarily political and military. Accordingly, we read of them administering justice (Josh 22:32), leading in battle (Num 1:16, 44; 10:4; etc.), dividing the land (17:4), and negotiating with outsiders (Josh 9:18–19). Speiser ("Background and Function," 115) rightly comments "The נשיא represents (in Exod 22:27) the chief political authority, comparable to later מלך." Similarly, Halpern, *Constitution of the Monarchy*, 214. Furthermore, the non-military interpretation of נָשִׂיא also overlooks the fact that the most militaristic figure in the entire book of Ezekiel, Gog of Magog, is introduced three times as a "chief prince" (נְשִׂיא רֹאשׁ, 38:2, 3; 39:1).

At the same time, this interpretation overplays the religious/liturgical role of the נָשִׂיא. The fact that "princes" provided offerings for the altar and the dedication of the tabernacle in Num 7 does not mean theirs was a sacral office. It means simply that they represented and acted on behalf of their tribes and clans. Where they are actually involved in cultic activity, the sacrifices are for themselves, not on behalf of the community (Lev 4:3, 31, 35). Indeed, when they attempted to seize a more significant role in the cult this was denied them (Num 16:1–3).

87. The reading of LXX and Papyrus[967] in verses 22 and 24 may reflect an early reading of the text, perhaps a harmonization with verse 25, which declares expressly that "My servant David shall be their נָשִׂיא forever." A similar phenomenon may account for Ezek 28:12, where מֶלֶךְ is also rendered as ἄρχων by LXX, though in this

responsible for the change may simply have recognized that this מֶלֶךְ is in fact a king. Not only do political entities identified as מַמְלָכוֹת, "kingdoms" (Greek reads βασιλείας) require a מֶלֶךְ at the head, but this is also virtually required by the reference to that nation as גּוֹי, which is by definition ruled by a king, rather than an עַם, "people." For the moment Ezekiel offers no hints of the king's identity. He deals only with the issue of principle: a nation (גּוֹי) is by definition a monarchy (מַמְלָכָה), which must by definition be ruled by a royal figure, a מֶלֶךְ.[88] If the emphasis on a single ruler symbolizes the nation's new unity, MT's reading of מֶלֶךְ instead of נָשִׂיא highlights the restoration of Israel to full nationhood.

The expansion of the covenant formula in verses 23b–24a concretizes the spiritual renewal described in verse 23a by announcing his appointment of David as "king" in Israel. As YHWH's servant (עֶבֶד) and as shepherd-king, he will tend the people after the divine model set out in chapter 34, and apparently inspire them with his own conduct (cf. Deut 17:19–20) to walk in the ways of YHWH as called for in the covenant and the Deuteronomic Torah (v. 24b).

With his five-fold affirmation of the eternality of the restoration in the second panel (24b–28), YHWH transforms this oracle into a powerful eschatological statement, envisaging an entirely new existence, where the old historical realities are considered null and void, and the new saving work of God is perceived as final.[89] For Ezekiel eschatological events are neither ahistorical nor supra-historical; they are based upon YHWH's past actions in history and represent a final solution to the present historical crisis. But the scope of his eschatological hope extends beyond a renewal of YHWH's covenant with his people, incorporating all the other promises upon which the Israelites had based their security: YHWH's covenant with David, his establishment of Jerusalem as the place for his name to dwell, and his special interest in the land of Canaan as his land, offered as a gracious fiefdom to Israel to administer on his behalf.

In spite of the prophet's avoidance of specifically messianic designations,[90] the messianic significance of this oracle is obvious. The principal features of Ezekiel's Messiah are reflected in the titles and role designations he bears. As David he is heir to the eternal dynastic promises

---

instance the influence derives from נָגִיד, "prince," in verse 2, which LXX renders as ἄρχοντι. So also Duguid, *Ezekiel and the Leaders*, 23.

88. Cf. Duguid, *Ezekiel and the Leaders*, 24–25.

89. Cf. Block, "Bringing Back David," 180–81.

90. So also Targum Jonathan, on which see Levey, *Targum of Ezekiel*, 4–5; Levey, *The Messiah*, 83–87.

made by YHWH to Israel's greatest king. As עֶבֶד, "my servant," he enjoys a special relationship with YHWH, ruling the people as his specially chosen agent. As נָשִׂיא, "prince, chieftain," he stands at the head of his people, not as a tyrannical ruler, but as one who has been called from their ranks to represent them. As מֶלֶךְ he symbolizes the nation's new unity. All other pretenders to the throne have been dismissed that Israel may be one nation (גּוֹי אֶחָד) under "one king" (מֶלֶךְ אֶחָד) occupying the land of Israel. As רֹעֶה אֶחָד, "one shepherd," he seeks the welfare of the flock, according to the pattern of YHWH himself (chapter 34). In all these roles, Ezekiel's Messiah symbolizes the realities of the new age. Remarkably, he plays no part in the restoration of the nation. He neither gathers the people nor leads them back to their homeland. Unlike other prophets, Ezekiel does not speak of the Messiah as an agent of peace[91] or righteousness;[92] these he attributes to the direct activity of God. The Messiah's personal presence symbolizes the reign of YHWH in the glorious new age.

THE נָשִׂיא IN EZEKIEL 40–48

We conclude this discussion of the transformation of Ezekiel's royal vision with a few summary comments about the נָשִׂיא in chapters 40–48.[93] Here the נָשִׂיא functions, not as a tribal chieftain, nor as a military leader, but as the leader of the people in the context of highly developed centralized economic and religious structures. We might summarize his role and function as follows:

1. Although the outer eastern gateway is forever closed to human traffic, the נָשִׂיא alone may sit in the gateway and eat his sacrificial meals there before YHWH (44:1–3).[94]

2. The נָשִׂיא is assigned a special territorial grant, separate from the tribal allotments, consisting of two large tracts of land on either side, east and west, of the sacred reserve (45:7–9; 48:21).

91. Isa 9:5–6[6–7]; 11:6–9; Mic 5:5[6]; Jer 23:6; Zech 9:9–10.

92. Isa 5–6; 11:2–5; Jer 23:5–6. On the relationship of Ezekiel's Messiah with other biblical portraits, see Moenikes, "Messianismus," 289–306.

93. For my discussion of this enigmatic figure see Block, "Bringing Back David," 183–88 (reproduced below, pp. 74–93).

94. The notion of "sitting before YHWH" is relatively rare in the Hebrew Bible: Judg 20:26; 21:2; 2 Sam 7:18 = 1Chr 17:16; 1 Kgs 8:25; 2 Chr 6:16.

3. The נָשִׂיא must provide the prescribed animals, grain, and oil for sacrifices, which are to be offered on his and the people's behalf (45:21–25).

4. On weekly Sabbaths and new moon celebrations the נָשִׂיא shall stand in the inner court to watch the priests presenting the offerings on his behalf. Forbidden to step out onto the most sacred space of the inner court, he must prostrate himself on the threshold of the gate (46:1–7, 12).

5. At the appointed festivals, the נָשִׂיא must enter the sacred precinct with the rest of the lay worshippers. However, unlike the נָשִׂיא, the common folk may not turn around inside the precinct and exit via the gate through which they entered (46:8–10).

6. The נָשִׂיא may present additional voluntary offerings to YHWH, but they must be presented like the Sabbath and new moon offerings, while he watches from inside the east gate. After the offerings are completed he must leave this gate and it shall be shut behind him (46:12).

7. The נָשִׂיא may apportion his property to his sons as their permanent possessions, but if he awards any of his land to his servants, in the year of liberation it must return to the prince (46:17).

8. The נָשִׂיא may not confiscate property of the people and give it to his sons as their own territorial grants (46:18).

My earlier conclusions regarding the role of the נָשִׂיא in Ezekiel's closing vision still stand.[95] The primary concern in this vision is not political, but cultic. Unlike 31:23–24 and 37:22–24, the issue here is not the return of David, but the presence of YHWH. The role of the נָשִׂיא is facilitative, not regally symbolic. Unlike past kings, who perverted the worship of YHWH for selfish ends and/or sponsored the worship of other gods, this נָשִׂיא is charged with promoting the worship of YHWH in spirit and in truth. Uniquely in this vision, with its radically theocentric portrayal of Israel's future, the נָשִׂיא emerges as a religious functionary, serving the holy community of faith, which itself is focused on the worship of the God, who dwells in their midst. Where the presence of God is recognized, there is purity and holiness. Ezekiel's נָשִׂיא is not responsible for the administration of the cult. Not only does he not participate actively in the ritual; unlike previous kings, but he also does not build the temple, design

95. "Bringing Back David," 187–88.

41

the worship, or appoint the priests; these prerogatives belong to YHWH. While departing from the historical roles of David and Solomon, this agrees with the image of the נָשִׂיא in 34:23–24, who is installed as under-shepherd by YHWH only after the latter has personally rescued Israel. In this ideological presentation the נָשִׂיא functions as YHWH's appointed lay patron and sponsor of the cult, whose activity ensures the continuance of harmonious relations between deity and subjects. The God of Israel has fulfilled his covenant promises, regathering the people and restoring them to their/his land. More important, he has recalled the people to himself and established his residence in their midst. Now let them celebrate, and let the נָשִׂיא lead the way.

Conclusion

In Ezekiel's mind, the kings of Israel, specifically David and his descen-dants, were YHWH's specially chosen agents appointed to govern his people in his place, and thereby secure their well-being.[96] Ezekiel's oracle against Israel's kings in 34:1–10 shares the theocratic vision of Deu-teronomy, in which the king's primary role is to represent YHWH by embodying covenant righteousness and promoting the well-being of those in his charge. His position within the tri-partite covenantal relationship may be illustrated as follows:

---

96. Just as at the cosmic level אָדָם, as the image of God, was charged to govern the world as God's viceroy (Gen 1:26–28; Ps 8), so at the national level the Davidic kings were appointed as vice-regents of YHWH, charged to govern as YHWH would, were he personally present.

Figure 2: The Role of the King in Israel's Administrative Order

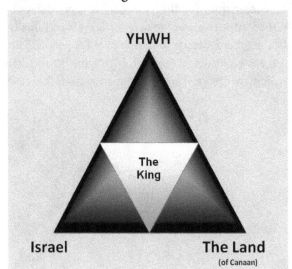

But in Ezekiel's mind the ideal and reality of the history of Israel's monarchy were miles apart. His comments about past kings tend to go in two directions.

On the one hand, in the past Israel's kings have failed miserably in their obligations as leaders of the people. For Ezekiel the dominant problem with Israel's monarchs was arrogance and the abuse of their role as מֶלֶךְ, expressed by violently exploiting their subjects for personal gain (34:2b–6; 45:8–9). Instead of promoting the health of the people, the hearts of Israel's kings were lifted high over their brothers (cf. Deut 17:20), and they terrorized and exploited them ruthlessly for selfish ends (19:3, 6–7). Indeed, in the final statement of that part of this pastoral oracle that concerns the shepherds of Israel, YHWH declares his determination to rescue his people from their own leaders (34:10).

In this event the king of Babylon plays a crucial role. Ezekiel envisions Nebuchadnezzar not only as a divine agent of judgment on the nation for their rebellion against him, but also as an agent of deliverance, rescuing the people from their oppressors, and providing a refuge for the exiles in Babylon while YHWH's fury rages all around at home. At the same time, in a remarkable twist, the coda of 17:22–24 portrays Nebuchadnezzar as the agent through whom the dynasty is rescued. Jehoiachin is removed to Babylon so that at the appropriate time, when YHWH has reconstructed the covenantal triangle, a representative of the Davidic house is available.

This sets the stage for the final restoration oracles, according to which, having brought the remnants of all the tribes back to their ancestral homeland and reestablished justice among the people, YHWH will finally install the ideal David as shepherd, prince, and king over his people. The ideational portrayal of the נָשִׂיא in the final vision highlights his facilitative role in ensuring that deity, people, and land permanently enjoy the ancient ideals.[97]

97. I am grateful to Jason Gile and Charlie Trimm for their helpful comments on an earlier draft of this essay.

3

The Tender Cedar Sprig

Ezekiel on Jehoiachin[1]

Introduction

IF HISTORIANS AND BIBLICAL scholars do not overlook or undervalue the significance of King Jehoiachin in Israel's history in general,[2] they certainly pay little attention to the contribution offered by the book of Ezekiel to reconstructing a historical portrait of this man. The standard dictionaries typically limit their treatment of Jehoiachin to a passing note that the exilic prophet dates events according to the exile of Jehoiachin (Ezek 1:2).[3] However, it would be remarkable if this was all Ezekiel had

---

1. This essay was originally published in *Hebrew Bible and Ancient Israel* 1 (2012) 173–202. I am grateful for the assistance Matthew Patton has offered through various stages in the composition of this paper. Of course, any errors of substance or infelicities in logic and composition are my own.

2. The *Dictionary of the Old Testament: Historical Books* (edited by B. T. Arnold and H. G. M. Williamson) lacks an article on Jehoiachin.

3. (1) Kim ("Jehoiachin," 207) does not even provide the reference; (2) Liver ("Jehoiachin," 106–7) concludes (puzzlingly) from Ezek 1:2 that Jehoiachin's family retained leadership of the Babylonian exiles; (3) Foulkes ("Jehoiachin," 744–45) adds that this suggests some viewed him rather than Zedekiah as the legitimate king of Judah; (4) Berridge ("Jehoiachin," 662–63) adds a parenthetical reference to the lamentation in 19:1–9, with a non-committal comment, "where many commentators believe that the king of verses 5–9 is Jehoiachin"; (5) Schultz, "Jehoiachin," 976; (6) Wiseman, "Jehoiachin," 737–38.

to say about him. After all, the prophet and the king apparently were *schleppt* off to Babylon together—presumably both against their will[4]—along with thousands of fellow notable Judaeans.[5] It is possible that the Judaean exiles by the River Chebar (Akkadian *Nār Kabaru*) communicated with those in Babylon and its environs.[6] After all, Ezekiel was a prominent (albeit often discounted) prophetic figure in the community of exiles, and Jehoiachin was eventually elevated in the city of Babylon to a significant place among captured kings who shared his fate.[7]

The possibilities increase in the light of the recent discovery of more than thirty tablets from a place called al-Yāḫdah (*[uru]ia-a-ḫ-u-du*), "the city of Judah," which was located near Borsippa in the immediate vicinity of Babylon.[8] The earliest of these is dated in the thirty-third year of Nebuchadnezzar (572/571 BCE). We cannot tell whether the residents of al-Yāḫdah came in the 597 BCE deportation or with a new wave of deportees after the fall of Jerusalem eleven years later. However, this toponym provides a link with a ration text from Nebuchadnezzar's thirteenth year (592 BCE) that identifies Jehoiachin as "king of Judah (*Ia-a-ḫu-du*)." If people in Jerusalem were in contact with the exiles (Jer 29–30), conversations

4. Second Kings 24:12 suggests Jehoiachin surrendered to Nebuchadnezzar voluntarily, but the verb לקח clearly places him at the mercy of the Babylonians.

5. 2 Kgs 24:6–17; 2 Chr 36:8–10; Jer 29:1–2; 37:1–2; 52:30.

6. It is generally assumed this colony was located near Nippur, some eighty kilometers southeast of Babylon. For general discussion, see Block, *Ezekiel 1–24*, 84. This conclusion is reinforced by a cache of fifth-century-BCE tablets known as the Murashu Documents unearthed in Nippur that bear the names of many who were obviously Judaean. See generally Stolper, "Murashū, Archive of," 927–28; Stolper, "Fifth Century Nippur," 83–132; Stolper, "A Note on Yahwistic Personal Names," 25–28; Zadok, *Jews in Babylonia*; Coogan, *West Semitic Personal Names*; Coogan, "Patterns in Jewish Personal Names," 183–91. Since they derive from the Persian period, not surprisingly they provide no evidence for contact between the population of Nippur and Babylon. Although the Akkadian designation *nār kabari* was applied to at least three different canals (see Zadok, "Notes on Syro-Palestinian History," 727), Ezekiel's Chebar probably ran through a suburb east of Nippur, within sight of the ziggurat of Enlil, which had for centuries been the hub of Mesopotamian religion. Thus Petter, *Ezekiel and Mesopotamian City Laments*, 110–11, based on research by Douglas R. Frayne communicated personally.

7. For the biblical evidence, see 2 Kgs 25:27–30; Jer 52:31–34; for extra-biblical evidence, see Weidner, "Jojachin," 925–26; *ANET*, 308. For further discussions, see Bea, "Jojachin in Keilschrifttexten," 78–82; Gerhards, "Begnädigung Jojachins," 64–66; Wiseman, *Nebuchadnezzar and Babylon*, 81–84.

8. The tablets are in the process of publication. Three have already been published by Joannès and Lemaire, "Trois tablettes cunéiformes," 17–34. For a preliminary report of the remainder, see Pearce, "New Evidence for Judaeans," 399–411.

were probably carried on among the exiles who resided in different colonies, including those in the city of Babylon itself.⁹ Apart from these ration tablets, the only unequivocal extra-biblical reference to Jehoiachin is found in the Babylonian Chronicle of the third year of Neriglissar:¹⁰

> The seventh year, in the month of Kislev, the king of Akkad mustered his troops, Marched on Ḫatti, and set up quarters facing the city of Yeḥud. In the month of Adar, the second day, he took the city and captured the king [Jehoiachin]. He installed there a king of his choice [Zedekiah]. He collected its massive tribute and went back to Babylon.¹¹

9. It is not clear how Daniel fits into this picture or what historical weight may be given to the traditions preserved in the book. While the calendrical issues are formidable, the opening statement suggests Daniel was taken to Babylon in Jehoiakim's third year (Dan 1:1), identified by Jeremiah as his fourth year (Jer 46:2). According to the Babylonian Chronicle, in 605 BCE Nebuchadnezzar was leading his father Nabopolassar's forces in the west. Upon the latter's death, Nebuchadnezzar hurried home to claim his father's throne, perhaps taking Daniel and his companions with him, though it is also possible he may have taken them back the next year, along with a massive amount of tribute after a season of campaigning. For text and translation of the Babylonian Chronicle, see Glassner, *Mesopotamian Chronicles*, 228–29. For discussion of the chronological issues involved, see Wiseman, *Nebuchadnezzar and Babylon*, 12–24. In any case, if Daniel was elevated to prime ministerial status by 597, he could have had a hand in securing for his Judaean countrymen favorable locations for settlement (like Joseph had done for his brothers in Egypt), which contributed to their rapid integration into the Babylonian economy, as witnessed by both the al-Yāḫdah and Murashū documents. He may even have contributed to the favorable treatment rendered Jehoaichin by both Nebuchadnezzar and his successor Evil-Merodach. Ezekiel's references to Daniel (Ezek 14:14, 20; 28:3) are admittedly puzzling. Most scholars reject identifying this Daniel (spelled consonantally as *dn'l*, rather than *dny'l*) with the Daniel of the book. However, the alternatives are as problematic as the traditional interpretation. See Block, *Ezekiel 1–24*, 447–50. While the historical value of Susanna, one of the Apocryphal additions to Daniel set in Babylon during the Judaean exile (587–538 BCE), is dubious, it identifies the heroine as the wife of a rich man named Joakim, who had a paradisiacal garden adjoining his house. Because he was the most honored of all (the exiles), the Jews would come to him (for counsel? support?). The LXX of 2 Kings regularly renders Jehoiachin's name as Ιωακιμ, including 2 Kgs 24:6, which also refers to Jehoiakim as Ιωακιμ (cf. also Jer 52:31 and Ezek 1:2). See further note 22 below.

10. Jar handles from Judah with the seal inscription, לאליקם נער יוכן, "Eliakim *na'ar* Yaukin," once thought to identify King Jehoiachin have now been discredited. See Garfinkel, "The Eliakim Na'ar Yokan Seal Impressions," 74–79; Rainey, "A Rejoinder," 61; Mykytiuk, *Identifying Persons*, 23–39.

11. BM 21946, as translated by Glassner, *Mesopotamian Chronicles*, 231.

Correlating biblical and extra-biblical data, we may date Jehoiachin's exile to the turn of the year (2 Chr 36:10), probably in the month of Nisan of Nebuchadnezzar's eighth year (2 Kgs 24:12), that is, mid-April, 597 BCE. While for Jehoiachin this event meant the end of his tenure as king of Judah, for Ezekiel it had personal and professional significance. It meant the end of his professional dreams—or so he will have thought, until 593 BCE, when YHWH called him to prophetic priestly service (Ezek 1:4—3:27).[12] The purpose of this essay is not to clarify all the issues related to the tenure and life of Jehoiachin, but to inquire what contribution the book of Ezekiel might make to that picture.

JEHOIACHIN'S NAME AND TITLE

The name Jehoiachin appears in the book of Ezekiel only in Ezek 1:2. However, since this verse was inserted by a late editor to clarify the enigmatic reference to "the thirtieth year" in verse 1,[13] it contributes little to an understanding of the prophet Ezekiel's disposition toward Jehoiachin. But since it is clearly part of the Ezekielian tradition, it deserves brief comment. The gloss identifies Jehoiachin by title and name: הַמֶּלֶךְ יוֹיָכִין, "the king Jehoiachin." Within this book both elements are extraordinary.

First, as part of Ezekiel's polemic against the historical kings of Judah, especially those who ruled in the nation's waning decades, the prophet rarely uses the word מֶלֶךְ. He prefers to identify Israel's past rulers as נְשִׂיאִים, "princes," rather than מְלָכִים, "kings" (see Table 1 above). While opinions on why Ezekiel avoided the term, מֶלֶךְ, when speaking of Israel's kings vary, it seems that in his mind the expression represented independence and arrogance, while נָשִׂיא reflected a more modest status of the rulers as vassals of YHWH.[14] Ezekiel did not have a problem with the monarchic institution in principle, but with the way those who sat on

---

12. Although Ezekiel is generally recognized as the priestly prophet, his role is probably more accurately defined as "prophetic priest."

13. For discussion, see Block, *Ezekiel 1–24*, 85–89.

14. He links נָשִׂיא with עֶבֶד, "servant, vassal," in 34:23–24 and 37:24–25, and refers to past kings as נְשִׂיאַי, "my princes," in 45:8. Ezekiel also recognizes the last kings as vassals of earthly foreign rulers: Zedekiah was a vassal of Nebuchadnezzar (12:10; 17:16 [he was "made king" (הַמְלִךְ) by Nebuchadnezzar]; 21:30[25]); Jehoiakim was a vassal of the king of Egypt (19:4–9). However, 17:16 cautions against overstating the distinction. If נָשִׂיא actually bears a stronger nuance of vassalage, Ezekiel would more naturally have used הִשִּׂיא, "to install, set up," as prince. Cf. 1 Kgs 11:34, where YHWH says, כִּי נָשִׂיא אֲשִׁתֶנּוּ כֹּל יְמֵי חַיָּיו, "For I will make him prince all the days of his life."

the throne of David exercised their power. Within Ezekiel's theocratic perspective, YHWH was Israel's real king, and the occupants of the throne, the descendants of David, were his vassals. However, because they had historically acted contrary to the divine will (Deut 17:14–20) and "done the evil (הָרַע) in the eyes of YHWH,"[15] Israel's kings did not deserve the title מֶלֶךְ.[16]

It is somewhat ironical that the person responsible for this note should have referred to Jehoiachin as מֶלֶךְ, not only because the prophet was hesitant to honor any of the Judahite kings with this title, but especially because he occupied the throne a mere one hundred days.[17] This was scarcely long enough to get used to the crown. We do not know when the editor of the book of Ezekiel added this note, but calling him הַמֶּלֶךְ, "the king," even though he had been removed from the throne and ignominiously exiled from his capital and his land alike, agrees with the indigenous Babylonian ration list mentioned above. Although this administrative text is short, it identifies Jehoiachin as *šar*, "king," five times, at least four of which read more fully, "king of Judah" (*šar* ^mat^*Ia-a-ḫu-du/Ia-ku-du*).[18]

Second, it is surprising that Jehoiachin's name should appear at all. The present form of the name, יוֹיָכִן, occurs only here. Elsewhere it appears as יְהוֹיָכִין,[19] יְכָנְיָהוּ (Jer 24:1), יְכָנְיָה,[20] and כָּנְיָהוּ.[21] All are variations of the sentence name meaning "YHWH has established."[22] In contrast to Jeremiah,

---

15. Although Ezekiel never uses the expression, his colleague Jeremiah does (52:2), and the deuteronomistic historian uses it at least eighteen times (1 Kgs 15:26, 34; 22:53; 2 Kgs 8:18, 27; 13:2; 14:24; 15:9, 18, 24, 28; 17:2; 21:2, 20; 23:32, 37; 24:9, 19 (cf. 2 Chr 21:6; 22:4; 33:2, 22; 36:5, 9, 12).

16. For further discussion, see Block, "Transformation of Royal Ideology," 208–46 (reprinted above, pp. 11–13).

17. According to 2 Chr 36:9 "Jehoiachin was eight years old when he began to reign; he reigned three months and ten days in Jerusalem." 2 Kings 24:8 rounds off his reign to three months.

18. In the fifth he is identified as *ya-ku-ú-ki-nu mār šarri ša ya-ku-du*, which Weidner ("Jojachin," 926) deemed a scribal error.

19. 2 Kgs 24:6, 8, 12, 15; 25:27; 2 Chr 36:8–9; Jer 52:31.

20. 1 Chr 3:16–17; Esth 2:6; Jer 27:20; 28:4; 29:2.

21. Jer 22:24, 28; 37:1; Lachish Letter 3:15 (perhaps Arad 49:4).

22. Noth, *Die israelitische Personennamen*, 202; Fowler, *Theophoric Personal Names*, 98. The name appears in Akkadian as *Ia-'-ú-kin*. LXX renders it either as Ιεχονια/Ιεχονιας/αν/ου (1 Chr 3:16–17; 2 Chr 36:8–9; Jer 22:24, 28; 24:1; 27:20 [LXX 34:20]; 29:2 [LXX 36:2]; 35:4 [28:4]; Esth 1:1) or Ιωακιμ (2 Kgs 24:6, 8, 12, 15; 2 Kgs 25:27; Jer 37:1 [LXX 44:1]; 52:31; Ezek 1:2). In the New Testament, Matt 1:11–12 reads Ιεχονίας/ν.

who identifies his royal contemporaries by name 100 times, and earlier kings more than twenty times,[23] Ezekiel never mentions a historical king by name. To be sure, David's name occurs four times (34:23, 24; 37:24, 25), but in each instance the prophet has in mind a future king, who will be installed by YHWH and will serve the nation as shepherd and as a symbol of their unity. The only monarch the prophet identifies by name is Nebuchadnezzar, a foreigner.[24]

It is difficult to assess the significance of these details added by the editor in Ezek 1:2–3. It may reflect his own respect for Jehoiachin, or perhaps he has captured the hope the name represents for the prophet.

JEHOIACHIN'S STORY

Before we explore Ezekiel's disposition toward Jehoiachin, we need to establish the historical context within which the prophet offers his assessment of this monarch. From elsewhere we learn that Jehoiachin was the son of Jehoiakim, and grandson of Josiah. Jehoiakim (originally Eliakim) had been seated on the throne in Jerusalem in place of his father Jehoahaz, by Pharaoh Neco in 609 BCE.[25] Within a little more than a decade after Josiah's death, the Judaeans would see four different kings succeed each other in rapid succession. Jehoahaz (609) was installed as king by the people, but ruled a scant three months before he was removed and taken to Egypt by Pharaoh Neco (2 Kgs 23:30–33; 2 Chr 36:1–3). Jehoiakim (609–597) was installed in his place as a puppet of the Egyptians (2 Kgs 23:34—24:7; 2 Chr 36:4–8). After defeating the Egyptians at Carchemish in Jehoiakim's fourth year (605), the Babylonian forces under Nebuchadnezzar appeared for the first time in the Levant (Hamath). However, upon word of the death of his father, Nebuchadnezzar hurried home to claim the throne. He returned the next year asserting control over Samaria and the coastal region as far as Ashkelon. Jehoiakim's response to Nebuchadnezzar's arrival on his doorstep is unclear. The narrative provided in Jer 36 suggests a fast was proclaimed, presumably to plead with YHWH to ward off the Babylonians, but Jehoiakim rejected the response that YHWH sent through his prophet Jeremiah. Apparently within a year or two the

23. His contemporaries: Josiah (18x), Jehoahaz (1x, as Shallum, 22:11), Jehoiakim (22x), Jehoiachin (10x, also as Coniah and Jeconiah), Zedekiah (49x); earlier kings, David (14x), Solomon (1x), Hezekiah (3x), Manasseh (1x), Amon (2x).

24. Ezek 26:7; 29:18, 19; 30:10.

25. All dates given are based on Galil, *Chronology of the Kings of Israel*, 108–26.

Babylonians were able to establish control over Jerusalem. The Egyptians and Babylonians resumed their hostilities in 601/600 BCE, and Jehoiakim made the fatal mistake of allying with the Egyptians.[26] Nebuchadnezzar responded by besieging Jerusalem and capturing Jehoiakim, who apparently died as they were preparing to take him away to Babylon (cf. 2 Kgs 24:2–6; 2 Chr 36:5–8).[27] In his place Nebuchadnezzar installed Jehoiachin.

Jehoiachin ruled long enough for the biblical narrator to be able to characterize his reign as "doing the evil in the sight of YHWH," his divine Sovereign, just as his father had done (2 Kgs 24:9; 2 Chr 36:9), and for Nebuchadnezzar to punish him for his misconduct. According to the Babylonian Chronicle cited above, the siege of Jerusalem began in the late fall (Babylonian Kislev = late November to early December) and lasted through Ṭebet and Šebat. Jerusalem surrendered and Jehoaichin was captured on 2 Adar, which is 2 Nisan in the calendar of Judah, the second day of the new year (Esth 3:7). Counting back three months and ten days (2 Chr 36:9) from 2 Adar, brings us into the month of Kislev, which suggests that Jehoiakim was captured at the beginning of this siege. Nebuchadnezzar appears to have installed Jehoiachin as his puppet in the hopes that Jerusalem would accept his overlordship—which apparently proved false. The correlation of these dates also means that Jerusalem was under siege throughout Jehoiachin's tenure as king. Had Jehoiachin cooperated, the siege would surely have been lifted. Apparently he did not submit to his Babylonian overlord, and 100 days into his reign Nebuchadnezzar had had enough. When he arrived in Jerusalem, Jehoiachin surrendered and Nebuchadnezzar sent him to Babylon, where he would spend the rest of his life, and apparently be buried.[28]

But what does Ezekiel the prophet make of this man? I shall explore the question by considering Ezekiel's disposition toward Jehoiachin's past, and his disposition toward his future.

---

26. Josephus (*Ant.* 10.6.2) suggests Jehoiakim stopped paying tribute to Babylon. For discussion of the relationship between the Babylonians and Judah between Nebuchadnezzar's invasions of the latter in 605/604, 601/602, and 598/597, see Lipschits, "Babylonian Domination," 36–67; Albertz, *Israel in Exile*, 45–69.

27. On which, see Lipschits, "'Jehoiakim Slept with his Fathers . . .'" 1–33; Seitz, *Theology in* Conflict, 105–20.

28. This reconstruction is admittedly speculative. Jehoiachin's only recorded actions involve "doing the evil in the sight of YHWH" (2 Kgs 24:9; 2 Chr 36:9)—which involves rebellion against YHWH—and "he 'went out' (אֵצֵ֤) to the king of Babylon," along with his mother and his courtiers, commanders, and officers (2 Kgs 24:12).

EZEKIEL'S VIEW OF JEHOIACHIN'S PAST

Jehoiachin in Ezekiel's Date Notices

Although the historian of 2 Kgs 24:14–16 does not mention priests among the thousands of professional and skilled men whom Nebuchadnezzar deported to Babylon, the narrative of Jer 29:1–2 lists elders, priests, and prophets, along with the king and his court, artisans, and smiths. Ezekiel was not yet ordained to the priestly ministry, but as an exiled member of the priestly clan he shared with Jehoiachin the stress and ignominy of deportation. In both 33:21 and 40:1, Ezekiel employs the expression that the editor responsible for Ezek 1:2 used to refer to Jehoiachin's exile (גָּלוּת) in first person, dating significant events expressly to "our exile" (גָּלוּתֵנוּ).[29] These notes contribute to the profoundly autobiographical character of the book and explain in part why Ezekiel's date notices break from the normal convention of dating events according to the year of the reigning monarch.[30] At the same time, they reinforce the impression of Ezekiel's contempt for Zedekiah,[31] while hinting at the significance of Jehoiachin's exile for the Davidic house. However, Ezekiel never suggests that Jehoiachin's spiritual disposition changed from the assessment offered by Israel's historians (2 Kgs 24:9; 2 Chr 36:9).[32]

29. Cognates to גָּלוּת occur elsewhere in the book. גּוֹלָה is used for the "exile" itself (Ezek 12:3–4, 7, 11; 25:3), while הַגּוֹלָה occasionally refers to the community of exiles (Ezek 1:1; 3:11, 15; 11:24–25). The verb גָּלָה (qal) is used in the sense of "to go into exile" (12:3; 39:23, qal), and הִגְלָה (hiphil) for "to send into exile" (39:28).

30. Ezekiel 24:1–2 is the exception that proves the rule. Here treating the exile of Jehoiachin (and Ezekiel) as the *terminus a quo* creates impossible chronological problems with the other date notices in the book, but particularly 33:21–22. The similarities between this date notice and 2 Kgs 25:1 (= Jer 52:4) suggest the editor of Ezekiel's oracles may have tried to highlight the significance of this date by following the official paradigm for date notices. See further Block, *Ezekiel 1–25*, 772–74; Galil, *Chronology*, 110–11.

31. For full discussion of Ezekiel's disposition toward Zedekiah, see Lang, *Kein Aufstand*.

32. Although Jeremiah pronounces woe on Jehoiachin in Jer 22:24–30, he does not explicitly charge him with any crimes. The closest he comes is to mention his dread of Nebuchadnezzar (v. 25).

Jehoiachin in Ezekiel's Riddle of the Cedar Sprig (17:3–4, 22a)

Apart from allusions to Jehoiachin's exile in the date notices, the exiled king is the subject of two of Ezekiel's prophecies, the riddle of chapter 17 and the dirge of chapter 19. No text illustrates Ezekiel's ambivalence toward Israel's monarchy as dramatically as his metaphoric riddle in chapter 17.[33] The chapter has a curious structure, involving a two-part riddle followed by a two-part interpretation. Based on the subject matter, the four parts exhibit the following chiastic arrangement:

A The Riddle of the Cedar Sprig (vv. 3–4)
  B The Riddle of the Vine (vv. 5–10)
  B' The Interpretation of the Riddle of the Vine (vv. 11–21)
A' The Interpretation of the Riddle of the Cedar Sprig (vv. 22–24)

Although the chapter actually involves two riddles that appear together, the interpretation of the second riddle follows immediately after the riddle itself, as we would expect, but the interpretation of the first is oddly delayed until the end. Technically, only the first short segment and verse 22 pertains to Jehoiachin. The remainder of the interpretation concerns a future far beyond him.

Although Jehoiachin is Ezekiel's main concern in the first segment, the primary character in the first phase of this extended and complex metaphor is a great eagle (v. 3). Throughout the ancient world eagles served both as a positive symbols of strength (Isa 40:31) and royal splendor,[34] but also as a fearful symbols of terror. Esarhaddon's boast, "Like a furious eagle I spread my pinions to destroy my enemies,"[35] illuminates the meaning of Hosea's reference to the Assyrian hordes as "an eagle coming against the house of YHWH" (Hos 8:1). Ezekiel's nearer predecessor, Habakkuk, had described the Babylonians as "an eagle swooping down to devour" (1:8).[36] But this eagle is different: he is cast as a genuinely benevolent figure, plucking off a sprig of a cedar (that is about to be cut down?), taking it away to Babylon, and planting it there, apparently in very favorable circumstances.

---

33. The opening line indicates the genre of the text: חוּד חִידָה וּמְשֹׁל מָשָׁל, "Compose a riddle and make up a fable."

34. With Sennacherib's reference to the eagle as "the prince of the birds" (Luckenbill, *Annals of Sennacherib*, 36), compare Pindar's "king of the birds" (*Olympian Odes* 13.21).

35. Borger, *Inschriften Asarhaddons*, §44. Cf. also §65.

36. Cf. also Deut 28:49; Jer 4:13; 48:40; 49:22; Lam 4:19; and the reduction of Nebuchadnezzar to the level of the symbol of his pride in Dan 4:30–33.

While it is obvious the prophet is speaking of a particular and special bird, it may not have been so obvious to Ezekiel's audience whom this eagle represented. Could this be YHWH, who both narrative and hymnic tradition says had carried Israel on his eagle's wings and brought them to himself (Exod 19:4; cf. Deut 32:11)?[37] Or was this some human monarch? In addition to serving as a symbol of strength and terror, in the ancient Near East the eagle was a common military and royal symbol, being attested on ensigns as early as the Old Babylonian city of Lagash and as late as the Persian and Roman periods.[38] Kings were often portrayed as cherub-like figures with eagle's wings.[39]

By having the great eagle fly to Lebanon, where he plucked off the top of a cedar, Ezekiel has adapted and transformed a stock phrase, "cedars of Lebanon."[40] The association of these cedars with the royal constructions in Jerusalem[41] encourages a connection with the dynasty. However, in an act quite uncharacteristic of eagles, the magnificent bird snipped off the "crown"[42] and carried the shoot of fresh growth[43] off to a foreign land, identified enigmatically as a "land of merchants" (אֶרֶץ כְּנַעַן) and a "city of traders" (עִיר רֹכְלִים). On first hearing, one's impulse is to associate these expressions with Israel's native land, to which the former expression always refers outside this book[44] and which from earliest times was associated

37. These texts are reminiscent of the Etana Legend in which the shepherd Etana is carried to heaven on the wings of an eagle. Cf. ANET, 114–18, esp. 118; Dalley, *Myths from Mesopotamia*, 189–202.

38. See Lang, *Kein Aufstand*, 33–38.

39. Compare the description of the King of Tyre as a cherub in 28:14.

40. Judg 9:15; Isa 2:13; 14:8; Ps 29:5; 104:16; cf. 1 Kgs 5:12[14]; Isa 37:24, "the cedar in Lebanon" (Ezek 31:3 [cf. vv. 15–16]; Ps 92:13; cf. 1 Kgs 5:13[4:33]; 2 Kgs 14:9), "the cedar from Lebanon" (Ezek 27:5; cf. Ezra 3:7). Cf. also the paralleling of "Lebanon" and "cedars" in Jer 2:23; Zech 11:1; Cant 5:15. References to foreigners importing cedar lumber from Lebanon are common: Israel (1 Kgs 5:22–28[8–14]; 2 Chr 2:7–15; Cant 3:9); Egypt (*ANET*, 243), Assyria (Isa 37:24), Babylon (*ANET*, 307).

41. One of Solomon's royal buildings was called "the house of the forest of Lebanon" (1 Kgs 7:2).

42. The expression צַמֶּרֶת, "crown," occurs only in Ezekiel. Here and in verse 22 it is paralleled with רֹאשׁ, "peak." In 31:3, 10, 14 the צַמֶּרֶת צָמָר of the tree is very high, reaching into the clouds. The form, derived from צֶמֶר, "wool," may have been suggested by the woolly appearance of clouds around the treetops. Cf. the place name Zemaraim, "twin peaks" (?) in Josh 18:22.

43. The parallel expression רֹאשׁ יְנִיקוֹתָיו (from יָנַק, "to suck") concretizes the image of צַמֶּרֶת by referring to the fresh growth of the evergreen, which is still tender and easily plucked off by a bird.

44. Gen 17:8; 45:25; Exod 6:4; 16:35; Lev 14:34; 18:3; 25:38; Num 13:2, 17; 32:32;

with cities.[45] Situated between the anchors of the Fertile Crescent, with Egypt to the south and Aramaeans, Hittites, Assyrians, and Babylonians to the north and east, occupants of the land of Canaan played an important mercantile role.[46] By this interpretation the benevolence of the great eagle is obvious: he takes the sprig and plants it back in the homeland. Although the identification of Babylon with Lebanon is a stretch, if those in Ezekiel's audience connected the sprig with Jehoiachin and the eagle with Nebuchadnezzar, as in the case of his sign act in chapter 12, some may have interpreted the riddle positively as a prediction of Jehoiachin's [and their own] imminent return to the homeland.

However, there can be no doubt about the true referent in אֶרֶץ כְּנַעַן and a עִיר רֹכְלִים, since the prophet has previously glossed אֶרֶץ כְּנַעַן with כַּשְׂדִּים, "Chaldeans," that is, "Babylonia" (16:19).[47] Given Babylon's location on the Euphrates, this city probably played a significant mercantile role in ancient Mesopotamia. Even so, for Jehoiachin and Ezekiel and his immediate audience Babylon was the land of exile. What sense does he intend for "land of merchants" and "city of traders?" Since a city is by definition a dwelling or group of buildings surrounded by defensive walls for the protection of the residents, in contrast to the fields out there where crops and vineyards are planted, the purpose of bringing the sprig to this city presumably was to protect it, as merchants protect their goods in warehouses within the walls of the city. In any case, both the image of the bird and his actions are painted in positive noble strokes, in stark contrast to the second eagle (Egypt) and the vine (Zedekiah) in verses 5–21.

As already observed, unlike the central core of this chapter, which consists of a second metaphor (vv. 5–10) and then follows this up immediately with an interpretation (vv. 11–21), the opening scene lacks an interpretation, leaving the reader to ponder over its significance—until the coda in verses 22–24. While many delete the coda as a post-exilic

---

33:51; 34:2; Deut 32:49; Josh 5:12; 22:11, 32; 24:3; 1 Chr 16:18; Ps 105:11.

45. Num 13:19, 28; Deut 1:22; 6:10; 9:1; 20:16; Josh 10:2, 19, 20; 11:12–14, 21, etc.

46. The mercantile significance of כְּנַעַן is most obvious in Hos 12:8 and Zeph 1:11, but the gentilic כְּנַעֲנִי means "traders" in Prov 31:24; Isa 23:8; and Zech 14:21. On רכל, meaning "traders, vendors," see 1 Kgs 10:15; Ezek 27:2, 13, 15, 17, 20, 22–24; Nah 3:16; Cant 3:6; Neh 3:31–32; and 13:20. Ezekiel capitalizes on this role for his metaphorical portrayal of Tyre as a merchant ship in Ezek 27. The Tyrians and the rest of the Phoenicians represented all that remained of the original Canaanites.

47. Ezekiel uses the word כַּשְׂדִּים as a toponym elsewhere in Ezek 11:24; 23:16, and in a gentilic sense ("Chaldaeans") in Ezek 1:3; 12:13; 23:14–15.

insertion,[48] without it the riddle of verses 3–4 remains unresolved. Like the interpretation of the riddle concerning the vine, verses 22–24 declare that behind the actions of the magnificent eagle we are to see the actions of YHWH. Ultimately he is the one who plucks a shoot from the top of the cedar, and sets it (in a secure place), until the time is right to retrieve it and plant it on a high and lofty mountain.

But whom does this sprig, this foremost of the fresh young twigs of the cedar (רֹאשׁ יְנִיקוֹת) represent? If the cedar represents the Davidic dynasty, the freshness of the sprig suggests either a youthful king or one whose tenure was cut off before his reign could be established and mature, that is, shortly after assuming the throne.[49] These qualifications could apply either to Jehoahaz, the twenty-three year old son of Josiah who reigned only three months before he was taken away to Egypt (2 Kgs 23:31–34), or to Jehoiachin, the eighteen-year-old son of Jehoiakim, who also reigned only three months before he was taken away to Babylon (2 Kgs 24:8–16). However, since Ezekiel's interpretation of the riddle of the vine identifies the magnificent eagle with the king of Babylon, expressly declaring that he came to Jerusalem and took its king (and the princes) back to Babylon, the sprig obviously refers to Jehoiachin. We cannot fully establish the significance of his transplant to Babylon until we have considered the rest of the coda. For the moment, we note simply that, contra 2 Kgs 24:9 and 2 Chr 36:9,[50] so far this riddle has not suggested a negative reason for his removal from the cedar and his deportation to Babylon. On the contrary, the reference to "the land of merchants" and the "city of traders" opens the door for a beneficent rather than punitive purpose.[51]

---

48. For a defense of its inclusion see Block, *Ezekiel 1–24*, 549–50.

49 Compare the characterization of the sprig as רַךְ, "tender," in verse 22 with Prov 4:3–4, "When I was a son with my father, tender (רַךְ), and my mother's favorite, he taught me and said to me, 'Let your heart hold fast my words; keep my commands, and live.'"

50. Both texts declare that Jehoiachin "committed the evil in the eyes of YHWH." This dim view of Jehoiachin is also shared by Jeremiah (Jer 22:24–30). On the other hand, if our identification of the first branch of 19:10–13 with Jehoiachin is correct, then even in Ezekiel's mind Jehoiachin is implicated in the pervasive hubris of the Davidic house and punished for this arrogance by destruction by fire.

51. According to 2 Kgs 25:27–30, Nebuchadnezzar's successor Evil-Merodach also had a favorable view of Jehoiachin.

Jehoiachin in Ezekiel's Dirge over the Vine (Ezekiel 19:10–14)

Ezekiel's second oracle involving Jehoiachin is part of a larger literary unit concerning the last kings of Judah in chapter 19. Unlike the metaphorical riddle in chapter 17, the decipherment of the images in this text is complicated by the absence of an interpretation.[52] The preamble to chapter 19 identifies this text as a dirge,[53] but in reality it also exhibits features found in riddles (חִידָה; cf. 17:2) and parodies.[54] Ezekiel has taken the form of a קִינָה and infused it with alien content. This is not only a funeral song, but also a riddle that deals enigmatically with a living reality—the fate of the Davidic dynasty.

The preamble to the dirge announces that this oracle concerns the princes (נְשִׂיאִים) of Israel generally. The dirge itself concerns a pride of lions, specifically a mother lioness and two of her cubs. But whom do these lions represent? More precisely, what is the lioness?[55] One's first impulse is to identify the lioness as Hamutal, the wife of Josiah and mother of Jehoahaz and Zedekiah (2 Kgs 23:31; 24:18). However, this interpretation is excluded by the portrayal of her second cub in verses 5–9, which most identify as Jehoiakim, who is identified elsewhere as the son of Zebidah, the daughter of Pedaiah of Rumah (2 Kgs 23:36). Perhaps the lioness functions symbolically for Judah or the Davidic dynasty,[56] but then Ezekiel should have used the masculine, לָבִיא. The choice of the feminine, לְבִיָּא, suggests the referent must be feminine, probably Jerusalem, which, like other geographic names, is consistently identified as feminine in the

---

52. The secularity of this dirge is striking; YHWH is not mentioned at all, not even in the preamble. For fuller discussion of the dirge's portrayal of Jehoahaz and Jehoiakim, see Block, "Transformation of Royal Ideology," 215–20; reprinted above, pp. 10–42.

53. Hebrew קִינָה is a technical term for a special kind of musical composition, composed and sung at the death of an individual (2 Sam 1:17; Amos 5:1; 2 Chr 35:25; Jer 7:29; 9:9 [10]). The fact that ten of the eighteen occurrences of the word in the Old Testament are found in Ezekiel reflects the general tone of his ministry. Petter (*Ezekiel and Mesopotamian City Laments*) has argued recently that Ezekiel's usage of the lament genre provides the key to the themes and structure of the book. Outside this text, קִינָה identifies dirges over the falls of both Tyre (26:7) and its king (27:2, 32; 28:12), as well as both Egypt (32:16) and the Pharaoh (32:2).

54. Yee ("Anatomy of Biblical Parody," 565) defines a parody as "the literary imitation of an established form or style."

55. Note the form of the opening question and its answer: מָה אִמְּךָ לְבִיָּא, "What is your mother? A lioness!"

56. This was our interpretation in *Ezekiel 1–24*, 604.

book.[57] If this is correct, Ezekiel minimizes their genealogical participation in the dynasty of David and highlights their geographical location.

The first of the lioness' two cubs (vv. 3–4) obviously refers to Jehoahaz, the immediate successor to Josiah, since he was the only king of Judah taken to Egypt (2 Kgs 23:34). Although Jehoahaz reigned only for three months, it was long enough for the deuteronomistic historian to characterize him as one "who did the evil in the sight of YHWH" (i.e., defection from YHWH to other gods) just as his predecessors had done (2 Kgs 23:31b).[58] In Ezekiel's view, Jehoahaz was a violent ruler, who developed a particular appetite for human flesh. His notoriety spread quickly to the surrounding nations, who combined forces to capture him and drag him off with hooks to Egypt. Ezekiel is silent on why this upstart lion was taken to Egypt, but the geographic reference offers the first concrete clue to the human behind the symbol.[59]

Though some suggest that Ezek 18:10–13 applies to Jehoiakim,[60] in our view the second part of this dirge (vv. 5–9) contains the clearest reference in Ezekiel to this king, the son of Josiah by a second wife, Zebidah (2 Kgs 23:36). Scholars have identified the second lion variously as Jehoiakim, Jehoiachin, and Zedekiah,[61] or as a combination/fusion of Jehoiakim and Zedekiah.[62] On balance, Jehoiakim is the strongest candidate,[63] though for rhetorical reasons Ezekiel seems to play loose and free with the historical record, especially with the origins and the end of his reign. Nevertheless, within Ezekiel's lifetime, Jehoiakim ruled tyrannically like this lion, ruthlessly exploiting his people for selfish ends, until he was captured by the Babylonians.[64]

57. So also Odell, *Ezekiel*, 237–39.

58. Jeremiah has a short note on Jehoahaz (Shallum, Jer 22:10–12), but he adds nothing to the picture.

59. Cf. Jeremiah's vague reference to Shallum being taken captive and dying in the land of his captors.

60. See Laato, *Josiah and David Redivivus*, 172–74.

61. For discussion of the merits of each candidate see Block, *Ezekiel 1–24*, 604–6; Begg, "Identity of the Princes," 358–65.

62. See further Begg, "Identity of the Princes," 364. Greenberg (*Ezekiel 1–20*, 355–56) treats verses 5–9 as a composite portrait, but does not identify the kings.

63. Two recent commentators have gone separate ways on this issue: Darr, "The Book of Ezekiel," 1270, follows our approach; Odell (*Ezekiel*, 235–36) is non-committal.

64. According to the dirge this lion was captured by a hunter and taken to the king of Babylon to stifle his roaring on the mountains of Israel. But the picture of the lion devouring human prey, laying waste the landscape, and terrifying the inhabitants with

Without warning, in verse 10 the subject of the dirge changes from a zoological metaphor (a pride of lions) to a horticultural figure (a vine). The interpretation of verses 10–14 is complicated by numerous textual problems, further disintegration of the *qînâ* meter, and the less obvious correlation with historical events. Nevertheless, this dirge displays important links with the preceding on at least four counts: (1) its secular fable tone, without any reference to God; (2) its portrayal of the primary figure (lioness, vine) as the mother (אִמֶּךָ) of the secondary figures (cubs, branches); (3) its focus on a pair of kings, in this instance Jehoiachin (vv. 10–13) and Zedekiah (v. 14);[65] (4) its echoes of Jacob's oracle concerning Judah in Gen 49:8–12.[66]

Exhibiting strong lexical links with chapter 17, verses 10–14 describe an extra-ordinary plant, planted beside abundant waters (מַיִם רַבִּים) and producing fine fruit and thick foliage. It sent out special kinds of branches: מַטּוֹת עֹז, "strong staves," and שִׁבְטֵי מֹשְׁלִים, "scepters of rulers," which represent "the official insignia of a tribal chieftain."[67] Its crown reached high into the clouds and could be seen for miles around. However, it was uprooted, dried up, and burned. Whereas vines normally grow near the ground (cf. 17:6), this plant is a monstrosity, sending its profusion of branches into the sky. If Ezekiel's audience had linked this image with the riddle of chapter 17, they might have interpreted its wild growth as a representation of hubris, which is answered by divine judgment.

Despite the links with 17:1–10, an important shift in the symbolic significance of the vine is evident. Whereas the previous plant had represented an individual king (Zedekiah), in this instance, the vine (mother) represents either the tribe/nation of Judah, from which more than one

---

his roaring accords with the image of Jehoiakim's oppressive rule as painted by the Jeremiah (Jer 22:13–23). And when Ezekiel describes the exploitative and self-serving character of past rulers in 34:2b–6, the freshest illustration in his mind will have been Jehoiakim. See further my discussion in *Ezekiel 1–24*, 604–6.

65. Cf. Block, *Ezekiel 1–24*, 609–10; similarly Begg, "Identity of the Princes," 367–69, though he suggests the shift from Jehoiachin to Zedekiah occurs between verses 12 and 13. Darr ("Ezekiel," 1273) follows Begg, but her interpretation rests on a misreading of וְעַתָּה, "And now," as וְאַתָּה, which she renders as "but it/she" (instead, read "but you").

66. For further discussion, see Botha, "Socio-Cultural Background," 249–65, esp. 256.

67. Thus Milgrom, *Numbers*, 143, on Aaron's rod (Num 17:16–26[1–11]). Ezekiel's reference is reminiscent of Jer 48:17, which pairs מַטּוֹת עֹז, "a mighty scepter," with מַקֵּל תִּפְאָרָה, "a magnificent rod." Psalm 110:2 links the same expression with the Davidic dynasty.

ruler sprouts, or the city of Jerusalem, since Ezekiel portrays the גֶּפֶן as feminine and the vine as the "mother" of its branches.[68] But she has abandoned her natural function as a producer of grapes and assumed the posture of a huge tree, a symbol of the arrogance of the nations.[69] In this story, the self-aggrandizement provokes the wrath of YHWH, who punishes her by uprooting and humiliating her, subjecting her to the east wind (the Babylonians), and transplanting her in a foreign land. By this interpretation, this segment of the dirge indicts not only Judah's kings, but also Jerusalem herself and the nation she represents.

It seems best to interpret the strong branches of this part of the dirge as a figure for the Davidic dynasty, the succession of royal rulers who have sprouted from the tribe of Judah in Jerusalem, with the מַטּוֹת, "staves," that serve as שִׁבְטֵי מֹשְׁלִים, "scepters of rulers," representing not one but two kings. The first, Jehoiachin, was torn off, withered and burned (removed from the throne), and then transplanted with the vine in the desert. וְעַתָּה, "But, nevertheless," in verse 13 introduces a contrastive and parenthetical situation.[70] The strong branch (the dynasty) has been uprooted, hurled to the ground, dried up, and burned (vv. 11–12); "nevertheless it is planted (שְׁתוּלָה) in the desert, in a dry and thirsty land." But how can a branch that has been burned be planted? Only if a twig has been cut off before it withered. This statement corresponds to 17:5: "He brought it [the topmost shoot of the cedar] to a land of merchants; in the city of traders he set it." In contrast to the idealized image of Jehoiachin's exile painted in chapter 17, now Ezekiel's portrayal is more realistic. Planting a twig in the desert raises questions of viability. Will it flourish? Whereas Ezekiel had asked this question explicitly with reference to the vine in 17:9–10 and given an emphatically negative response in 17:11–21, here the query remains unanswered. Instead, in 19:14 he returns to the image of the burned up strong branch: it was completely consumed, without a branch, let alone scepter, surviving—a reference to Zedekiah's end.

By this interpretation the two dirges involving lions and branches of a vine present the last four kings of Judah according to their historical order: Jehoahaz, Jehoiakim, Jehoiachin, and Zedekiah.[71] If this understanding of verses 10–14 is correct, then, in contrast to Ezekiel's portrayal of the sprig in 17:3–4, 22, the prophet is here less committal about the fate

---

68. Thus Odell, *Ezekiel*, 240–41. Compare Israel's portrayal as a vine in chapter 15.

69. Cf. the portrayal of Assyria and Egypt as huge cedars in chapter 31.

70. Cf. *DCH*, 6.638, §11n (16).

71. So also Begg, "Identity of the Princes," 366–69.

of the dynasty than he was in the earlier text. While Jehoiachin's removal to the desert raises questions of his viability, the fact that this branch has been planted gives reason for hope for the dynasty. However, again in contrast to chapter 17, Ezekiel does not develop this motif here. His rhetorical point is that in the face of the Babylonian threat neither those who remain behind in Jerusalem nor the exiles in Babylon may look to the Davidic ruler on the throne as a symbol of security for Judah and Jerusalem. Both nation and dynasty are doomed.

JEHOIACHIN'S FUTURE IN EZEKIEL

If Ezekiel's discussion of Jehoiachin's past is veiled in metaphorical imagery, the prophet's vision of the deposed and deported monarch's future is even less clear. Of course, this is not surprising, since the future can never be seen with the clarity with which one sees the past—not even by a prophet. Ezekiel's sign act recorded in Ezek 12:1–7 might initially have given hope to the exiles who apparently continued to view Jehoiachin as their king. In full view of the people, the prophet packed his knapsack, dug a hole in the wall of his house, and crawled out through it. With their reader-response hermeneutic, some in his primary audience probably interpreted this as a symbolic act predicting his (and their own) imminent return to Jerusalem. But Ezekiel dashed these hopes with the divine interpretation, which went in a completely different direction. The rhetorical aim of this piece of "street theater"[72] is to dash the Judaeans' hope for rescue from the Babylonian threat, a hope that is based on the presence of a descendant of David on the throne in Jerusalem (2 Sam 7). Ezekiel had represented the prince (הַנָּשִׂיא) and his countrymen who remain behind in Jerusalem. Rather than anticipating Jehoiachin's release, it predicts Zedekiah's capture. Not only will the king himself perish, but through YHWH's agent, Nebuchadnezzar, and his three-fold weapons—sword, famine, pestilence (v. 16)—YHWH himself will destroy the nation, in fulfillment of the covenant curses in Leviticus 26 and Deuteronomy 28. The oracle makes clear that the king is actually the target of YHWH's hunt (v. 13; cf. 17:19–21).

If there is no hope for Zedekiah, what prospects could there be for Jehoiachin? Ezekiel answers this question in the coda added to his riddle concerning the cedar sprig in 17:22–24. Paul Joyce rightly observes that this is the third of only four declarations of hope in the first twenty-four

72. Lang, "Street Theater," 307, characterizes Ezekiel's sign acts as "one-man street theater."

chapters.[73] Our earlier discussion of the riddle of the plants and the eagles had focused on verses 3–4, which had the magnificent eagle (Nebuchadnezzar) plucking off one of the topmost twigs (רֹאשׁ יְנִיקוֹת) and taking it to the land of merchants, the city of traders (Babylon). Ezekiel did not specify the eagle's purpose in transporting the sprig, though we interpreted this as a benevolent act that results in the sprig's preservation. The interpretation the coda provides for the riddle (vv. 22–24) confirms this conclusion.

Several features of the coda deserve comment. First, now Ezekiel portrays YHWH as the primary mover in the revival of the sprig. Whereas the riddle (vv. 3–4) had focused on the great eagle, who took hold of the top of the cedar, plucked off the highest fresh twig, and brought it to Babylon,[74] the riddle assumes the Babylonians are agents of YHWH. However, the coda has no room for secondary agents, and is emphatic in highlighting YHWH's role. YHWH declares, אֶשְׁתָּלֶנּוּ . . . אֲנִי וְשָׁתַלְתִּי אֲנִי אֶקְטֹף . . . וְנָתַתִּי . . . וְלָקַחְתִּי אָנִי, "I myself will take . . . and I will set . . . I will pluck . . . and I myself will plant . . . I will plant it" (vv. 22–23a). Ultimately, he was responsible for the removal of the sprig from the cedar in verses 3–4 as well. However, the nature of YHWH's action in setting (נָתַן) the sprig is unclear. Apparently this is a shorthand expression for the divine equivalent to the eagle's action in bringing the sprig to the land of merchants and depositing it (שִׂים) it in the city of traders (v. 4), presumably for safekeeping.[75] In any case, this action contrasts with the dry and thirsty desert in which the branch is planted in 19:13.

Second, Ezekiel introduces a new element, a tender sprig (רַךְ). The botanical imagery in verses 22–24 is reminiscent of the language of other prophets, who spoke of the scion who would revive the Davidic line as a חֹטֶר, "shoot," and a נֵצֶר, "branch" (Isa 11:1), or as a צֶמַח, "sprout" (Jer 23:5).[76] However, whereas Isa 11:1 creates an image of a stump that has been cut down as an act of judgment—though because of the irrepressible life of the roots new shoots emerge from the stump—here YHWH snips

73. Joyce, "King and Messiah in Ezekiel," 327. The other passages are 11:14–21, 16:59–63, and 20:4–44.

74. The use of the verb הֵבִיא, "to bring," rather than הוֹלִיךְ, "to take" (2 Kgs 24:15), describes the event from the Babylonian viewpoint (where Ezekiel and the exiles are found).

75. The verbs שִׂים in verse 4 and נָתַן in verse 22 function as virtual synonyms for שָׁתַל, "to transplant." Cf. the actions with respect to the vine (vv. 7, 8) and the sprig at the end (vv. 22, 23), as well as in 19:13.

76. Cf. also Jer 33:15; Zech 3:8; 6:12. These issues are widely discussed. Heskett, *Messianism*; Stromberg, "Root of Jesse" 655–69; Rose, *Zemah and Zerubbabel*.

the sprig from the top, without any reference to judgment. Apparently this is as an act of benevolence, ensuring the survival of a branch of the tree until the judgment has passed.

Although the coda maintains Jehoiachin's identification as "the top-most of its shoots" (רֹאשׁ יְנִיקוֹתָיו, vv. 4, 22), his attention is focused on a tender sprig that grows from the "topmost shoot" that was brought to Babylon and has apparently grown into a cedar in its own right. However, in a second act of planting, YHWH plucks off a sprig "from the very top of the cedar" (צַמֶּרֶת הָאֶרֶז הָרָמָה), which he identifies as רַךְ, "a tender one."[77] It may seem far-fetched at first, but we should consider whether Ezekiel's lexical choice points to a Josianic figure.[78] Some suggest that in 17:22 רַךְ, "tender shoot," serves as a harbinger of the messianic personage whom the prophet will present in greater detail in later salvation oracles.[79] However, Ezekiel's use of this word may also point backward, at least historically, if not literally. The word רַךְ links this text with 2 Kgs 22:19 (= 2 Chr 34:27), where the prophet Huldah acknowledges the tenderness (רַךְ) of King Josiah's heart,[80] demonstrated by his humble contrition before YHWH when he heard the curses written in the Torah. While the books of Kings in their present form obviously did not yet exist at the time of Ezekiel's oracle, undoubtedly written records of the accomplishments of the kings

---

77. Derived from רכך, "to be tender, soft," elsewhere רַךְ is usually used adjectivally, "soft, tender, delicate." Here it is used substantively, "the tender one." For the substantive use of the feminine counterpart, רַכָּה/הָרַכָּה, "tender woman," see Isa 47:1 and Deut 28:56, respectively (//עֲנֻגָּה, "delicate one"). In Job 40:27 רַכּוֹת denotes "soft, gentle words." In Deut 28:56 רֹךְ is used as an abstraction, "delicacy." See further *HALOT*, 1236–37.

78. Josiah is the only person in the Old Testament recognized as totally devoted to YHWH according to the paradigm of Deut 6:4–5. In 2 Kgs 23:25 the narrator asserts that there was no other king in Israel who turned to YHWH "with all his heart/mind (לֵבָב), with all his being (נֶפֶשׁ), and with all his possessions (מְאֹד), according to the entire Torah of Moses."

79. Ezek 34:23–24; 37:24–25. For a discussion of the messianic interpretation, see Laato, *Josiah and David Redivivus*, 162–64. Since LXX omits the word, Vg. offers the earliest versional attestation of an outrightly messianic interpretation. Compare Tg.'s subdued paraphrase: "I myself will bring near a child from the kingdom of the house of David which is likened to the lofty cedar, and I will establish him from among his children's children; I will anoint (ארבי) and establish him by my Memra on a high and exalted mountain." On the non-messianic eschatology of the Targum to Ezekiel, see Levey, "Targum to Ezekiel," 144–45.

80. יַעַן רַךְ־לְבָבְךָ, "because your heart was tender." Although רַךְ לְבָבְכֶם/לֵבָב means "to be fearful, faint-hearted" elsewhere (Deut 20:3; Isa 7:4; Jer 51:51, all associated with יָרֵא; also 2 Chr 13:7), this sense is excluded here.

63

who preceded Zedekiah were available to those interested in reading them.[81] Even if they were not, Josiah's reputation as a pious ruler and his devotion to YHWH were well known.

By embedding chapter 18 between two metaphorical portrayals of Israel's kings in chapters 17 and 19, the compiler and editor of Ezekiel's prophecies has invited readers to consider the three case studies of chapter 18 as allusions to Josiah (vv. 5–9), Jehoiakim (vv. 10–13), and Jehoiachin (vv. 14–20) respectively.[82] By this interpretation Jehoiachin is cast in a remarkably favorable light—in stark contrast to the historian's assessment in 2 Kgs 24:9,[83] and Ezekiel's own portrayal in 19:10–14, where the prophet implicates him in the pervasive hubris of the Davidic house and announces his punishment for it by fire.[84] However, in this context Ezekiel

81. Cf. the concluding comment to the life of Josiah by the chronicler in 2 Chr 35:26–27, "Now the rest of the acts of Josiah and his faithful deeds (חֲסָדָיו) in accordance with what is written in the Torah of YHWH, and his acts, first and last, see, they are written in the Book of the Kings of Israel and Judah." If F. M. Cross is correct that the primary edition of the Deuteronomistic History was composed in Josiah's time in support of the king and his reform (*Canaanite Myth and Hebrew Epic*, 284–85), then Ezekiel could have had access to a written assessment of Josiah as a person and his reign.

82. Thus Zimmerli, *Ezekiel 1*, 72; Laato, *Josiah and David Redivivus*, 162–64. Laato argues (ibid., 358) that the point of chapter 18 in its present context is that Jehoiachin (Jekoniah) remains the legitimate heir to "the Davidic throne (as suggested in Ezek 17:22–24) despite the curse uttered in Jer 22:24–30. Jekoniah is responsible only for what he himself has done not for what his father has done. If he returns to YHWH and does not follow his father's evil acts he will prosper." That the chapter should open with a righteous man (Josiah) followed by a wicked son (Jehoiakim), and a potentially righteous grandson (Jehoiachin) Laato takes as support for his thesis that the redactor of Ezekiel viewed righteous Josiah as a *typos* for the coming Messiah described in 17:22–24. Cf. ibid., 203, 360–61.

83. However, the historian notes that Nebuchadnezzar's successor, Evil-Merodach, viewed Jehoiachin favorably.

84. Jeremiah shares Ezekiel's negative disposition to Josiah's successors, including Jehoiachin. On Jeremiah's disposition toward Jehoiachin, See Laato, *Josiah and David Redivivus*, 94–100; Job, *Jeremiah's Kings*, 79–100. However, my student, Matthew Patton, has called for a more nuanced reading of Jeremiah, noting: (1) In Jer 22:24–30, Jehoiachin is lamented, rather than castigated—in contrast to Jehoiakim, who is explicitly castigated and whose demise is unlamented in the previous verses; Jehoiachin is even compared to a precious seal. (2) Jer 24:1–10 explicitly names Jehoiachin among the exiles who are considered to be "good fruit," in contrast to Zedekiah, who is named among the bad figs. (3) In Jer 27:20–22, YHWH not only promises that the vessels from the temple and the palace that went into exile with Jehoiachin will return, but speaks expressly of visiting (פָּקַד) them, hinting at positive possibilities for Jehoiachin. (4) Jer 52:31–34 is ambiguous, but not lacking in positive features.

is not characterizing Jehoiachin as רַ֫ךְ; nor is he alluding to Jehoiachin's piety. Rather, the expression applies to a sprig that grows from Jehoiachin, presumably a descendant to come. Obviously the topmost twig from the cedar of Lebanon that the great Eagle has brought to "the land of merchants," "the city of traders" (v. 4), has flourished, for it has now grown into a cedar (אֶ֫רֶז) in its own right. Skipping over the sprig's exile in the land of merchants, YHWH takes a tender shoot (רַךְ) from the top of the cedar and plants it on a very high mountain, where it grows into a tall tree and provides a home for every kind of bird.[85] The tree itself is an enigma. On the one hand, it is a stately cedar (אֶ֫רֶז אַדִּיר), but on the other hand, it yields fruit for food and evokes admiration for its magnificence.[86]

Third, with Ezekiel's reference to planting the tree on the high mountain of Israel, and especially its growth into a fruitful and stately tree under which birds of every kind will rest, he adapts a well-known extra-biblical and biblical motif of the cosmic tree. Typically this tree is portrayed as a huge plant with its crown reaching into the heavens and its roots going down to the subterranean streams from which it draws its nourishment.[87] Although cuneiform texts do not discuss the tree, in Assyrian iconography the tree functions as an imperial symbol, representing "the divine order maintained by the king as the representative of the god Aššur, embodied in the winged disk hovering over the tree."[88] It is possible that Ezekiel was introduced to the "cosmic tree" motif for the first time in Babylon,[89] but the present passage may also have been inspired by Isa 11:1–10, where the

---

85. Hebrew כֹּל צִפּוֹר כָּל־כָּנָף, literally, "every bird, every wing," recalls Gen 7:14.

86. The triad of expressions, עָנָף, "boughs," פְּרִי, fruit," and אַדִּיר, "stately, noble," invites comparison with the eagle's intentions for the vine in verse 8, though this is an entirely different type of plant.

87. We should not associate the tree with the "Tree of Life" in a paradisiacal garden. Cf. Wallace, "Tree of Knowledge and Tree of Life," 658. For studies on the tree as a symbol of an ordered world in the face of the threat of death in ancient Near Eastern written and visual sources alike, see Winter, "Lebensbaum," 57–88. See also Gowan, *When Man Becomes God*, 102–6. Cf. also Frese and Gray, "Trees," 27–28; more recently, Walton, *Ancient Near Eastern Thought*, 175–76. On the cosmic tree in this text, see Metzger, "Zeder, Weinstock und Weltenbaum," 197–229; Metzger, "Weltenbaum," 1–34.

88. Parpola, "The Assyrian Tree of Life," 167. As reinforcement for this conclusion, Parpola observes that the king sometimes takes the place of the tree between the winged genies. In these contexts the king represented the realization of the cosmic order in man. He was "a true image of God, the Perfect Man" (ibid., 168).

89. See the more detailed development of the symbol in 31:1–18 (of Egypt); in Daniel 4 the world tree represents Nebuchadnezzar.

elements of a newly sprouted messianic shoot, the mountain of YHWH, and peaceful coexistence with wild animals are all conjoined. Ezekiel's tree is planted on "the high mountain of Israel" (הַר מְרוֹם יִשְׂרָאֵל), a clear allusion to Mount Zion (cf. Isa 2:2–4; Mic 4:1–3). The birds of every kind that nest in the tree symbolize neither the nations of the world nor enemies of Israel (the former are represented by the trees of the field in v. 24), but the population of the earth who come as refugees and find shelter in its boughs and presumably eat from its fruit. This interpretation is reinforced by 31:6, which adds the beasts of the field to the birds of the sky among the creatures that find security in and under the boughs of the tree:

> In its branches all the birds of the sky made their nests;
> And under its boughs all the wild animals bore their young,
> While in its shadow lived all the great nations.[90]

In both texts the nations are separated from the creatures, suggesting at best that the birds and beasts represent the population of the earth that have been abused by the rulers of the nations. Alternatively, the reference to every kind of bird nesting in its shade may simply highlight the tree as a symbol of security for all. Although this mountain will become increasingly significant in later oracles, only here in this book are the motifs of Davidic line and Zion brought together—though without mentioning either by name.[91] In so doing the prophet reminds the exiles that YHWH had not forgotten his covenant with David (2 Sam 7). The dynasty would survive the deportation; it would be revived within the context of its original founding, and its protective influence would be felt around the world.

In a move exceptional for Ezekiel,[92] the last verse highlights the universal impact of the tree with a complex version of the recognition

90. Cf. Isa 16:1–5; Amos 9:11–12; Zech 9:9–10. Similarly, Laato, *Josiah and David Redivivus*, 163. The nations are represented by all the trees of the field that acknowledge YHWH in the next verse. At best, these birds represent the kings of the earth (cf. the portrayal of the kings of Babylon and Egypt as in the riddles).

91. The mountain motif is absent from both 34:23–24 and 37:22–25. Verse 22 comes close, but instead of focusing on Zion/Jerusalem, Ezekiel neutralizes the David-Zion connection by referring to "the mountains of Israel" rather than "the mountain of Israel." The present association is reminiscent of both Ps 78:68–73 and 132:10–18, each of which juxtaposes the election of David and the establishment of his dynasty with the choice of Mount Zion as YHWH's dwelling place. However, Ezekiel studiously avoids the name Zion, probably because it had been so badly misused in official theology and because of the shame priests and kings had brought to the place. On the concept of Zion as a world mountain, see Clifford, *Cosmic Mountain*, 131–60.

92. The universalistic vision of this coda contrasts with Ezekiel's pervasive parochialism that also characterizes texts involving the restoration of David as shepherd of

formula. One might have expected that when all the trees, that is, the dynasties of the earth as embodiments of the nations, observe this tree's splendor and productivity, and experience the protection it offered, they would fall down before it in homage and submission. But this oracle is not about Davidic imperialism; it is about YHWH's cosmic sovereignty and fidelity, which is highlighted by four sensitively constructed parallel lines:

> I bring down the high tree,
> I make high the low tree;
> I dry up the green tree,
> And I make the dry tree flourish (17:24).

These gnomic declarations recall many similar statements in the Old Testament.[93] For a concrete illustration of bringing down the high, the listeners need look no farther than Zedekiah, whose fate had been described in verses 19–21 and whose end will be declared with the same combination of verbs in 21:31[26]. As for the low being lifted up, this could refer to Jehoiachin, who will be elevated in the Babylonian court (2 Kgs 25:27–3). However, in long range terms this was a very modest elevation, scarcely matching the growth of the cosmic tree and in any case involving no concomitant bringing down of Nebuchadnezzar. Rather, it refers to the restoration and elevation of what Jehoiachin represents. He may be currently languishing in captivity in Babylon, but his line and the line of David will live. His scion will be restored to the throne of Israel, and elevated to the status of universal king.

To the exiles Ezekiel's words may have seemed like an impossible dream, but they are guaranteed in the final three lines. YHWH has spoken; he will act. The foundation for this oracle is found in his covenant with David, communicated four centuries earlier by Nathan the prophet (2 Sam 7). Not only had YHWH promised him eternal title to the throne of Israel, but David had also recognized its cosmic significance when he interpreted Nathan's oracle as "the instruction for humanity" (תּוֹרַת הָאָדָם, 2 Sam 7:19).[94] YHWH had not forgotten his ancient word. Nor would

---

Israel (34:23–24; 36:24–25).

93. Involving שָׁפֵל and גָּבַהּ, 1 Sam 2:7; 2 Sam 22:28 = Pss 18:28[27]; 75:8[7]; 147:6; Isa 2:11, 12, 17; 26:5; also Sir 7:11. The most common pairing of roots involves שפל and רום. Other variations of the pair occur in Isa 10:33; 57:15; Pss 138:6; 147:6; Job 5:11; Eccl 10:6.

94. Even though the syntax of the statement is clear, scholars have struggled with it, noting especially the divergences from the corresponding utterance in 2 Chr 17:17. See McCarter, *II Samuel*; Stoebe, *Das zweite Buch Samuelis*, 231. For possible

he betray this new word, issued through Ezekiel, in the interests of the dynasty. It would not only survive the exile; its best years lay in the future.

Earlier the prophet had disputed the claims of those who had escaped the deportation of 597 BCE, and therefore argued that this was a sign of YHWH's favor toward them. In their minds, because they were left behind in Jerusalem, they were secure in the "pot" (11:3), and the exiles' deportation was obvious proof that YHWH had abandoned them (11:15). Ezekiel responded by declaring that Jerusalem should not be viewed as a pot protecting the people from danger, but as a trap holding them for the outpouring of divine fury (11:5–12), and the exile should be interpreted, not as a sign of divine rejection, but of election.[95] YHWH had removed them from Jerusalem to spare them the conflagration to come, and brought them to Babylon where he personally became their "small sanctuary."[96] Our text suggests that just as the remnant of the exiles represented the hope and future of the nation, so Jehoiachin represented the hope and future of the dynasty. The enemies of Israel may wreak their havoc on the people, the land, the temple, and the dynasty, but Babylon would provide refuge both for the exiles and for a remnant of the house of David.[97]

The riddle of chapter 17 suggests that Ezekiel envisioned Nebuchadnezzar as more than a divine agent of judgment on the nation for their rebellion against him; he was also an agent of preservation, who provided a refuge for the exiles in Babylon while YHWH's fury raged all around at home, and rescued the Davidic house by bringing Jehoiachin to Babylon. In a truly remarkable twist, the coda of 17:22–24 reinforces Nebuchadnezzar's role as the agent through whom the dynasty would be rescued. By removing Jehoiachin from the throne and taking him to Babylon before he

---

explanation for the differences and a solution to the text-critical issues, see Barthélemy, ed., et al., Critique textuelle de l'Ancien Testament, 1. Josué, Juges, Ruth, Samuel, Rois, Chroniques, Esdras, Néhémie, Esther, 457–58. For discussion of the significance of David's statement, see Gentry, "Rethinking the 'Sure Mercies of David,'" 288–91.

95. See my fuller discussion in Ezekiel 1–24, 350–56.

96. The precise significance of the comment in verse 16, "And I became to them a sanctuary in small measure (וָאֱהִי לָהֶם לְמִקְדָּשׁ מְעַט) in the lands where they had gone," is uncertain, but it should probably be related to 37:27, "My sanctuary shall be over them" (וְהָיָה מִשְׁכָּנִי עֲלֵיהֶם). Greenberg (Ezekiel 21–37, 757–58) rightly sees in the latter a transformation of the tabernacle primarily as a symbol of God's dwelling amidst Israel to a sheltering presence over them.

97. In this respect the role of Babylon is analogous to that of Egypt in the narratives of Genesis. In Gen 45:7–11 and 50:20–21, Joseph declares to his brothers that his presence in Egypt was part of God's plan to secure the existence of the chosen family while a famine devastated Canaan and the rest of the region.

destroyed Jerusalem he set the stage for Ezekiel's final restoration oracles. According to 34:23–24 and 37:21–28, in the future, after YHWH will have brought remnants of all the tribes back to their ancestral homeland and reestablished justice among the people, he will install the ideal David as shepherd, prince, and king over his people.

THE SIGNIFICANCE OF EZEKIEL'S PORTRAYAL OF JEHOIACHIN

The deportation of Jehoiachin in 597 BCE and the apparent collapse of the Davidic house with the execution of Zedekiah in 586 BCE raised doubts about YHWH's fidelity to his word in the minds of his people. Although neither Ezekiel nor any of the prophets hint at a latter-day spiritual renewal of Jehoichin comparable to that of his great-great-grandfather Manasseh,[98] Ezekiel's portrait of Jehoiachin offered hope for this man, but especially for the dynasty—a hope that seems to be reflected in the strange postscripts to both the book of 2 Kings and Jeremiah:[99]

> In the thirty-seventh year of the exile of King Jehoiachin of Judah, in the twelfth month, on the twenty-seventh day of the month, King Evil-merodach of Babylon, in the year that he began to reign, released King Jehoiachin of Judah from prison; he spoke kindly to him, and gave him a seat above the other seats of the kings who were with him in Babylon. So Jehoiachin put aside his prison clothes. Every day of his life he dined regularly in the king's presence. For his allowance, a regular allowance was given him by the king, a portion every day, as long as he lived. (2 Kgs 35:27–30 = Jer 52:31–34, *NRSV*)[100]

---

98. See 2 Chr 33:18–19 and the Apocryphal "Prayer of Manasseh."

99. The paragraph concludes both the MT and LXX versions of Jeremiah.

100. Jeremiah adds, עַד־יוֹם מוֹתוֹ, "until the day of his death." Although the Chronicler ends his history of Israel with Cyrus' decree authorizing the Jews in exile to return to Jerusalem (2 Chr 36:22–23), he is silent on this episode. Goulder ("Behold My Servant Jehoiachin," 186–87) identifies Jehoiachin with צַדִּיק עַבְדִּי, "my righteous servant," who makes many righteous in Isaiah 53. While the possible links between Isaiah 53 and what we know from elsewhere about Jehoiachin are striking, and although Jehoiachin suffers the pain of exile with his countrymen, in the end it is unlikely that the person whom Israel's historians describe as being deported for "doing evil in the sight of YHWH" should bear the sins of his people in a substitutionary or sacrificial sense.

Although some interpret this text pessimistically, that is, that it offers no hope for the restoration of the Davidic dynasty,[101] others see here a positive sign for the future of the royal house.[102] Volkmar Fritz aptly observes,

> This short and quite vague epilogue helps to soften the end of the Deuteronomistic History a little, in that it now finishes with an act of mercy that allows hope for the continuation of the Davidic dynasty without voicing specific expectations. The end is still the destruction of Judah, interpreted by the Deuteronomistic Historian as the fulfillment of the divine judgment. The epilogue does nothing to change this, but by referring to King Jehoiachin as still being alive, it not only saves from despair but introduces a glimmer of hope for the future. As opposed to the unknown fate of the blinded rebel Zedekiah, the treatment of Jehoiachin by Evil-merodach gives rise to a more positive image of the future. The influence of those expectations linked to the Davidides is reflected in the hopes arising from the fact that Zerubbabel, Jehoiachin's grandson, is made governor of Judah at the beginning of the Persian hegemony (cf. Haggai 1).[103]

But this raises the question: Why would this action by the Persian king be interpreted so positively? Was it only because of the memory of the dynastic promise to David in 2 Sam 7? Or were there other influences?

The historians' dating of this event may provide a clue. According to 2 Kgs 25:27 and Jer 52:31, Evil-merodach elevated Jehoiachin shortly after he assumed the Babylonian throne. The exact date is specified as the twenty-seventh day of the twelfth month (Adar) of the thirty-seventh year of Jehoiachin's exile,[104] which computes to 561–560 BCE.[105] Although

---

101. See especially Noth, *Deuteronomistic History*, 142–44; Cogan and Tadmor, *II Kings*, 329–30.

102. For a positive and hopeful interpretation of 2 Kgs 25:27–30, see among others von Rad, *Studies in Deuteronomy*, 86, 90–91; Goulder, "Behold My Servant Jehoiachin," 175–90; Provan, "Messiah in Kings," 71–76; Provan, *1 & 2 Kings*, 87–93; Hobbs, *2 Kings*, 368–69. For surveys of scholarship on 2 Kgs 25:27–30, see Murray, "Of All the Years," 245–47; and Janzen, "An Ambiguous Ending," 39–58.

103. Fritz, *1 & 2 Kings*, 426.

104. וַיְהִי בִשְׁלֹשִׁים וָשֶׁבַע שָׁנָה לְגָלוּת יְהוֹיָכִין מֶלֶךְ־יְהוּדָה בִּשְׁנֵים עָשָׂר חֹדֶשׁ בְּעֶשְׂרִים וְשִׁבְעָה לַחֹדֶשׁ. The slight variation in the date given in Jer 52:31 (thirty-seventh year, twelfth month, twenty-fifth day of the month; cf. LXX, 37.12.20) is inconsequential for this discussion.

105. So also Sweeney, *I & II Kings*, 469; Lundbom, *Jeremiah 37–52*, 535. Nebuchadnezzar died in October 562 BCE, and was succeeded by his son, Evil-merodach (Akkad. Amēl-Marduk), who ruled only for two years. The cuneiform records provide

Ezekiel's riddle concerning the tender sprig is undated, since all the oracles in Ezekiel 1–24 were delivered before the fall of Jerusalem in 586 BCE (cf. Ezek 24:1; 33:21), Jehoiachin's elevation occurred ca. twenty-five years after the prophet had delivered the oracle in Ezekiel 17.[106] It is possible that the postscripts to 2 Kings and Jeremiah were inspired by the coda of Ezekiel's riddle; the editors of these books may have interpreted the promotion of Jehoiachin in Babylon as a hopeful sign that could lead to the tender sprig being planted on the high and lofty mountain of Israel (17:22–23).

This possibility is strengthened by the Ezekielian style and tone especially of the date notice in 2 Kgs 25:27 = Jer 52:31. Many have noted how awkwardly this *postscriptum* fits at the end of 2 Kings.[107] Without warning the narrator shifts his attention from the small group of Judaeans who had fled to Egypt in the wake of the assassination of Gedaliah in 586 to a totally disconnected event in Babylon that happened more than two decades later and that involved a long forgotten deposed king. The conclusion to Jeremiah is equally awkward. In the previous paragraph (Jer 52:28–30) the narrator had summarized the scope of Nebuchadnezzar's deportations of Jews from Jerusalem, offering separate numerical totals for the first (597 BCE) and second (586 BCE) deportations. This paragraph abruptly introduces events that happened twenty-five years later without any attempt at integration.

Even as we note the awkwardness of this *postscriptum* in its narrative contexts, we observe unmistakable links with Ezekiel, especially in

---

no information on Evil-merodach's death, but Berossus reports that he was assassinated by his brother-in-law, Neriglissar. See further, Sack, "Evil-merodach," 679; *idem*, *Amēl-Marduk*—562–560 BC.

106. I assume the coherence and essential integrity of chapter 17, including the coda. Even if Ezekiel added the coda later, it probably should not be dated later than 571 BCE, the date given for Ezekiel's latest dated oracle (Ezek 29:17). For a defense of the pre-586 date for the coda, see Lang, *Kein Aufstand*, 84–88.

107. According to Cogan and Tadmor (*II Kings*, 330), the *postscriptum* was added "by an exilic writer who brought the narration of Jehoiachin's life up to date." Earlier (ibid., 329) they had noted, "This passage appears nonintegral to the book of Kings, it contains none of the phraseology typical of Deuteronomistic editing, nor does it articulate any of the historiographic tenets of the Deuteronomic school." However, some have compared this paragraph with the account of the elevation of Mephibosheth in 2 Sam 9:9–13. See Schipper, "'Significant Resonances' with Mephibosheth," 521–29. Konkel, *1 & 2 Kings*, 666, observes that "Both Mephibosheth and Jehoiachin seem to represent a dynasty that survives, but is incapable of functioning as a royal order. The parallels to Mephibosheth suggest that Jehoiachin is testimony to the survival of Israel, even in exile."

the opening date notice. First, the form of the date notice corresponds precisely to the form that is standard in Ezekiel; events are dated from the deportation of Jehoiachin, rather than the accession of the current ruler.[108] The differences are evident when we compare this notice with others within these chapters: 2 Kgs 25:1, 8; Jer 52:4, 12.[109] Second, although Jeremiah shares Ezekiel's penchant for dating oracles, the precision of the present date notice contrasts with Jeremiah's. Whereas Ezekiel regularly dates oracles by year, month, and date, Jeremiah usually dates them by year, and occasionally by month, but apart from Jer 52:31, never by day.[110] Third, the expression for "exile" (גָּלוּת) in the date notice, is typically Ezekielian, occurring elsewhere only in Ezek 1:2; 33:21; and 40:1.[111] Fourth, both 2 Kgs 25:27 and Jer 52:31 identify Jehoiachin as "King of Judah" (מֶלֶךְ־יְהוּדָה). This is extraordinary, since at the time of this event Jehoiachin was far away in Babylon and had not occupied the throne of Judah for twenty-five years. However, the identification agrees with Ezek 1:2 and, as we observed earlier, with the way people in Babylon were identifying him.[112] While we do not know the source of the rest of this *postscriptum* (2 Kgs 25:27b–30; Jer 52:31b–34), given these links, it is reasonable to suppose that the editors responsible for their insertion at the ends of the deuteronomistic history and Jeremiah were familiar with Ezekiel's prophecies in some written form. They might, therefore, naturally have linked Jehoiachin's elevation with Ezekiel's oracle of the tender sprig, in which case this oracle would have fueled readers' optimism concerning

108. This observation is not compromised by the synchronizing note, "in the year he [Evil-merodach] began to reign" (בשנת מלכתו; 2 Kgs 35:27; Jer 52:31), which is added later.

109. See also Jer 39:2. Apart from 1:1, which is enigmatic and general, and 3:16, which is linked to 1:2–3, the date notices tend to follow the stereotypical pattern found in 8:1, וַיְהִי בַּשָּׁנָה הַשִּׁשִּׁית בַּשִּׁשִּׁי בַּחֲמִשָּׁה לַחֹדֶשׁ, "It happened in the sixth year in the sixth [month] on the fifth [day] of the month." Cf. 20:1; 26:1; 29:1; 29:17; 30:20; 31:1; 32:1; 32:17; 33:21; 40:1. The anomalous character of 24:1 has been noted above.

110. By year: 25:1; 26:1; 27:1; 32:1; 36:1; 45:1; cf. 46:2 (date of an event, rather than an oracle); 49:34 (the year is missing; "early in the reign of Zedekiah"); by month: 28:1; 36:9; 41:1. Jeremiah 39:2 includes the day, but the reference is to an event rather than an oracle. Of more than three dozen date [more properly year] notices in 1–2 Kings, notices including the year, month, and date occur only in chapter 25 (vv. 1, 8, 27).

111. Elsewhere the word is used as a collective for exiles: Amos 1:6, 9; Isa 20:4; 45:13; Jer 24:5; 28:4; 29:22; 40:1; Obad 20. However, the cognate verb, גָּלָה, "to go into exile," and it causative *hiphil* counterpart, הִגְלָה, "to send into exile," are very common. See *HALOT*, 191–92.

112. Cf. the reference to *šar* ᵐᵃᵗ*Ia-a-ḫu-du/Ia-ku-du*, in the Babylonian ration tablet, *ANET*, 308.

the future of the Davidic dynasty. With the emergence of Zerubbabel, the grandson of Jehoiachin, as a leader of the returning exiles, these hopes were fanned into flame.[113]

CONCLUSION

Although Ezekiel is transparent in his contempt for Zedekiah, his disposition toward Jehoiachin is not so clear. YHWH's charge in 19:1 to take up a lament for the princes of Israel seems to lump Jehoiachin together with Jehoahaz, Jehoiakim, and Zedekiah. Employing the metaphor of lion cubs, the dirge portrays the first two as violent man-eating animals (vv. 2–9). Changing the metaphor from that of a pride of lions to a massive vine, the second half of the lament accuses the latter two of hubris, for which the vine is plucked up, and burned (vv. 10–14). This characterization renders Laato's proposal to associate the righteous grandson in Ezek 18:14–18 with Jehoiachin[114] unlikely. However, it appears that Ezekiel was able to distinguish between the man and what the man represented. He interpreted Jehoiachin's exile to Babylon as a ray of hope for the future of the dynasty. YHWH had brought down the high tree and dried up the green tree; he was able also to exalt the low tree and make the dry tree flourish. Not only was he able to accomplish this; he bound himself by his word to do so: "I am YHWH; I have spoken; I will act" (17:24). He will not forget his ancient word to David.[115]

---

113. Ezra 2–5; Neh 7:7; 12:1, 47; Hag 1:1, 12, 14; 2:2, 4, 20–23; Zech 4:6–10. Cf. Matt 1:12–13; Luke 3:27.

114. Laato, *Josiah and David Redivivus*, 172–74.

115. 2 Sam 7:13, 16; Ps 89:28–29, 34–37[27–28, 33–36].

4

Bringing Back David

Ezekiel's Messianic Hope[1]

INTRODUCTION

Many readers know the prophet Ezekiel primarily for his fantastic visions and bizarre behavior. However, in circles where prophecy conferences are in vogue, he is perceived as the Old Testament eschatologist par excellence. His restoration oracles in chapters 34–37, the Gog Oracle in chapters 38–39, and the final vision of the restored temple and environs in chapters 40–48 offer a picture of Israel's future unique in style and unmatched for its detail. However, the exilic prophet displays a special interest in one particular aspect of Israel's glorious future, the person and role of the Messiah,[2] the subject of this paper. Before we focus on the relevant texts several general features of his treatment of this topic deserve notice.

1. This essay was originally published in *The Lord's Anointed: Interpretation of Old Testament Messianic Texts*, edited by P. E. Satterthwaite, R. S. Hess, and G. J. Wenham, 167–88. Grand Rapids: Baker, 1995.

2. Levey (*The Messiah*, xix) defines "messianism" as

> "the predication of a future Golden Age in which the central figure is a king primarily of Davidic lineage appointed by God. . . . It was believed that during the time of the Messiah the Hebrew people will be vindicated, its wrongs righted, the wicked purged from its midst, and its rightful place in the world secured. The Messiah may not always be the active agent in these future events, but his personality must

The Scarcity of References to the Messiah

Although more than one fourth of Ezekiel's preserved prophecies look forward to Israel's glorious tomorrow, overt references to the Messiah in the book are remarkably few.[3] The topmost crown of the cedar, identified as רַךְ (sprig, shoot) in 17:22 may serve as a harbinger of the figure to be developed later,[4] but obvious messianic allusions are rare elsewhere in the judgment oracles against Israel/Judah (chs. 4–24) and the oracles against the foreign nations (chs. 25–32).

A second allusion to the Messiah has been recognized 29:21. In an oracle against a foreign nation (Egypt) and supportive of a foreign king (Nebuchadnezzar), Ezekiel concludes his pronouncement with an enigmatic reference to "a horn" (קֶרֶן) that YHWH will cause to sprout (צָמַח) for the house of Israel. Literally, the noun denotes an animal's horn, and is often used synonymously with שׁוֹפָר, though the latter usually refers more specifically to a ram's horn. Since horns are the focus of many creatures' power, קֶרֶן naturally functions figuratively for "strength." Accordingly, YHWH hereby offers hope to the exiles. The fact that the fulfillment of the prophecies against Tyre was delayed for more than a decade does not mean YHWH has forgotten his promises to Israel or his debt to Nebuchadnezzar. When the prophet and his people see him settling this outstanding account they may take heart that YHWH's long-standing account with Israel (albeit of a different nature) will also be settled.

But the issue has another side. The mixed metaphor, in which קֶרֶן is used with צָמַח, occurs in one other text, Ps 132:17, where YHWH promises to "cause a horn to sprout for David." This link provides the basis for the long-standing messianic interpretation of our text. But most scholars reject the messianic assessment, on the grounds that the idea of a royal messianic deliverance is not important in Ezekiel, and that the notion would in any case be intrusive in this context. However, neither argument is entirely convincing. On the one hand, Ezekiel does in fact make

always be present, at least as the symbol of the glorious age which will be ushered in."

3. The messianic interpretation of specific texts like Ezek 34:23–24 is implicit in LXX and Peshitta, and overt in the Vulgate and the Rabbinic *Gen. Rab.* 97, but the Targum refuses to recognize the Messiah anywhere in Ezekiel.

4. LXX omits the word. Compare the horticultural designations for the Messiah elsewhere: חֹטֶר ("shoot") and נֵצֶר ("branch") in Isa 11:1 and צֶמַח ("sprout") in Jer 23:5; 33:15; Zech 3:8; 6:12. For a recent messianic interpretation of 17:22–24, see Laato, *Josiah and David Redivivus*, 154–64.

several clear messianic pronouncements; on the other, a reference to a Davidic scion at this point is no more surprising than the presence of the verse itself. Furthermore, since this is Ezekiel's latest recorded oracle, the resurfacing of earlier ideas is not surprising.

Elsewhere messianic hints are scarce. Even in the restoration oracles unequivocal references to the Messiah occur in only two contexts, 34:22–23 and 37:22–25. Some dispute the messianic role of the prince (נָשִׂיא) in chapters 40–48. Only by inference can he be identified as a Davidide, and his role is described in other than royal terms.

The Reinterpretation of Genesis 49:10 in Ezekiel 21:23–32[18–27]

At least one earlier text, which was probably interpreted messianically by the people, Ezekiel reconstrues and applies to the contemporary political crisis. The oracle concerning Nebuchadnezzar, the wielder of the divine sword against Judah (21:23-32[18–27]), ends with a sinister reinterpretation of Gen 49:10, an ancient promise concerning Judah's hegemonic position within Israel.[5] Rereading מִשְׁפָּט, "right, claim,"[6] as "judgment," the prophet identifies the person to whom the task of "judgment" is delivered as Nebuchadnezzar. He hereby envisions the imminent fall of Jerusalem, an event in which no Messiah shall interfere. Ezekiel has taken an ancient word, on which his audience had staked their hopes, and transformed it

---

5. The messianic/christological interpretation of עַד־בֹּא אֲשֶׁר־לֹו הַמִּשְׁפָּט וּנְתַתִּיו, dates back to LXX ἕως οὗ ἔλθῃ ᾧ καθήκει καὶ παραδώσω αὐτω, "until the one comes for whom it is fitting, and I will give it to him," on which see Monsengwo-Pasinya, "Deux textes messianiques," 356–76. Lust ("Messianism and Septuagint," 188–91) interprets the Septuagintal rendering as a "priestly messianic expectation as opposed to a royal Davidic messianic expectation." Most Christian interpreters after Jerome have interpreted אֲשֶׁר־לֹו הַמִּשְׁפָּט as a theological interpretation of Shiloh in the patriarchal prophecy. See Keil, *Biblical Commentary on Ezekiel*, 1:305; Hengstenberg, *Christology of the Old Testament*, 687. For more recent proponents of the messianic interpretation see Taylor, *Ezekiel*, 165; Cazelles, "Shiloh," 239–51; Alexander, "Ezekiel," 844–45; Cooper, *Ezekiel*, 215.

For a non-messianic interpretation of Gen 49:10 see Pili ("Posibili casi di metatesi," 457–71), who proposes reversing the letters of שילה as הליש, giving the meaning, "Till the lion comes to whom the obedience of the peoples shall belong"; cf. Gen 49:9. Lang (*Kein Aufstand*, 119), follows Caquot ("La parole sur Juda," 5–32), in recognizing in Shiloh an abbreviation for Solomon.

6. Elsewhere the word means "justice" (18:5, 19, 21; 27; 33:14, 16, 19), "judgment" (23:24), "custom" (23:24), "design" (42:11). Cf. Wevers, *Ezekiel*, 160; Lust, *Congress Volume*, 184–86.

into a frightening prediction of doom.[7] To Ezekiel, Gen 49:10 is not about tribute and subordination of the world to Judah, but the judgment of Judah by that world's principal representative.[8]

Ezekiel's Messianic Hope and Judgment Oracles

Ezekiel's messianic hope represents the inverse of a fundamental aspect of his judgment oracles. In the face of the Babylonian invasion, Israelite[9] confidence was founded upon an official orthodoxy resting on four immutable propositions, four pillars of divine promise: the irrevocability of YHWH's covenant with Israel (Sinai), YHWH's ownership of the land of Canaan, YHWH's eternal covenant with David, and YHWH's residence in Jerusalem, the place he chose for his name to dwell. But Ezekiel's overriding purpose in chapters 4–24 is to transform his audience's perception of their relationship with YHWH, exposing delusions of innocence, and offering a divine understanding of reality. Deliberately he demolishes the pillars on which official orthodoxy had constructed its notions of eternal security. However, once Jerusalem has fallen and the old illusions of spirituality have been destroyed, the prophet can look forward to a new day, based upon the same immutable promises of YHWH. The earlier problem with official orthodoxy was not its theological structures but its misapplication of truth. He had been systematic in tearing down the illusory pillars of orthodoxy in his judgment oracles; he would be equally systematic in reconstructing those pillars in his restoration oracles. These reconstruction pronouncements included the reaffirmation of YHWH's ancient promises to David. In both, the judgments and the restoration, the word of YHWH is affirmed: not only the immediate word, whose fulfillment confirms Ezekiel's status as a true prophet but especially the ancient word, declared through Nathan to David in 2 Sam 7.

The Near Eastern Context

Ezekiel's messianic vision is at home in the ideological and cultural milieu of ancient Mesopotamia. If his portrayal of the departure of YHWH from

7. Cf. Fishbane, *Biblical Interpretation*, 502–3.

8. Cf. Moran, "Gen. 49,10," 424–25.

9. Like Ezekiel, we use the term Israelite as a theological and ethnic designation for the so-called people of YHWH, whether they be the original twelve tribes, the kingdom of Judah, or the remnant of exiles.

the temple and the devastating effects of the divine abandonment of the land displays striking links with other Babylonian and Assyrian accounts of divine abandonment, the same is true of his vision of his nation's restoration. In several ancient texts the divine appointment of a human king represents a fundamental element, if not the climax of the normalization of the relationship between a deity and his land people.[10] Accordingly, Ezekiel's anticipation of a new (messianic) king over his own people would have been understood by ancient Israelite and outsider alike.

Ezekiel's Nationalistic Perspective

Whereas the messianic visions of other prophets were inclusivist, incorporating peoples and lands beyond Israel, Ezekiel's perspective is narrowly exclusive, parochial, nationalistic. The goal in YHWH's restorative activity does indeed have international implications, viz., the universal recognition of his person and the vindication of his name, but this will be achieved through the total restoration of Israel. This must necessarily involve the regathering of the population from the lands where they have been scattered, their return to the homeland, which has been physically rejuvenated, and the people's fundamental spiritual revitalization.[11] Since the territorial transformation envisioned by the exilic prophet does not extend beyond the borders of Israel,[12] naturally his Messiah is also a national ruler.

Having made these preliminary observations we may examine Ezekiel's messianic hope more closely by focusing on the two texts cited earlier, and then make some observations on the role of the נָשִׂיא in the concluding temple vision.

EZEKIEL 34:23–24

Ezekiel's first explicit reference to the Messiah occurs near the end of an extended restoration oracle in which YHWH poses as a benevolent

---

10. The "Prophetic Speech of Marduk" II:20ff. (see Borger, "Gott Marduk," 3–24); Esarhaddon's account of the rebuilding of Babylon (*ARAB* 2, 242–47 §§640–51; Borger, *Die Inschriften Asarhaddons*, 37 A:16–40); the Prayer of Adad-guppi (*ANET*, 560–62); the Cyrus Cylinder (*ANET*, 315). For discussion of these texts in this context see Block, *Gods of the Nations*, 134–48.

11. See especially 36:16–38.

12. A point convincingly argued by Darr, "The Wall around Paradise," 271–79.

divine shepherd, rescuing his beleaguered human flock from the tyranny of exploitative rulers and bullying members within the flock (34:1–31). Without warning the attention moves from YHWH's negative activity, viz., resolving problems within the flock, to exciting new positive actions on Israel's behalf, culminating in the appointment of a human shepherd over them and the restoration of peace and security (vv. 23–31).[13] The covenant formula, which summarizes the goal of YHWH's salvific actions, appears at the beginning (v. 24) and at the end (vv. 30–31), providing a framework for interpreting the intervening material. The two principal motifs dealt with here, the appointment of David as (under-)shepherd of YHWH's flock, and the covenant of peace, are fundamental to the Jewish messianism that would flourish in the intertestamental period.[14] The repetitive and staccato style of verses 23–24 reflects Ezekiel's increasing excitement as he approaches the climax of the oracle. These verses are packed with vital information on the new shepherd's status within Israel. First, this ruler will be neither self-appointed nor elected by the people, but chosen by YHWH himself.[15] Like his contemporary Jeremiah, Ezekiel perceives Israel as a theocracy.

Second, the shepherd will be singular. The reference to "one shepherd" (רֹעֶה אֶחָד) goes beyond Jer 23:4, which has YHWH installing responsible shepherds (plural) to replace the present exploitative and irresponsible rulers. In announcing a single ruler YHWH seeks a reversal of the division of Israel into northern and southern kingdoms that occurred after the death of Solomon (1 Kgs 11–12). Like the rest of the prophets, Ezekiel perceived the nation as one and recognized as legitimate only the dynasty reigning from Jerusalem.[16]

Third, the shepherd will be David. Ezekiel's identification of the divinely installed king as David is based on a long-standing prophetic tradition, although this ruler is explicitly identified as David only twice

---

13. For the conjunction of these motifs see also Jer 23:1–8; 30:8–11; 33:12–26.

14. See Levey's definition of "messianism" in n. 1 above.

15. A principle established already in the "Mosaic Charter for Kingship," Deut 17:14–20. הֵקִים ("raise up"), in the sense of "install in office," with YHWH as the subject, is applied in the Old Testament to the appointment of prophets (Deut 18:15, 18; Jer 29:15; Amos 2:11), judges (Judg 2:16, 18), priests (1 Sam 2:35), kings (1 Kgs 14:14; Jer 30:9), watchmen (Jer 6:17), deliverers (Judg 3:9, 15), shepherds (Jer 23:4, 5; Zech 11:16), and even adversaries (1 Kgs 11:14).

16. He will expand on this notion in 37:15–24, where the term אֶחָד occurs no fewer than eleven times.

outside this book.[17] On the one hand, the eighth-century prophet Hosea had looked forward to the day when the sons of Israel would "return and seek YHWH their God and David their king."[18] On the other, however, Ezekiel's diction is closer to Jer 30:8–10, which also combines the appointment of David with the anticipated restoration of the nation. There is no thought in these prophecies of the resurrection of the historic king, as some kind of David *redivivus*. Ezekiel's use of the singular "shepherd" and his emphasis on אֶחָד ("one") also preclude the restoration of the dynasty in the abstract, that is, simply a series of kings. He envisions a single person, who may perhaps embody the dynasty, but who occupies the throne himself.

Although Ezekiel's hope of a divinely appointed shepherd king in the context of national restoration agrees with common Near Eastern thinking, his specific prediction of a revival of the nation's original royal house[19] contrasts with the general nature of extra-Israelite expectations.[20] Having earlier foretold and witnessed the fall of the Davidic house (ch. 17), Ezekiel now declares its restoration. His pronouncement is based upon YHWH's covenant with David, announced by Nathan the prophet in 2 Sam 7:8 (1 Chr 17:7). Significantly for our discussion, David's divine election had earlier been described as a call "from the pasture (הַנָּוֶה), from following the flock, to be ruler (נָגִיד) of YHWH's people Israel."[21] YHWH's affirmation of

17. Jer 23:5 speaks of raising up for David "a Righteous Branch" (צֶמַח צַדִּיק, cf. 33:15); Amos 9:11, of restoring (הֲקִים) "the fallen hut of David." Compare Isa 9:5–7[6–8], which speaks of the child upon the throne of David, Isa 11:1, referring to "a shoot from the stump of Jesse" (חֹטֶר מִגֵּזַע יִשָׁי; cf. "the root of Jesse" [שֹׁרֶשׁ יִשַׁי] in v. 10). Gross ("Israel's Hope," 125–26) follows Hossfeld (Untersuchungen zu Komposition und Theologie, 230ff. and 284ff.) in deleting the reference to David as a late intrusion, dependent upon Ezek 37:24–25.

18. The statement is commonly deleted as a late Judaean insertion. Cf. Zimmerli, *Ezekiel 2*, 219; Wolff, *Commentary on Hosea*, 63. For a contrary opinion see Andersen and Freedman, *Hosea*, 307.

19. Excluding the failed Saulide experiment.

20. The *ex eventu* reference to Cyrus with the archaic title "King of Elam" in the "Dynastic Prophecy," provides the nearest analogue. Cf. Grayson, *Babylonian Historical-Literary Texts*, 24–57. The "Prophetic Speech of Marduk" (II:19–34) refers to the promised king simply as "a king of Babylon." For the text see Block, *By the River Chebar, Excursus A*, 100–107; also available in Block, *Gods of the Nations*, 155–62; Longman III, *Fictional Akkadian Autobiography*, 234. Other "Akkadian Prophecies" define the tenures of a series of kings, but refer to them generically as šarru. Cf. Grayson and Lambert, "Akkadian Prophecies," 12–14.

21. Note the popular awareness of David's divine election reflected in 2 Sam 5:2: "YHWH said to you, 'You will shepherd (תִּרְעֶה) my people Israel, and you will be a

the eternality of the Davidic covenant[22] had provided the basis for all the prophetic hopes.[23] However, the capture of Zedekiah and the collapse of the Davidic house in 586 BCE raised doubts about YHWH's ability and/or will to keep his word. Ezekiel hereby announces that the ancient promise has not been forgotten. YHWH will fulfill his irrevocable promise and his unfailing covenant to the house of David as the sole legitimate dynasty in Israel.

Fourth, the shepherd will be the servant of YHWH. Ezekiel's repetition of עַבְדִּי ("my servant") simultaneously presents an intentional contrast with the self-seeking shepherds of verses 1–10 and recalls the traditional view of David's willing subordination to YHWH.[24] Moreover, in the Old Testament עֶבֶד־יְהוָה ("servant of YHWH") also functioned as an honorific title for those who stood in an official relationship to God, often with the implication of a special election to a task.[25] David's own standing

---

ruler (נָגִיד) over Israel.'" Compare the psalmist's celebration of the same notion in Ps 78:70–72:

> He chose David, his servant,
> and took him from the sheepfolds.
> From caring for the nursing ewes he brought him
> to tend (לִרְעוֹת) Jacob, his people,
> Israel his own possession.
> He tended (רָעָה) them with integrity of heart;
> With his skilful hands he led them.

22. The word עוֹלָם appears eight times in 2 Sam 7:13, 16, 24–29. See especially verse 13 ("I will establish the throne of his kingdom forever") and verse 16 ("Your dynasty and your kingdom will endure before me forever; your kingdom will be established forever").

23. A fact reflected most clearly in Jer 33:17, 20–21, 25–26, but enthusiastically celebrated by the psalmist in Ps 89:29–30, 34–37[28–29, 33–36].

24. עַבְדִּי is used of David thirty-one times in the Old Testament. See 2 Sam 3:18; 7:5, 8, 26; etc. (see BDB, 714). The title is also applied to Hezekiah (2 Chr 32:16), Zerubbabel (Hag 2:23), and "my servant the Branch" (Zech 3:8; cf. 6:12).

25. Accordingly the patriarchs served as the bearers of the divine revelation, promise and blessing (Abraham, Gen 26:24 and Ps 105:6, 42; Isaac, Gen 24:14 and 1 Chr 16:13; Jacob, Exod 32:13 and Deut 9:27); Moses served as YHWH's agent of deliverance and the mediator of the divine covenant (so designated forty times: Exod 14:31; Jos 1:2, 3, 13, 15; Num 12:7–8, etc.); the Levitical singers performed as official benedictors for YHWH (Pss 113:1; 134:1; 135:1) and the prophets functioned as YHWH's officially commissioned spokespersons (Ezek 38:17; 2 Kgs 17:13; Dan 9:6, etc.). For references see BDB, 714. Even the non-Israelite Job was a servant of YHWH, modeling the divine ideals of piety and (unwittingly) functioning as a vehicle through whom the pattern of divine-human relationships was vindicated before Satan (Job 1:8; 2:3; 42:7–8).

is expressed most clearly by YHWH himself, who identifies him as "David my servant, whom I have chosen" (1 Kgs 11:34).

Fifth, the shepherd will be a נָשִׂיא ("prince") in the midst of his people. Ezekiel's use of the archaic title נָשִׂיא contrasts with Hosea and Jeremiah, who had both spoken explicitly of "David their king." However, it is consistent with his efforts elsewhere to downplay the roles of Israel's monarchs,[26] and harks back to 1 Kgs 11:34, where it is said of Solomon, "I will make him prince (נָשִׂיא) all the days of his life for the sake of David my servant." In chapters 40–48 Ezekiel will apply the title to the official sponsor and patron of the cult, but usually the term functions primarily as a political designation. Ezekiel's preference for נָשִׂיא over מֶלֶךְ ("king"), the normal designation for Israel's rulers, is not intended to deny this person's true kingship but to highlight the distinction between him and the recent occupants of the office. The prophet emphasizes the ruler's identification with the people by noting that he will not only be "prince over Israel" (v. 23),[27] but "prince in their midst." Officially the נָשִׂיא may be "the promoted one,"[28] but in view of his presence in the midst of (בְּתוֹךְ) Israel, some view him simply as *primus inter pares.*[29] One may perhaps recognize here an ironical allusion to Deut 17:19–20, which had prescribed for Israel's kings the reading of the Torah "to prevent their hearts from being exalted about their kinsfolk." However, both his status as shepherd among sheep and the expression "prince over them" suggest authority as well as identification.[30] In this arrangement, YHWH is the divine patron of the people; David is his representative and deputy. Ezekiel's announcement of the appointment of a new David for Israel was intended to instill new hope in the hearts of the exiles. Contrary to appearance, the demise of the Davidic house in 586 BCE did not reflect divine impotence or indifference to previous commitments. These events had not only fulfilled previous prophetic utterances,[31]

26. Compare the use of the term in 7:27; 12:10, 12; 19:1; 21:17, 30[12, 25]; 22:6; 26:16; 27:21; 30:13; 32:29; 37:25; 38:2, 3; 39:1, 18. Except for the reference to Jehoiachin as מֶלֶךְ in 17:12, and David in 37:22–24, Ezekiel reserves this title for foreign kings of Egypt, Babylon, and Tyre.

27. Cf. "princes of Israel" in 19:1; etc.

28. נָשִׂיא derives from נָשָׂא ("lift up"). Except for 7:27, when Ezekiel juxtaposes נָשִׂיא with the people of the land, the term refers to the king (45:16, 22; 46:2–3, 8–9). For studies of the word see Hammershaimb, *Some Aspects,* 54; Levenson, *Theology of the Program,* 55–74; Niehr, "נָשִׂיא nāśî'," 44–53; Duguid, *Ezekiel and the Leaders,* 10–18.

29. So Hossfeld, *Untersuchungen zu Komposition und Theologie,* 272.

30. So also Duguid, *Ezekiel and the Leaders,* 49.

31. Ezek 12:1–16; 17; 19.

they set the stage for a dramatic and new act of YHWH. The decadence of the old order had been removed; now the people are challenged to look forward to a new day when YHWH's Davidic servant will be reinstated in accordance with his eternal and irrevocable covenant.

The texts from Hosea and Jeremiah cited above hinted at an inseparable link between the election of David and the status of Israel as the people of YHWH.[32] A similar development is evident in 34:24, which ties YHWH's national covenant with Israel to the dynastic covenant with David. Indeed a comparison of the national covenant formula and Ezekiel's statement suggests that the prophet perceives the appointment of David as נָשִׂיא as an aspect of the fulfillment of the national pledge, "I will be your God and you shall be my people." The echo of the first line of this covenant is obvious in the first statement of verse 24.[33] Reminiscence of line 2 will be delayed until verse 30. But how is Ezekiel's assertion that "My servant David will be prince among them," related to this formula? The answer is found in the prepositional expression, בְּתוֹכָם ("in their midst"), which recalls an auxiliary affirmation often viewed as a part of the covenant formula, "I will dwell in your midst."[34] For Ezekiel, the prince is more than a political or military functionary, effecting the restoration; his role begins after the restoration has been achieved by God, at his initiative, and in his time.[35] In short, he symbolizes the presence of YHWH in the midst of his people.

The messianic promise of David the prince taking his place among the people of Israel is sealed with an expanded version of the divine self-introductory formula. The statement is deliberately inserted to reinforce confidence in the present prophetic pronouncement and YHWH's irrevocable commitment to David, the promise celebrated in Ps 89:34–38[33–37]. Accordingly, YHWH's restoration of his flock and the appointment of David is not motivated primarily by pity for the bruised and battered sheep of Israel, but from his covenant with his people (cf. Deut 4:31). The goal of the restoration is the reestablishment of that covenant in its full force and scope. The Messiah, who will function as a servant of YHWH

32. Both Hos 3:5 and Jer 30:9–10 speak of "YHWH their God and David their king."

33. Compare וַאֲנִי יְהוָה אֶהְיֶה לָהֶם לֵאלֹהִים ("And I, YHWH, shall be their God," v. 24) with Ezekiel's version of the formula: וַאֲנִי/אָנֹכִי אֶהְיֶה לָהֶם לֵאלֹהִים (11:20; 14:11; 36:28; 37:23, 27).

34. Cf. Gen 17:7; Exod 29:45–46; Lev 26:12–13; etc.

35. Caquot, "Le messianisme," 18–19.

and symbol of the new reality must come from the house of David, a theme to be developed more fully in 37:15–28.

EZEKIEL 37:22–25

The second reference to the restoration of the Davidic dynasty occurs in the interpretation of a sign act involving two pieces of wood on which are inscribed the names Judah and Joseph. Ezekiel is instructed to unite these two sticks as a symbolic gesture promising the eventual reunification of all the tribes of Israel in one nation (37:16–28). The interpretation proper (vv. 21–28) offers an anthology of Ezekielian restoration ideas,[36] bringing his salvation oracles to a fitting conclusion. This verbal explanation divides into two parts (vv. 21–24a; 24b–28), each with its own covenant formula (vv. 23, 27): verses 21–24a are preoccupied with the reunification of the nation under one king; verses 24b–28 with the eternality of YHWH's restorative acts. Accordingly, the specification of one shepherd over all of Israel in verse 24a belongs to the preceding, rather than that which follows, and the identification of David as מֶלֶךְ ("king") in verse 24a ties in with the use of the same word in verse 22, but contrasts with Ezekiel's preferred designation for Israel's rulers, נָשִׂיא, in verse 25. This division of verses 21–28 results in two panels of approximately equal length.[37]

According to the first panel, Ezekiel's interest is not in creating "a single piece of wood" (עֵץ אֶחָד) from two pieces (עֵצִים), but "a single nation" (גּוֹי אֶחָד) from two nations (שְׁנֵי גוֹיִם) (v. 22). The preference for the term גּוֹי over עַם ("people") is deliberate. The latter, a warm relational term, with undertones of kinship, would have been appropriate in another context, but here the concern is the restoration of Israel as a *nation*, which requires the use of גּוֹי.[38] Given prevailing ancient Near Eastern perceptions, by affirming Israel's ethnic, territorial, political, and spiritual integrity Ezekiel paints a remarkably comprehensive picture of a mature nation.

Ezekiel stresses the restoration of Israel's political integrity by announcing the reversal of 931 BCE, when a single people had *de facto* become two nations. For the moment omitting any reference to David, the factual statement of verse 22b was called for by the previous notice

36. For a summary, see Lust, "Ezekiel 36–40," 526–27; cf. Friebel, *Jeremiah's and Ezekiel's Sign-Acts*, 367.

37. In MT the first panel consists of seventy-two words; the second, sixty-eight.

38. See Block, "Nations," 492; "People," 759–60. For a fuller study of these terms see *idem, Foundations of National Identity*, 12–127.

that Israel would be constituted a single nation (גּוֹי אֶחָד). The emphasis is on the singularity of the monarchy: a single king will rule over all the tribes; never again would there be two nations (גּוֹיִם), which is to say two kingdoms (מַמְלָכוֹת). If the emphasis on a single ruler symbolizes the nation's new unity, the present preference for מֶלֶךְ over נָשִׂיא highlights the restoration of Israel to full nationhood.[39] The use of the latter expression here would have suggested less than complete restoration. For the moment Ezekiel offers no hints of the king's identity. His concern is principle: a nation (גּוֹי) is by definition a monarchy (מַמְלָכָה), which must be ruled by a king (מֶלֶךְ).[40]

In verse 23 the promise of spiritual rejuvenation is expressed in terms of a healthy relationship between Israel and her patron deity. Arguing from effect to cause, the prophet begins by announcing the symptoms of the new spiritual reality: the nation will be rid of the defilement resulting from the people's idolatry, disgusting practices, and acts of rebellion. Echoing 36:25–28, the process of purification involves the divine rescue of the Israelites from their "apostasies," their purification, and the renewal of the covenant, expressed by citing the covenant formula, "They shall be my people and I will be their God." The expansion of the covenant formula in verse 24a concretizes the spiritual renewal by announcing his appointment of David as "king" in Israel.[41] By identifying the king by name YHWH not only affirms the eternality of his original promise to David

---

39. In the face of Ezekiel's decided preference for נָשִׂיא ("chieftain, prince"), scholars have long stumbled over the present choice of מֶלֶךְ, and many emend the text here and in verse 24 accordingly, with support from LXX which reads ἄρχων. On the Septuagintal reading, see Lust, "Exegesis and Theology," 217–21; Rofé, "Qumranic Paraphrases," 171–73. Cf. Boehmer, "mlk und nś," 112–77; Hammershaimb, "Ezekiel's View," 51–63; Schunck, "Die Attribute," 651, n. 23. מֶלֶךְ occurs thirty-seven times in the book, twenty-five of which refer to foreign kings: e.g., the kings of Babylon (17:12; 19:9; 21:23–25; 26:7), Egypt (29:2–3), Tyre (28:12), Edom (32:29), the earth (28:17), the coastlands (27:35). Outside of this context, מֶלֶךְ occurs in 1:2 (of Jehoiachin); 7:27 (unnamed and parallel to נָשִׂיא); 17:12 (of Jehoiachin, removed by the king of Babylon); 43:7, 9 (three times, of Israel's past paganized kings). While Ezekiel's hesitancy to designate Israelite kings as מְלָכִים may reflect a basic anti-monarchic stance, the emendation proposed for this text overlooks the fact that מֶלֶךְ provides a better contextual correlative for גּוֹי, especially in the face of the following association of מַמְלָכוֹת and גּוֹיִם. Furthermore, LXX renderings of מֶלֶךְ vary. Only 1:2 and 17:12 translate βασιλεύς; 7:27 drops the reference; 43:7a, 7b, 9 read ἡγούμενοι; the present context (37:22a, 22b, 24) reads ἄρχων.

40. Cf. Duguid, *Ezekiel and the Leaders*, 24–25.

41. The addition seems awkward, but the occurrence of a similar phenomenon in 34:23 cautions against its deletion.

(2 Sam 7:16); he also discredits past rulers who have wrongly claimed the title, "king of Israel," particularly the Josephite/Ephraimite rulers of the northern kingdom. As in 34:23–24, the king's special relationship with YHWH is reflected in the designation, עַבְדִּי ("my servant"). Whereas all the northern kings and many of their Judaean counterparts, especially Ezekiel's contemporaries, had been driven by self-service, this new ruler will embody the ideals established in Deut 17:14–20, submitting to the overlordship of YHWH. As shepherd-king, he will function as the agent of YHWH's reign and the symbol of the nation's unity, exercising watch-care after the divine model set out in chapter 34.

No formal break separates the two panels of this oracle, but as already observed, the theme shifts dramatically from the unification of the nation to the permanence of the restored deity-nation-land relationships This is highlighted by the five-fold occurrence of עוֹלָם, which, as E. Jenni has argued, denotes fundamentally "the remotest time,"[42] either the remote past or the distant future. But along with the sense of duration, the word bears nuances of permanence, durability, inviolability, irrevocability, and immutability, and in so doing points to the definitive nature of the coming salvation.[43] The specific affirmation in verse 25 that "David my servant shall be their prince forever (לְעוֹלָם)" addresses the previous problem of the mortality of even good kings in Israel. Unlike the original David, and his honorable successors like Hezekiah and Josiah, all of whom died, in the future the failure and the moral inconsistency of succeeding rulers will be remedied.

With his five-fold affirmation of the eternality of the restoration, YHWH transforms this oracle into a powerful eschatological statement, envisaging an entirely new existence, where the old historical realities are considered null and void, and the new salvific work of God is perceived as final.[44] For Ezekiel eschatological events are neither ahistorical nor suprahistorical; they are based upon YHWH's past actions in history and represent a final solution to the present historical crisis. But the scope of his eschatological hope extends beyond a renewal of YHWH's covenant with

42. Jenni, "עוֹלָם ʿōlām," 228–30. For a full study see Jenni, "Das Wort ʿōlām in Alten Testament."

43. Jenni, "עוֹלָם ʿōām," 239.

44. The nearest Hebrew equivalent to Greek ἔσχατος, "last" (cf. Kittel, "ἔσχατος," 697–98) is אַחֲרִית. This word combines nuances of finality and newness, as evidenced by Jeremiah's characterization of the eschatological covenant as both "everlasting" (בְּרִית עוֹלָם, 32:40) and "new" (בְּרִית חֲדָשָׁה, 31:31). See further Schunck, "Eschatologie der Propheten," 119; von Rad, Old Testament Theology, 2:112–19.

his people, incorporating all the other promises upon which the Israelites had based their security: YHWH's covenant with David, his establishment of Jerusalem as the place for his name to dwell, and his special interest in the land of Canaan as his land, offered as a gracious fiefdom to Israel to administer on his behalf. In contrast to the following prophecy against Gog, which fixes the time of the battle with this northern foe in the distant future with a variety of temporal phrases,[45] no hints concerning the time of fulfillment are given. These events are deemed eschatological, therefore, not because they are expected to transpire at the end of history but because they are new and they are final—their effects guaranteed to continue forever.

According to verses 24b–25, Israel's renaissance will be demonstrated in a new commitment to the will of YHWH as the divine patron, their occupation of the hereditary homeland forever, and their enjoyment of the rule of David, YHWH's servant, forever. Shifting attention away from political reunification in the first panel, Ezekiel reverts to his preferred designation for Israel's kings, נָשִׂיא (cf. vv. 22, 24a), and defines his role spiritually as "servant of YHWH for them," rather than politically as "king over them" (v. 24). The term נָשִׂיא alludes to the prince's ties with the people and his function as regent under YHWH, and prepares the way for chapters 40–48, where the person with this title functions primarily as religious leader. Just as Israel's title to the hereditary homeland is based upon YHWH's gift to "his servant" Jacob, so the pledge of a new ruler is based upon his promise to another servant, David. The language is obviously dependent on 2 Sam 7, where David is twice identified by YHWH as עַבְדִּי, "my servant" (vv. 5, 8), and where he acknowledges this role no fewer than ten times.[46] This link is strengthened by the description of the new David's tenure as "eternal" (עוֹלָם occurs eight times in the earlier text).[47] YHWH's covenant with the dynasty may have been suspended, but it has not been forgotten. He hereby dismisses unequivocally the conditionality of past occupancy of the throne.[48] What happened to Zedekiah in 586 BCE will

---

45. "Many days hence"(יָמִים רַבִּים, 38:8), "on that day" (בַּיּוֹם הַהוּא, 38:10, 14, 18, 19; 39:11), "in the future years," (בְּאַחֲרִית הַשָּׁנִים, 38:8), "in the future days" (בְּאַחֲרִית הַיָּמִים, 38:16), "the day when I manifest my glory" (יוֹם הִכָּבְדִי, 39:13), "from that day onward" (מִן־הַיּוֹם הַהוּא וָהָלְאָה, 39:22).

46. 2 Sam 7:19, 20, 21, 25, 26, 27 [*bis*], 28, 29 [*bis*].

47. 2 Sam 7:13, 16 [*bis*], 24, 25, 26 (all עַד־עוֹלָם); 29 [*bis*] (לְעוֹלָם). David expresses his consciousness of the eternality of this covenant in his charge to his subjects and to his son Solomon in 1 Chr 28:4, 7, 8, 9.

48. D. Bloesch's description of the new covenant (Jer 31:31–34; Ezek 34:25) ("All

never happen again. In verses 26–27 the attention returns to YHWH, who, as the source of Israel's renewal, promises to make a [re]new[ed] covenant with Israel.

Taken as a whole, this oracle reinforces Ezekiel's exalted view of YHWH—he is faithful to his ancient and modern prophetic word and promises his eternal covenant of peace out of concern for his reputation—as well as his realistic view of God's people. Against the grain of centuries of history and deep-seated prejudices, YHWH extends his grace to the whole house of Israel—not only Judah, but Joseph and his confederates as well. He rescues them not only from sin, but from their divisive past. By renewing the eternal covenant and establishing his residence in the midst of the nation, all tribes enjoy equal access to the divine patron, and participate in the benefactions that emanate from him.

This oracle also reinforces Ezekiel's complex view of the Messiah. In spite of the prophet's avoidance of specifically messianic designations,[49] the messianic significance of this oracle is obvious. The principal features of Ezekiel's Messiah are reflected in the titles and role designations he bears. As David he is heir to the eternal dynastic promises made by YHWH to Israel's greatest king through the prophet Samuel.[50] As עַבְדִּי ("my servant") he enjoys a special relationship with YHWH. Not only is the Messiah's role primarily religious; he also derives his authority by divine appointment rather than personal acumen or democratic election. As נָשִׂיא ("prince, chieftain") he stands at the head of his people, not as a tyrannical ruler, but as one who has been called from their ranks to represent them. As מֶלֶךְ ("king") he symbolizes the nation's new unity. All other pretenders to the throne have been dismissed that Israel may be "one nation" under "one king" occupying the land of Israel. As רֹעֶה אֶחָד ("one shepherd"), a fifth title added in verse 24 to remind his audience of the new dynastic disposition, he will seek the welfare of the flock, protecting and nurturing them after the pattern of YHWH himself (ch. 34), and in fulfillment of the

---

Israel Will Be Saved," 132) apply to the Davidic as well: "It is unconditional in that it proceeds out of the free grace and mercy of God, but its efficacy is contingent on faith and obedience." While David recognized an element of contingency in his charge to Solomon (1 Kgs 2:4; cf. also Ps 132:13 and 1 Chr 28:9), YHWH's threat of discipline in 2 Sam 7 does not suggest cancellation of title to the throne. Ps 89:4–5, 29–38[3–4, 28–37] speaks specifically of an eternal and irretractable covenant.

49. So also the Targum, on which see Levey, *Targum of Ezekiel*, 4–5; Levey, *The Messiah*, 83–87.

50. 2 Sam 7. In this regard Ezekiel follows long-standing prophetic tradition: Amos 9:11; Hos 3:5; Isa 8:23–9:6[9:1–7]; 11:1–5; Mic 5:1–4[2–5]; Jer 23:5–6.

ancient Mosaic charter for kingship.[51] In all these roles, Ezekiel's Messiah symbolizes the realities of the new age. Remarkably, he plays no part in the restoration of the nation. He neither gathers the people nor leads them back to their homeland. Unlike other prophets, Ezekiel makes no mention of the Messiah as an agent of peace[52] or righteousness,[53] these being attributed to the direct activity of God. The Messiah's personal presence symbolizes the reign of YHWH in the glorious new age.[54]

THE נָשִׂיא ("PRINCE") IN EZEKIEL 40–48

The נָשִׂיא in Ezekiel's concluding vision is an enigmatic figure. On the one hand, the title links him with the person described in 34:24 and 37:25. But the portrait of this person is less than ideal, and in the narrative of the vision the prophet provides no clear hints of a Davidic connection, the basis of all messianic hopes. The privileges and responsibilities of the נָשִׂיא in Ezekiel's new order are described in a series of scattered fragments: 44:3; 45:7–8 and its echo in 48:21; 45:21—46:12.[55] Based on these texts the following observations concerning the role and function of the נָשִׂיא may be made:

1. Although the outer eastern gateway is forever closed to human traffic, the נָשִׂיא alone may sit in the gateway and eat his sacrificial meals there (44:1–3).[56]

51. Deut 17:14–20.

52. Isa 9:5–6[6–7]; 11:6–9; Mic 5:5[6]; Jer 23:6; Zech 9:9–10.

53. Isa 9:5–6[6–7]; 11:2–5; Jer 23:5–6. On the relationship of Ezekiel's Messiah to other biblical portraits see Moeinikes, "Messianismus," 289–306.

54. For a critique of Laato's forced thesis that the model of kingship of Ezekiel's new David derives from the royal ideology prevailing in Josiah's time (*Josiah and David Redivivus*, 177–89), see Becker's "Review of *Josiah and David Redivivus*," 250–55.

55. Many follow Gese (*Verfassungsentwurf*, esp. 108–23) in isolating 44:1–3, 45:21–25, and 46:1–10, 12 as a discreet נָשִׂיא stratum. Laato (*Josiah and David Redivivus*, 189–96) offers a recent modification of Gese's theory. For a convincing critique of this approach see Duguid, *Ezekiel and the Leaders*, 27–31. The abruptness of the notice and the fact that 44:3b is largely repeated in 46:8 have raised questions concerning the authenticity of this verse. For discussion see Zimmerli (*Ezekiel 2*, 439). However, the present passing reference to the נָשִׂיא, to be followed by a later fuller treatment, represents another example of the "resumptive exposition" that characterizes the book and may well have characterized Ezekiel's rhetorical style.

56. לֶחֶם, literally "bread," but here used in a broader cultic sense.

2. The נָשִׂיא is assigned a special territorial grant, separate from the tribal allotments, consisting of two large tracts of land on either side, east and west, of the sacred reserve (45:7–9; 48:21).

3. The נָשִׂיא must provide the prescribed animals, grain, and oil for the purification, whole burnt, and grain offerings, which are to be offered on his and the people's behalf (45:21–25).

4. On weekly sabbaths and new moon celebrations the נָשִׂיא shall enter the eastern gateway of the inner court through the vestibule, stand by the post of the gate,[57] that is the jamb between the vestibule and the series of guard recesses,[58] to observe the priests presenting the offerings on his behalf. Forbidden to step out onto the most sacred space of the inner court, he must prostrate himself on the threshold of the gate (46:1–7, 12).

5. At the appointed festivals the נָשִׂיא must enter the sacred precinct with the rest of the lay worshippers, who are permitted to enter the outer court through either the northern or the southern gate. However, unlike the נָשִׂיא, the common folk may not turn around inside the precinct and exit via the gate through which they entered (46:8–10).

6. The נָשִׂיא may present additional voluntary offerings to YHWH, but they must be presented in the same way as the Sabbath and new moon offerings, with him observing from the inner east gate. After the offerings are completed he must leave this gate and it shall be shut behind him (46:12).

7. The נָשִׂיא may present portions of his property to his sons as their permanent possessions, but should he wish to award any of his land to his servants, in the year of liberation (שְׁנַת הַדְּרוֹר) it must return to the prince (46:17).[59]

8. The נָשִׂיא is barred from confiscating property of the people and giving it to his sons as their own territorial grants (46:18).

57. The architectural vocabulary changes from chapter 40, מְזוּזָה, "doorpost," replacing אַיִל, though מְזוּזָה had been used of the doorposts of the temple (41:21; 43:8; 45:19) and the inner gate (מְזוּזַת שַׁעַר, 45:19; 46:2).

58. See 40:28–37.

59. Whereas his contemporary, Jeremiah, applied the term דְּרוֹר to the "release" of persons (Jer 34:8, 15, 17), in the present ordinance Ezekiel modifies a Mosaic custom of "proclaiming release" (קְרָא דְּרוֹר) every fiftieth year at which time all enslaved Israelites were to return to their patrimonial holdings (אֲחֻזָּה).

What is to be made of all these regulations? Recently some have read the Ezekielian Torah as a fundamentally anti-monarchic polemic.[60] Whereas under the old order kings had built temples, appointed cult officials, assigned ritual duties, offered sacrifices, and encroached upon sacred space with their private buildings (43:7–8), this ordinance assigns the civil ruler a third rank, two or three rungs below deity: Zadokite priests have access to YHWH, and the Levitical priests may serve within the courts, but the נָשִׂיא is repulsed. He must eat his meals at the gate.[61] Furthermore, in this vision the temple is deliberately separated from the royal palace complex (43:8; 48:19). The capital "city" is not the king's private preserve but belongs to the entire house of Israel, and severe restrictions are placed on the prince's management of land.

But do these details reflect a basically anti-monarchic stance in Ezekiel's final vision? We think not. One must distinguish between the monarchy in principle and the conduct of Israel's monarchs in history. In the light of the general ancient Near Eastern association of mature nationhood with kingship structures,[62] and also in view of specific traditional monarchic expectations[63] and the eternality of the Davidic covenant (2 Sam 7), it is inconceivable that Ezekiel would have opposed the monarchy *per se*. On the contrary, as we have seen, in 37:16–25 (cf. 34:23–25) he combines ancient tribal and Davidic covenantal traditions to promise specifically the return of David as king over all the tribes of Israel.[64] Furthermore, reconfiguring power structures is no guarantee that the abuses of the past will be resolved. Ezekiel's final vision does not eliminate hierarchical institutions; it redefines how existing structures will work in his new order.

60. J. Z. Smith, *To Take Place*, 61–62; Stevenson, *Vision of Transformation*, 109–23, 151–54.

61. Interpreting נָשִׂיא as equivalent to פֶּחָה, "governor," Tuell (*Law of the Temple*, 119) interprets נָשִׂיא as "a title descriptive of the cultic task of the *nśy*." He continues: "For the post-exilic priestly establishment this was of paramount concern, and reminiscent of Israel's ancient and honorable past, yet lacking dynastic or imperial overtones"; hence, he argues, it was not offensive to the Persian overlords.

62. Reflected in 1 Sam 8:5, 19. On this subject see Block, *Foundations of National Identity*, 493–585.

63. Note the expectation of kings in the patriarchal promise (Gen 17:6, 16; 35:11); the association of the scepter with Judah (Gen 49:10); the Balaam oracles (Num 24:7, 17); the Deuteronomic "charter for kingship" (Deut 17:14–20).

64. This fact may be denied only by excising the term מֶלֶךְ from the text. See the note above.

Past scholars have correctly recognized the special status of the נָשִׂיא in Ezekiel's final vision.[65] He is clearly an exalted figure, far more important than the "princes" of the premonarchic period. But does this mean Ezekiel identifies this נָשִׂיא with the messianic figure described in 34:23–25 and 37:22–25? Though some would argue that denying this link drives a wedge between the נָשִׂיא in chapters 40–48 and the נָשִׂיא in earlier chapters,[66] the view that the presentation of this figure in the latter chapters is in continuity with earlier references must answer several important objections.

First, Israelite messianic expectations were by definition monarchic in character, and immutably based upon YHWH's dynastic covenant with David. Why then are chapters 40–48 silent on the Davidic connection? They seem indeed to portray the נָשִׂיא as an honorable figure, but without apparent political power.

Second, Israelite messianism insisted on a close link between the Messiah and Jerusalem/ Zion. Why then does Jerusalem seem to be out of the picture in Ezekiel's final vision? The prince and his land are deliberately separated from the city bearing the name "YHWH is there" (48:35) and the temple, YHWH's true residence.

Third, Israelite messianism perceives the Messiah as sovereign over the entire universe. Why then does this vision not only tie him down to the land of Israel? It also places severe restrictions on the rights of the נָשִׂיא. YHWH may authorize him, even invite him to eat before him in this gate, but as a mortal he must enter by another way. Only YHWH may enter through the eastern gate.

Fourth, and perhaps most seriously, elsewhere (including Ezekiel's own statements in 34:23–24 and 37:27–25) Israel's Messiah is always portrayed in glorious idealistic terms. Why is the portrait of the נָשִׂיא in the Ezekielian Torah so shockingly realistic? Not only must offerings be presented on his behalf; specific ordinances warn him not to exploit and abuse his subjects like Israel's kings had done in the past (46:18).

These objections, however, may be answered from several directions. First, although one might expect a consistent use of a technical term like נָשִׂיא throughout the book, Ezekiel has a habit of using the same expressions with different nuances.

65. J. Wright ("A Tale of Three Cities," 17) comments: "The east gate legitimates the prince's power, equating him with the divine presence within the society."

66. Levenson, *Theology*, 75–101. Laato, *Josiah and David Redivivus*, 196, recognizes the temple mountain, the restoration of the temple, and the important role of the Messiah in this restoration, as links between the pro-נָשִׂיא traditions of chapters 40–48 and chapters 34 and 37.

Second, dramatic shift in genre is evident between the earlier restoration oracles[67] and the idealistic final vision. Whereas the former are closely tied to history, anticipating a wholesale reversal of the events surrounding the fall of Jerusalem in 586 BCE, the latter is contrived, idealized, symbolic, and many of its features are unimaginable.[68] Contrary to common popular opinion, the description of the temple is not presented as a blueprint for some future building to be constructed with human hands.[69] This vision picks up the theme of divine presence announced in 37:26–27 and describes the spiritual reality in concrete terms, employing the familiar cultural idioms of temple, altar, sacrifices, נָשִׂיא, and land. In presenting this theological constitution for the new Israel, YHWH announces the righting of all old wrongs and the establishment of permanent healthy deity-nation-land relationships Ezekiel's final vision presents a lofty ideal: Where God is, there is Zion. Where God is, there is also order and the fulfillment of all his promises.

Third, the primary concern in this vision is not political, but cultic. The issue is not the return of David, but the presence of YHWH. Accordingly, the role of the נָשִׂיא is facilitative, not regally symbolic. Unlike past kings, who perverted the worship of YHWH for selfish ends and/or sponsored the worship of other gods, this נָשִׂיא is charged with promoting the worship of YHWH in spirit and in truth. Uniquely in this visionary with its radically theocentric portrayal of Israel's future, the נָשִׂיא emerges as a religious functionary, serving the holy community of faith, which itself is focused on the worship of the God who dwells in their midst. Where the presence of God is recognized, there is purity and holiness. Ezekiel's נָשִׂיא is not responsible for the administration of the cult. Not only does he not participate actively in the ritual; he does not build the temple, design the worship, or appoint the priests; these prerogatives belong to YHWH. This agrees with the image of the נָשִׂיא in 34:23–24, who is installed as undershepherd by YHWH only after the latter has personally rescued Israel.[70] In this ideological presentation the נָשִׂיא functions as YHWH's appointed lay patron and sponsor of the cult, whose activity ensures the continuance of harmonious relations between deity and subjects. The God of Israel has fulfilled his covenant promises, regathering the people and restoring them

67. Chapter 34 is a genuine salvation oracle; 37:15–28 an interpreted sign-act.

68. A subject dealt with in my paper "Envisioning the Good News," read to the Evangelical Theological Society in Chicago, November 18, 1994. See below, 157–73.

69. A point convincingly argued by Stevenson, *Vision of Transformation*, 11–30.

70. Cf. Duguid, *Ezekiel and the Leaders*, 50–55.

to their/his land. More important, he has recalled the people to himself, and established his residence in their midst. Now let them celebrate, and let the נָשִׂיא lead the way!

5

Gog and Magog in Ezekiel's Eschatological Vision[1]

INTRODUCTION

I had intended to include a general discussion of what is meant by the term "eschatology," and a survey of biblical expressions generally thought to carry eschatological meaning. However, space constraints have forced me to move immediately into the eschatological hope of Ezekiel, and concentrate on the place of the Gog oracle in this prophet's vision of Israel's future. There is enough here to engage us. This essay will consist of three major parts: (1) general observations in the light of which the Gog oracle should be interpreted; (2) general observations on the form and nature of the Gog oracle; (3) a summary interpretation of the oracle as I see it. I shall conclude with brief reflections on the theological significance of the Gog oracle for Ezekiel's immediate audience and for his readers today.

GENERAL OBSERVATIONS ON EZEKIEL'S ESCHATOLOGY

Before discussing the Gog oracle itself, there are six observations on Ezekiel's eschatological messages as a whole which need our consideration.

1. This essay was originally published in *"The Reader Must Understand": Eschatology in Bible and Theology*, edited by K. Brower and M. Elliott, 85–116. Leicester, UK: InterVarsity, 1997.

95

First, although we tend to think of the eschaton as the end of human history as we know it, Ezekiel actually envisions two ἔσχατα, both involving the nation of Israel and/or Judah, one imminent, the other in the distant future. Most of the oracles of judgment in chapters 4–24 concern the end of the nation of Judah as Ezekiel and his contemporaries knew it. But eschatological language dominates only one oracle, the three-fold alarm of the sentry in 7:1–27.[2] The prophet's emotions are at a fever pitch as he announces the end of the nation with the six-fold repetition of the word קֵץ/הַקֵּץ, "An end/the end!" (vv. 2–3, 6)[3] and ominous references to הַיּוֹם, "the day" (vv. 7 , 10, 12), and הָעֵת, "the time" (vv. 7, 12), which represent cryptic references to יוֹם יְהוָה, "the day of YHWH." Ezekiel's emphasis on the event's imminence in this oracle[4] represents his answer to his contemporaries' dismissal of the notion of YHWH's judgmental intervention in their history as a delusion (12:21–25) and/or as an irrelevant and remote eschatological event, having no bearing on the present generation (12:26–28).[5] But the end envisioned here is not a chronological end of time or the end of cosmic history; it is the end of a city's existence.

Whereas the judgment oracles in chapters 4–24 focus on Jerusalem's imminent eschaton, the restoration oracles of chapters 34–48 look beyond the judgment to the distant future, when the fortunes of the nation of Israel will turn around and the disastrous events of the imminent present will be reversed. Fragmentary messages of hope have indeed been sounded occasionally prior to the fall of Jerusalem to the Babylonians,[6] but the full

2. The three alarms which crescendo with increasing intensity consist of verses 2aβ–4, 5–9, and 10–27 respectively.

3. In this chapter LXX translates קֵץ as πέρας, which, like ἔσχατος, may be used of both spatial extremity and chronological termination. ἔσχατος occurs six times in the LXX version of Ezekiel. In 35:5 it translates Hebrew קֵץ, "end" (in the phrase בְּעֵת עֲוֺן קֵץ, "at the time of the punishment of the end"), which in this context refers to Jerusalem's imminent end. The remaining five occurrences are all found in the Gog oracle, where it is used spatially (for יַרְכְּתֵי צָפוֹן, "the remotest part of the north," 38:5, 15; 39:2), and temporally (for בְּאַחֲרִית הַשָּׁנִים, "in the latter years," 38:8; בְּאַחֲרִית הַיָּמִים, "in the latter days," 38:16).

4. Notice the language of imminence: בָּא/בָּאָה, "It has come" (nine times in verses 1–12); עַתָּה, "Now" (vv. 3, 8); הִנֵּה, "Behold, watch out!" (vv. 5, 6, 10a, 10b); יָצְאָה, "It has gone forth" (v. 10); הִגִּיעַ, "It has arrived" (v. 12); מִקָּרוֹב, "shortly" (v. 8); and קָרוֹב, "It is near" (v. 7).

5. Cf. Hoffmann, "Day of the Lord," 45–47. Elsewhere Hoffmann argues that קָרוֹב יוֹם יְהוָה is a juristic technical phrase first coined by Zephaniah to emphasize the legal aspect of the day of YHWH. It was primarily a day of judgment for the wicked. Cf. Hoffmann, "The Root QRB," 70–73.

6. Ezek 11:16–21; 16:60–63; 17:22–24; 20:39–44.

development of these themes does not occur until the imminent eschaton arrives with the news that the city has fallen (33:21–22).

Second, the eschatological nature of Ezekiel's restoration oracles is not as obvious as scholars generally assume. Overtly eschatological language is rare in chapters 34–48. Indeed, if explicit technical vocabulary is a criterion for identifying an oracle as eschatological, then only the Gog oracle (38:1—39:29) qualifies, and even here this is uncertain. References to the day of YHWH are absent altogether. The expression בַּיּוֹם הַהוּא, "on that day," does indeed occur four times (38:10, 14, 18; 39:11), but in none of these instances does it bear the technical sense of יוֹם יְהוָה, "the day of YHWH." The only possible eschatological signals are found in 38:8 and 38:16, which contain the phrases בְּאַחֲרִית הַשָּׁנִים, "in the latter years," and בְּאַחֲרִית הַיָּמִים, "in the latter days," respectively.[7] But these may arguably mean no more than "in the course of time, in the future,"[8] that is, when the conditions spelled out in 38:8 will have been fulfilled. Nowhere does the text suggest that the events envisioned "pertain to the end of time."

Third, Ezekiel's vision of Israel's future is founded upon the nation's ancient covenantal traditions,[9] all of which involve eternal promises made by YHWH to his covenant people. To *Abraham* YHWH promised on oath a series of benefactions with universal[10] and "eternal" (עַד־עוֹלָם) implications: to be God to him and his descendants,[11] innumerable progeny,[12] and the land of Canaan.[13] At *Sinai* YHWH entered into a covenant with the nation of Israel which promised for them a future of blessedness and prosperity.[14] To *David* and his descendants YHWH promised eternal title

---

7. מִיָּמִים רַבִּים, "after [literally "from"] many days," in verse 8 should probably also be included.

8. Cf. Seebass, "אַחֲרִית *achᵃrîth*," 210–12; Jenni, "אחר *'ḥr danach*," 116–17. Compare Dan 2:28 and 10:14, where "in the latter days" functions as a technical term for the eschaton.

9. For a helpful summary see Petersen, "Eschatology (OT)," 575–79. For more detailed discussions concerning various aspects of Israel's eschatology see Müller, *Ursprünge und Strukturen*; Preuss (ed.), *Eschatologie*.

10. E.g., Gen 12:3, "In you/your seed shall all the families of the earth (מִשְׁפְּחֹת הָאֲדָמָה) be blessed." (Cf. 18:18; 22:18; 26:4; 28:14).

11. Gen 17:7–8; 26:3–4; cf. 12:3a.

12. Like the dust of the earth, the sand on the seashore, and the stars of the sky. Cf. Gen 13:16; 15:1–6; 16:10; 17:4–6; 22:17–18; 26:4, 24; 28:14.

13. Gen 12:7; 13:14–15; 17; 15:7–21; 26:3; 28:13; 35:12. Cf. Ps 105:10 = 1 Chr 16:17.

14. Lev 26:1–13; Deut 28:1–14. Although the covenant curses warned against infidelity to the divine suzerain, the covenant held out the prospect of a renewal of the relationship if Israel would respond appropriately to their punishment. Lev 25:40–45;

to the throne of Israel.[15] Concomitant with this covenant with David was YHWH's choice of *Zion* as his eternal dwelling place.[16] While Ezekiel's contemporaries had based their eternal security on these covenantal promises, the prophet himself had employed a variety of rhetorical strategies[17] to expose the illusory nature of their claims, predicting that YHWH would abandon his temple,[18] the Davidic house would be removed from the throne,[19] YHWH would leave his people,[20] and they would be removed from the land.[21] But the story could not end with the fall of Jerusalem. After all, YHWH's promises were irrevocable and eternal.[22] When Jeru-

---

Deut 4:29–37; 29:29–30:20. The Sabbath granted Israel as a symbol of the eternality of the covenant. Note the use of בְּרִית עוֹלָם, "eternal covenant," in Exod 31:16 and Lev 24:8. David recognizes the eternality of this covenant in 2 Sam 7:24, 26. The phrase gains popularity in the prophets. Cf. Isa 55:3; 61:8; Jer 32:40; 50:5; Ezek 16:60; 37:26.

15. 2 Sam 7:13, 15, 25, 29a, 29b (= 1 Chr 17:12, 14, 23, 27a, 27b); cf. 1 Kgs 2:4; 8:25; 9:5; Pss 89:4–5, 29–30, 37–38[3–4, 28–29, 36–37]; 132:10–12. Cf. the later description of this as a בְּרִית עוֹלָם, "eternal covenant," in 2 Sam 23:5.

16. 1 Kgs 8:12–21; Ps 132:13–16; cf. Pss 48; 68:16–19[15–78]; 78:68–71; 87. Also 1 Kgs 8:12–13.

17. (1) Legal addresses (רִיב): 14:12–15:8; 16:1–63; 20:1–44; 22:1–16; 23:1–49; (2) disputations: 11:1–12, 14–21; 12:21–25, 26–28; 18:1–32; 24:1–24; (3) figurative addresses (מְשָׁלִים): 19:1–14; 21:1–22[20:45—21:17]; 22:17–22; (4) laments: 19:1–14; (5) interpreted sign-acts: 4:1–5:17; 12:1–20; 21:23–32[18–27]; (6) watchman-type judgment speeches: 6:1–14; 7:1–27; 22:23–31; (7) vision reports: 8:1—10:22; 11:22–25.

18. Ezek 8–11.

19. Ezek 12:1–16; 17:1–21; 19:1–14. Jeremiah is even more emphatic announcing that Jehoiachin's/Coniah's descendants will never occupy the throne again (Jer 22:30).

20. Ezek 23.

21. It may be argued that all the oracles in chapters 4–24 are directed at one or more of the pillars on which the nation's immediate hopes rested. Promise of land (Abrahamic covenant): 4:1–3, 9–17; 5:5–15; 6:1–7; 7:1–27; 11:1–21; 12:17–20; 14:12–23; 15:1–8; 16:1–63; 21:6–22[1–17]; 21:23–32[18–27]; 22:1–31; 23:1–49; 24:1–15. Promise of covenant relationship (Israelite/Sinaitic covenant): 3:16–21; 5:4, 16–17; 6:11–14; 14:1–23; 15:1–8; 16:1–60; 18:1–32; 20:1–44; 23:1–49; 33:1–20; 33:23–29. Promise of dynasty (Davidic covenant): 12:1–16; 17:1–24; 19:1–14; 21:30–32[25–27]. Promise of residence in Zion: 7:20–24; 8:1—10:22; 11:22–25; 24:16–27. On these pillars, see Figure 1 above.

22. Just as Ezekiel's judgment oracles had sought to demolish the pillars upon which official orthodoxy based Jerusalem's/Judah's security, so the restoration oracle of chapters 34–48 seek deliberately to reconstruct those pillars: promise of land (Abrahamic covenant): 11:17; 22:42; 34:25–29; 35:1—36:15; 36:33–36; 38:1—39:20; 47:1—48:7, 23–29; promise of covenant relationship (Sinaitic covenant): 11:18–21; 16:60–63; 34:1–31; 36:16–32, 37–38; 37:1–14; 37:15–21; 37:25–28; 39:21–29; promise of dynasty (Davidic covenant): 17:22–24; 34:23–24; 37:22–25; promise of residence in Zion: 22:40–41; 37:26–27; 40:1—46:24; 48:8–22, 30–35.

salem fell to Babylon the benefactions promised by those covenants had indeed been suspended, but the promises could not be annulled or permanently withdrawn. The deity-nation-land relationship had to be restored, and the Davidic ruler had to be reinstalled as king. These notions are at the heart of Ezekiel's eschatological hope.

Fourth, although the tone of Ezekiel's restoration oracles contrasts sharply with his earlier messages of judgment, familiar judgmental elements persist. The woe oracle against the leaders of Israel preceding the promise of a restored flock in 34:1–10 is reminiscent of the oracles against the false prophets and prophetesses in chapter 13. The oracle against Mount Seir/Edom before the promise of a restored land in 35:1–15 recalls the prophecies against the foreign nations in chapters 25–26. The lengthy Gog prophecy in chapters 38–39 shares many of these features as well.

Fifth, these extended salvation oracles provide further examples of what I refer to as typically Ezekielian resumptive exposition. Notions briefly introduced in the context of earlier judgment oracles[23] are picked up and expounded in great detail. There is no need to depreciate these fragments as later additions inserted under the influence of the fully developed oracles.[24] Not only had the covenant curses in Lev 26:40–45 held out the prospect of ultimate renewal after judgment;[25] the compassionate character of YHWH and his fidelity to his covenant necessitated it.[26] Furthermore, Ezekiel's predecessor and contemporary, Jeremiah, envisioned just such an event within seventy years.[27] It is preferable, therefore, to interpret the earlier statements as pre-586 BCE premonitions of Israel's final restoration.[28]

23. Ezek 11:14–21; 16:53–63; 17:22–24; 20:39–44; 28:24–26.

24. So also Boadt, "Function of the Salvation Oracles," 3.

25. Cf. also Deut 29:29—30:10.

26. Cf. Deut 4:25–31.

27. Jer 29:10–14, on which see Larsson, "When did the Babylonian Captivity Begin?" 417–23. Fishbane has rightly maintained (*Biblical Interpretation*, 480) that this passage is not to be dismissed as an *ex eventu* prophecy: (1) *ex eventu* proclamations could afford to be more precise; (2) in Israel's *Umwelt* the figure seventy was a commonly accepted typological number for the duration of exile. Cf. Borger, *Inschriften Asarhaddons*, 65 (episode 15). On this text see Luckenbill, "Black Stone of Esarhaddon," 167–68; Nougayrol, "Textes hépatoscopiques," 85. See also Whitley, "The Term Seventy Years Captivity," 60–72; Orr, "Seventy Years of Babylon," 304–6; Ackroyd, "Seventy Year Period," 23–27; Borger, "Additional Remark," 74; (3) the text fails to mention the reconstruction of the temple, an element that would certainly have been expected in an oracle after the fact.

28. Baltzer ("Literarkritische und literarhistorische Anmerkungen," 171), acknowledges that at least 11:14–21 dates to a time when the temple was still standing.

Sixth, Ezekiel's understanding of the sequence of events involved in Israel's restoration was conventional. It was not only based upon Israel's own perceptions of nationhood,[29] but also patterned after common ancient Near Eastern judgment-restoration traditions. Just as Ezekiel's portrayal of the sequence of human sin-divine wrath-divine abandonment-disaster/exile in his oracles of judgment followed established patterns,[30] so his structure of Israel's anticipated reconstruction finds numerous analogues in ancient literature. This structure typically included the following succession of motifs: (1) a change in the disposition of the deity; (2) the appointment of a new ruler; (3) the reconstruction of the temple; (4) the return of the deity; (5) the regathering of the scattered population; (6) the establishment of peace and prosperity.[31] For the prophet, and those responsible for collecting and arranging his oracles, the fateful year of 586 BCE did not mark the end, but the center of the nation's history and YHWH's dealing with her.[32]

In light of these observations, the arrangement and shape of Ezekiel's salvation oracles are both logical and traditional. Generically his hopeful messages divide into two major blocks. In the first (chapters 34–39) the good news is proclaimed; in the second (chapters 40–48) the good news is envisioned. But in both the focus is on YHWH's restorative actions, for the glory of his name, according to the following grand apologetic scheme:

1. Renewing YHWH's role as divine shepherd/King of Israel (34:1–31)

2. Renewing YHWH's land (35:1—36:15)

3. Renewing YHWH's honor (36:16–38)

4. Renewing YHWH's people (37:1–14)

5. Renewing YHWH's covenant (37:15–28)

6. Renewing YHWH's role as defender of his people (38:1—39:29)

7. Renewing YHWH's presence among his people (40:1—46:24)

8. Renewing YHWH's presence in the land (47:1—48:35)

29. Which demanded (1) the participation of the entire house of Israel (2) the renewal of the relationship between people and deity; (3) the return of the population to the homeland; (4) the installation of an indigenous (Davidic) monarchy. Cf. Block, "Nations," 492–95.

30. Cf. Bodi, *Ezekiel and the Poem of Erra*, 183–218.

31. For details see Block, "Divine Abandonment," 15–42 (reprinted in *By the River Chebar*, 73–99); see also my earlier discussion in *Gods of the Nations*, 132–48.

32. Cf. Baltzer, "Literarkritische und literarhistorische Anmerkungen," 181.

We must interpret the oracle against Gog in Ezekiel 38–39 within this cultural and literary context, a matter to which we now turn.

THE NATURE AND DESIGN OF THE GOG ORACLE

The boundaries of the Gog oracle are clearly defined by the word event formula in 38:1 and the signatory formula in 39:29. After the opening formula, which serves as a general heading for both chapters, the text divides into two remarkably symmetrical panels, consisting of 38:1–23 and 39:1–29. The intentionality of this symmetry is reflected in the close correspondence between the introductions of the two parts (38:1–4aα; 39:1–2aα) and their parity in length.[33] Although dramatic shifts in style and content and the insertion of numerous rhetorical formulae[34] create the impression of an extremely complex oracle, chapters 38 and 39 function as a diptych, two leaves of a single document.

Whereas previous scholarship has concentrated on reconstructing the literary evolution of the Gog oracle,[35] I follow recent holistic approaches[36] in accepting the fundamental integrity and coherence of chapters 38

33. Panel A (38:2–23) consists of 365 words; panel B (39:1–29) 357 words.

34. Most of these highlight this text as divine speech and/or emphasize the divine objective in the proclamation and the event: (1) new charge to the prophet to speak, which subdivide each of the major panels into two subsections (38:14; 39:17), yielding the following subsection: A¹ 38:2–13; A² 38:14–23; B¹ 39:1–16; B² 39:17–29; (2) the citation formula (38:3, 14; 39:1, 17); (3) the signatory formula, which may signal the conclusion of a paragraph (39:10, 20, 29), or function as rhetorical punctuation marks (28:18, 21; 39:5, 8, 13); (4) variations of the recognition formula, at the ends of paragraphs (38:15 [cf. the following citation formula]; 38:23 [the end of panel A]) or incorporated into the divine speeches (39:6, 7, 22, 28); (5) the logical particle, לָכֵן, "Therefore" (38:14; 39:25); (6) time notices: וְהָיָה בַּיּוֹם הַהוּא, "and it will happen in that day" (38:18; 39:11); מְיָמִים רַבִּים "after many days," and בְּאַחֲרִית הַשָּׁנִים "in the latter years" (38:8); and בְּאַחֲרִית הַיָּמִים, "in the latter days" (38:16) are chronological markers.

35. Often these studies end by identifying an Ezekielian core, and attributing the rest to a series of interpretative additions (*Nachinterpretation*) by the "School of Ezekiel." Zimmerli's (*Ezekiel 2*, 296–99) reduction of the basic text to 38:1–9 (minus significant glosses), 39:1–5, 17–20, is more generous than some, but he ascribes the remainder to a series of interpretative expansions, each addition commenting on the preexistent text. For evaluations of Zimmerli's treatment of these chapters see Scalise, *From Prophet's Word*, 114–34; Odell, "Are You He of Whom the Prophets Spoke?," 1–42. Hossfeld (*Untersuchungen zu Komposition und Theologie*, 402–508) limits the original core to 38:1–3a and 39:1b–5, the rest representing six stages of expansion: (1) 38:3b–9; (2) 39:17–20; (3) 38:10–16; 39:6–7, 21–22; (4) 38:17; 39:8–10; (5) 38:18–23; 39:11–13 (14–16?); (6) 39:23–29.

36. Astour admits the oracle contains doublets and glosses that betray subsequent

and 39 as a literary whole.[37] With respect to genre, ever since F. Hitzig first applied the term "apocalyptic" to the prophecies of Ezekiel,[38] it has been fashionable to interpret the Gog oracle as an example of this genre.[39] However, recent work on apocalyptic literature raises doubts about the propriety of this classification. It certainly does not fit the standard definition of "apocalyptic" offered by J. J. Collins:

> "Apocalypse" is a genre of revelatory literature with a narrative framework, in which a revelation is mediated by an otherworldly being to a human recipient, disclosing a transcendent reality which is both temporal, insofar as it envisages eschatological salvation, and spatial insofar as it involves another, supernatural world.[40]

---

elaboration, but he argues "the style and imagery of its basic parts are not different from those of the chapters which are generally accepted as genuine writings of Ezekiel" ("Ezekiel's Prophecy of Gog," 567). Hals (*Ezekiel*, 285) comments, "The efforts of Zimmerli and Hossfeld here are welcome as speculative attempts of considerable heuristic value in enabling the discovery of even further complexities, but they are not at all convincing as actual literary reconstructions." R. Klein (*Ezekiel*, 158) asserts that these chapters antedate 539 BC, and if such an early date can be accepted for all or part of the oracle, then the possibility remains that the prophet himself is responsible for the text. Odell ("Are You He of Whom the Prophets Spoke?") criticizes the work of previous form critics for severing the Gog oracle from the rest of the book of Ezekiel and artificially and arbitrarily divorcing prophecy, which represents a response to historical events, and theological reflection on prophecy, which is supposedly less tied to events. Contrast the approach of Ahroni ("Gog Prophecy," 1–27), who defends the unity of the oracle, particularly 38:1—39:24, but argues for a late, post-exilic date.

37. Though 39:25–29 may reflect later reflection, intentionally composed to integrate the oracle with its broader present literary context.

38. Hitzig, *Prophet Ezechiel*, xiv–xv.

39. According to Ahroni ("The Gog Prophecy," 11–13), its "totally unrealistic and imaginative" style, along with its hyperbole and fantasy, contrast sharply with the historical roots and the realism of the rest of the book. Furthermore, the cosmic dualism, represented by the conflict between YHWH and Gog, the obscurities, the symbolic language, the prominence of the number seven, the enigmatic nature of the names of peoples, all point to an apocalyptic genre, and the references to previous prophecy (38:17) and the expression, "the navel of the earth" (38:12), give supporting evidence for a late date. Becker ("Erwägungen," 137–49) interprets the entire book of Ezekiel as a late pseudonymous apocalyptic work.

40. Collins, "Towards the Morphology of a Genre," 9. Cf. his preceding paradigm of apocalyptic characteristics (ibid., 5–9), which exposes the tenuous nature of the links between Ezek 38–39 and other apocalyptic writings. See also his fuller discussion of apocalyptic texts in the following essay of the same volume, "The Jewish Apocalypses," 21–59. According to Hanson ("Apocalypse," 27; cf. Hanson, *Dawn of*

Beyond the issue of not fitting this definition of apocalyptic, we note that many substantive and stylistic characteristics found in true apocalypses are common in ordinary prophecy: conflict between YHWH and the enemies of Israel, the deliverance of his people, YHWH's sovereignty over the universe. Furthermore, the claim that this text transcends temporal and historical realities derives from inadequate attention to the social environment from which the prophecy derives and to which it speaks.[41] Expressions like "after many days/years" (38:8) and "in that day" (38:18; 39:11) thrust some elements of this prophecy into the distant future, and 38:18–23 introduces the notion of a cosmic shaking, but neither serves as a precursor to an ultimate eschatological salvation, nor a true consummation.[42] The focus remains on Israel's own salvation which, like Ezekiel's previous restoration oracles, results in the vindication of YHWH's holiness, and the nation's recognition of him. At issue is primarily the local problem: Gog and his hordes invading the land of Israel. The name Gog and the dominance of the number seven may be symbolic, but this is a far cry from the elaborate symbolism of Daniel or the New Testament book of Revelation. On these bases, the apocalyptic approach to the Gog oracle should be abandoned.

Some have interpreted the Gog oracle along the lines of Ezekiel's oracles against foreign nations in chapters 25–32. Having isolated 38:1–3a and 39:1b–5 as the original *Grundtext,* Hossfeld recognizes a structure similar to the first oracle against Egypt (29:1–6) and Seir (35:1–4), and dates the prophecy prior to the oracles of chapter 32, which were delivered in 587–586 BC.[43] But this interpretation can be maintained only by disre-

---

Apocalyptic, for a fuller study), apocalyptic involves a revelation given by God through a mediator (usually an angel, but cf. Jesus Christ in Rev 1:1–2) to a seer concerning future events, expressed either in terms of a cosmic drama or elaborate symbolism. On apocalyptic, see further Russell, *Method and Message,* 104–39; Morris, *Apocalyptic;* Ladd, "Apocalyptic," 151–61.

41. One of the primary criticisms leveled by Odell ("Are You He of Whom the Prophets Spoke?," 43–50) at many contemporary approaches.

42. So also Hals (*Ezekiel,* 284), contra Childs ("The Enemy from the North," 187–98) and Batto (*Slaying the Dragon,* 157–62), who characterizes the Gog oracle as "proto-apocalyptic," a metahistorical portrayal of the cosmic conflict between YHWH and chaos, symbolized by Gog.

43. Hossfeld's text (*Untersuchungen zu Komposition und Theologie,* 494–501) breaks down like this:

garding the final shape of the text and ignoring its present placement at the heart of the restoration oracles.[44] Furthermore, an oracle against an enig-

---

Introduction (38:1–3a):

Word Event Formula	The word of YHWH came to me as follows:
Address of the Prophet	Son of man,
Hostile Orientation Formula	Set your face toward Gog, prince of Meshech and Tubal,
Commissioning Formula	Prophesy against him and say,
Citation Formula	Thus has the Lord YHWH declared:

The Message (39:1b–5a):

Challenge Formula	
The Announcement	See, I am against you, O Gog, prince of Meshech and Tubal! I shall turn you around, and drive you on, and draw you up from the remotest parts of the north, and lead you to the mountains of Israel. I shall strike the bow from your left hand, and knock the arrows out of your right hand. On the mountains of Israel you will fall—you and all your hordes, and the peoples accompanying you—I shall hand you over as food to every kind of predatory bird, and every wild animal. On the open field you shall fall.

Conclusion (39:5b):

Conclusion of Divine Speech Formula Signatory Formula	For I have spoken, The declaration of the Lord YHWH.

Nobile ("Beziehung," 255–59) argues that the redactor of chapter 32 had the Gog oracle in front of him, and that the Gog-pericope appeared as the continuation and climax of the oracles against the foreign nations. In fact, the Gog oracle radicalizes the conflict between YHWH and the nations. However, it was separated from the oracles against the nations because its fulfillment lies in the more remote future. Its placement before the temple vision (40–48) was determined by literary-liturgical considerations. The new temple cannot be described without first accounting for the basis of its construction, *viz.*, YHWH's final victory over the cosmic forces of chaos (represented by the nations).

44. Although the form and structure of the *Grundtext* bear some resemblance to 32:1–6+ and 35:1–4, the pronouncements in 25:1–26:6 show that the basic structure of Ezekiel's oracles against the foreign nations follows that of typical judgment speeches: accusation (introduced by יַעַן, "because"), followed by the announcement of judgment (introduced with לָכֵן, "therefore"). Furthermore, as Odell notes ("Are You He of Whom the Prophets Spoke?," 37), since chapter 32 announces the demise of Meshech and Tubal, it is unlikely they could have risen to greatness so quickly after the defeat announced here.

matic entity like Gog would be out of place in the context of the rest of the prophecies against the foreign nations, all of whom are Israel's immediate neighbors, and whose own history had touched Israel's at many points. The form critics' identification of the basic text may indeed be correct, but this does not mean the remainder is not authentically Ezekielian. Since Gog and his forces represent foreign nations in opposition to YHWH, it is not surprising that this text displays many affinities with the former. But the differences in the final products are so pervasive, it is unwise to force the present oracle into that grid.

Although the general structure of the oracle proper (38:1—39:20) displays some resemblance to Ezekiel's judgment speeches, its complexity of style and content precludes formal classification on the basis of structure alone. The seven-fold occurrence of the recognition formula,[45] provides the most obvious clue to its genre and intention. The Gog pericope consists of a series of fragmentary proof-sayings which, when brought together in this fashion, result in a single, powerful proof-oracle. Above all else, this complex divine speech expresses YHWH's determination once and for all to reveal to the nations his holiness and to his own people his covenant loyalty.[46] Since both notions had appeared in an earlier fragment of theological reflection at the end of the oracle against Tyre (28:25–26), and since so many of the ideas raised there will be resumed and expanded here,[47] the Gog pericope offers one more example of typically Ezekielian resumptive exposition.[48]

45. 38:16, 23; 39:6, 7, 22, 23, 28. This represents a denser concentration than anywhere else in the book. Two of these formulae occur in their simplest form (28:23, 39:6); the remainder vary greatly from the simple modification of YHWH with "the Holy One in Israel" in 39:7 to the elaborate additions in 39:23 and 39:28.

46. The subject of the verb in the recognition formula shifts in the course of the oracle, from the nations, in the first four and the sixth, to Israel in the fifth and seventh. Significantly, nowhere is the divine aim declared to be Gog's acknowledgment of YHWH which highlights his role as agent through whom YHWH achieves his goal, rather than the primary concern of his activity.

47. The regathering of the nation (קָבַץ, cf. 38:8); the manifestation of YHWH's holiness (נִקְדַּשׁ, 38:16; 39:7, 25, 27); "in the sight of the nations" (cf. 38:16); Israel living securely in the land (יָשַׁב לָבֶטַח, cf. 38:8, 11; 39:26); YHWH executing judgments (עָשָׂה מִשְׁפָּטִים, 39:21); Israel recognizing YHWH as their God (cf. 39:21, 28).

48. Whereas the earlier text had referred to the objects of YHWH's judgment vaguely as כָּל הַשָּׁאטִים אֹתָם מִסְּבִיבוֹתָם, "all who scorn them (Israel) round about," these are now identified specifically as Gog and his allies. The offense, expressed by the verb שׁוּט/שָׁאט, "to scorn," is now described in detail as showing contempt for Israel dwelling at peace within her own land, and taking advantage of her defenseless state

For sheer vividness, imagery, and hyperbole, this oracle has few equals. These features alone caution against over-literalism in interpretation. The intention of this text may be best appreciated if it is approached as a satirical literary cartoon strip consisting of eight frames. As the unit progresses, the images become increasingly caricatured, climaxing in a bizarre picture of predatory birds and wild animals seated around a table, gorging themselves on human flesh (39:17–20). The sequence of events reflected in the frames may be outlined as follows:

Panel A: The Defeat of Gog	(38:2–23)
Frame 1: The Conscription of Gog	(38:2–9)
Frame 2: The Motives of Gog	(38:10–13)
Frame 3: The Advance of Gog	(38:1a–16)
Frame 4: The Judgment of Gog	(38:17–22)
Interpretative Conclusion	(38:23)
Panel B: The Disposal of Gog	(39:1–29)
Frame 1: The Slaughter of Gog	(39:1–8)
Frame 2: The Spoiling of Gog	(39:9–10)
Frame 3: The Burial of Gog	(39:11–15)
Frame 4: The Devouring of Gog	(39:17–20)
Interpretative Conclusion	(39:21–29)

Many of these frames subdivide further on stylistic and substantive grounds into separate sub-sections. While each sub-unit has an identity and character of its own, they are thoroughly integrated to create a sequence of events whose total impact is much greater than the sum of its parts.

SUMMARY EXPOSITION

A detailed frame-by-frame exposition of the Gog oracle is not possible here. A summary interpretation of the key elements of each frame will, therefore, have to suffice.

---

to satisfy their greed (38:10–14). But as exposition, the Gog oracle is not slavishly bound to the antecedent fragment. Nor does it offer a phrase-by-phrase commentary nor adhere to Western canons of logic and progression. The demand for the latter in particular has led astray many interpreters, who, by dissecting the text into a series of fragments, rob the oracle of its force.

Frame 1: The Conscription of Gog (38:2–9)

The first frame introduces the primary antagonist, Gog, prince, chief of Meshech and Tubal. There is no consensus on the interpretation of the name Gog, but this is not for lack of effort.[49] The most likely explanation derives Gog from Gyges, the name of the King of Lydia, mentioned in six inscriptions of Ashurbanipal (668–631 BCE),[50] and known elsewhere for his invention of coinage.[51] Gog's homeland is identified simply as "the land of Magog." Although both names may turn out to be artificial creations,[52] it seems best to interpret Magog as a contraction of an original *māt Gugi*, "land of Gog,"[53] an allusion to the territory of Lydia in western Anatolia.[54]

49. Proposed explanations include: (1) a mythological "locust giant," analogous to the scorpion man in the Gilgamesh Epic (*ANET*, 88; cf. Amos 7:1, which LXX read as גֹּבַי, "locust" [Gressmann, *Messias*, 129, n. 1]); (2) a personification of darkness (cf. Sumerian *gúg*, "darkness" [Heinisch, *Ezechiel*, 183]); (3) Gaga, a name that appears in EA 1:36–40, alongside Hanigalbat and Ugarit (Albright, "Gog and Magog," 381–82); (4) Gaga, a deity mentioned in the Ugaritic sources (cf. Cuffey, "Gog," 1056).

50. See Cogan and Tadmor, "Gyges and Ashurbanipal," 65, n. 1. The most important reference is found in *ARAB* 2.351–52.

51. On his legendary reputation see Herodotus, *Histories*, 1.8–13. Some treat Gog as a dynastic name, referring in this context to his great grandson, Alyattes, under whom Lydia had once again become the dominant power in western Anatolia. Myres ("Gog and the Danger," 213–19) suggested this oracle was prompted by the "Battle of Eclipse" between Lydia and Media in 585 BC. Cf. more recently, Diakonoff, *Predystorija armjanskogo*, 179 (as cited by Astour, "Ezekiel's Prophecy," 569–70).

52. Many have seen in the names a cipher for Babylon: von Ewald, *Commentary on the Prophets*, 792–93; Cooke, *Ezekiel*, 480. Boehmer ("Wer ist Gog?" 321–55) saw in מגג a cryptogram for Babylon, a reverse kind of "athbash" (cf. Jeremiah's שֵׁשַׁךְ, "Sheshach" [25:26; 51:41], which, by replacing the first letter of the alphabet with the last, the second with the penultimate letter, etc., yields בבל). Ezekiel's method is more complex. Replacing each letter in בבל by its successor yields גגם, which, when reversed, produces מגג. Unfortunately, like all interpretations which see in the Gog oracle a message directed at Babylon, this understanding flies in the face of Ezekiel's consistent perception of the Babylonians as agents, not the enemies of God.

53. So Astour, "Ezekiel's Prophecy of Gog," 569; Yamauchi, *Foes*, 23. Josephus (*Ant.* 1.123, followed by Gressmann, *Messias*, 123–24) identified Magog with the Scythians: "Magog founded the Magogians, thus named after him, but who by the Greeks are called Scythians." Van den Born ("Études sur quelques toponyms," 197–201; *Ezechiël*, 223) assumes a scribal error for ארץ המגא, an ancient abbreviation for ארץ המגדן, "the land of the Macedonian," from which he deduces Gog to be a pseudonym for Alexander the Great. The name has no geographic or ethnographic analogues in ancient Near Eastern literature, though Albright ("Gog and Magog," 383) proposed a blend with Manda, an abbreviation of Umman Manda, the common Mesopotamian designation for "barbarian."

54. In Gen 10:2 (= 1 Chr 1:5) Magog is a personal name identifying the second son

The first frame has Gog at the head of a powerful international alliance (קָהָל רָב) that includes four northern kingdoms: Meshek and Tubal (vv. 2–3),[55] and Gomer and Beth-Togarmah (v. 6),[56] and three southern accomplices: Paras,[57] Cush (Ethiopia), and Put (Libya). The conjunction of Paras, Cush, and Put here and elsewhere in the book[58] suggests this triad derives from a traditional list of allies of Egypt.

But what is the significance of this alliance? Any answer to the question must keep in mind three significant observations. First, in contrast to the addressees in Ezekiel's oracles against the foreign nations, the names listed all represent distant peoples, from the fringes of Israelite geographic awareness. Second, the number of allies totals seven, a prominent number in the Gog oracle as a whole.[59] The number symbolizes totality, completeness,[60] raising the conspiracy against Israel from a minor oppor-

---

of Japheth and brother of Gomer, Madai, Javan, Tubal, Meshech and Tiras. LXX reads a personal name here as well, preparing the way for later writings in which Gog and Magog become a fixed pair of names of persons involved in the final eschatological battle. Rev 20:8; *Sybilline Oracles* 3:319–20, 512; a fragment of the Targum *Pseudo-Jonathan* to the Pentateuch on Num 11:26 (cf. Levey, *Messiah*, 105–7); fifth-century Hebrew Apocalypse of Enoch 45:5.

55. To be identified with Muški and Tabal respectively, two eastern Asia Minor kingdoms well-attested in Akkadian sources.

56. To be identified with the Qimmiraia (Cimmerians) and Til-garimmu in Akkadian sources. For a full discussion of these names see Yamauchi, *Foes from the North*.

57. Paras is best understood either as an alternative, perhaps Egyptian, spelling for Pathros, "Southland" (cf. Isa 11:11), or the name of power with strong links to Tyre and Egypt (cf. Ezek 27:10), to date unattested in extra-biblical records. Cf. Odell, "Are You He of Whom the Prophets Spoke?," 103–6; Odell, "From Egypt to Meshech." The common identification of Paras with Persia is unlikely not only because it is anachronistic, but also because Ezekiel shows no interest whatsoever in Babylon's eastern neighbors. A later insertion is ruled out because the presence of Persia in a list of subordinates to Gog here and in 27:10 would have been quite unrealistic in any post 539 BCE situation.

58. In 27:70 Paras, Lud (Lydia), and Put are military partners of Tyre; in 30:5 Cush, Put, and Lud are listed among allies of Egypt.

59. Note the enemies' seven weapons (39:9), the seven years' worth of fuel these provide (39:9), the seven months needed for the burial of the enemies' remains (39:12). Ahroni ("The Gog Prophecy," 17) also identifies seven sections in the composition. Significantly the number of nations addressed in the collection of oracles against the nations in chapters 25–32, and those who accompany Egypt in Sheol in 37:16–32 also total seven. Nobile ("Beziehung zwischen Ez 32, 17–32 und der Gog-Perikope," 256–57) sees here evidence that the redactor of the latter text had the Gog pericope in front of him.

60. See Pope, "Seven, Seventh, Seventy," 294–95.

tunistic incursion to a universal conspiracy. Third, the names in Ezekiel's list form a merismic pattern: Meshech, Tubal, Gomer, and Beth Togarmah represent the northern extreme of the world known to Israel; Paras, Cush, and Put the southern extreme, reinforcing the impression that the entire world is ganging up on Israel.[61] At the head of this alliance, Gog represents a formidable foe, able to attack whenever and wherever he pleases.

But how different is the appearance from the reality. Verses 4–6 are emphatic in affirming YHWH's total control over the movements of Gog. This truth is announced in three short declarations: YHWH will turn Gog around, put hooks in his jaws, and lead him out. Here the mysterious region beyond the Taurus mountains is portrayed as the lair from which YHWH will lead Gog out like an animal on a leash. Verse 7 is cast as YHWH's formal summons to Gog and the forces assembled to him, with Gog clearly in charge.[62] But Ezekiel's audience may have taken comfort in verse 8, which explains that the summoning[63] of Gog and his forces is not to be expected in the near future, but "after many days," "in later years." Although LXX renders the latter expression with ἔσχατος, it is not clear that the end of time is in mind. The reference may be simply to a later time, when the historical phase of the exile is over and the new period of settlement in the land has arrived.

The rest of verse 8 offers further clarification of the timing of the summons for Gog. It will happen when the land itself will have recovered[64] from the destruction and slaughter of an invading army, and the popula-

---

61. Compare the use of similar rhetorical strategies in ancient Neo-Assyrian sources, particularly the following boast of Sargon II: "In the might and power of the great gods, my lords, who sent forth my weapons, I cut down all of my foes from Iatnana (Cyprus), which is in the sea of setting sun, as far as the border of Egypt and land of the Mushki (Meshech),—the wide land of Amurru, the Hittite land in its entirety . . . (*ARAB* 2 §54)." Cf. §§82, 96, 97, 99, and §183, which uses the expression "from Egypt to Muški." See the discussion by Odell, "Are You He of Whom the Prophets Spoke?" 101–2; Odell, "From Egypt to Meshech." But Odell's thesis that Gog's campaign represents a rebellion against Nebuchadnezzar, incurring the wrath of YHWH (just as Gyges' revolt against Ashurbanipal had incurred the wrath of Ashur), is unlikely because: (1) Nebuchadnezzar is entirely out of the picture in this oracle; (2) the Gog invasion is thrust into the distant future; and (3) the relationship between Ashurbanipal and Ashur is hardly parallel to YHWH's relationship with Nebuchadnezzar.

62. The meaning of the final clause in verse 7 is uncertain, but in the context לְמִשְׁמָר must carry a military nuance, presumably charging Gog with leadership over the vast forces allied with him by serving as their guardian.

63. On פָּקַד = "to summon, muster," in military contexts, see 23:21.

64. On מְשׁוֹבֶבֶת, a *polal* feminine participle of שׁוּב, see Holladay, *The Root šûbh in the Old Testament*, 106–7.

tion will have been regathered from many peoples of the diaspora and resettled securely[65] on the mountains of Israel. Since verse 8 functions as a shorthand version of Ezekiel's salvation oracles,[66] Gog's invasion presupposes the fulfillment of the salvation oracles in chapters 34–37. Verse 9 spells out YHWH's marching orders to Gog, instructing him to take all his assembled forces and attack the peaceful mountains of Israel like a furious storm cloud.

To summarize the opening frame, here YHWH is portrayed as a general mobilizing the forces of Gog and his allies for his own military agenda. Gog's invasion of the land represents a part of the calculated plan of YHWH for his people. But this raises several questions. How can Gog, whom verses 3–6 had portrayed as the enemy of YHWH, simultaneously play the role of YHWH's agent? How can YHWH employ foreign nations against his people, especially after he has re-established the eternal covenant relationship and restored the people to the land? In raising these questions this first frame sets the rhetorical agenda for the following frames of the prophecy against Gog.

Frame 2: The Motives of Gog (38:10–13)

A new citation formula signals the beginning of the second frame in which the focus shifts from YHWH's initiative to the private motivations of Gog. "Ideas" rise in his mind, and he devises evil schemes to bring calamity upon the unsuspecting land. Verse 11 emphasizes that the land is undefended, and its population undisturbed and secure. The text does not explain why the inhabitants of the mountains of Israel have taken no defensive precautions, but one may assume that they have finally put their confidence in YHWH's promises of eternal peace and prosperity, as spelled out in the previous restoration oracles. Verse 12 offers additional information on the state of the nation: its ruins have been repopulated in fulfillment of 36:10, 33; the people are regathered from their dispersion among the nations; the population is prospering with abundant livestock

65. The phrase יֹשֵׁב לָבֶטַח, which derives from Lev 26:5b–6, serves as a minor keyword in the oracle (cf. verses 11, 14; 39:26), describing the security offered by YHWH when the blessings of the covenant are operative and the divine patron stands guard over them.

66. Especially 36:1–15, addressed to the mountains of Israel and highlighting the restoration of its population, 36:24, 33–36 which speaks of regathering the people and rebuilding the ruins, and 34:25–29 which describes the scene of perfect peace and tranquility.

and other movable goods, in fulfillment of 34:26–27; and her people live on top of the world.[67]

Apparently oblivious of YHWH's hand, by his own confession Gog is motivated by a single passion: greed, the lust for loot and booty. But he is not alone in this. According to verse 13, Sheba, Dedan, and the merchants of Tarshish have been watching Gog's activity with great interest. The reason for their interest may be guessed from their names: Sheba and Dedan represent merchant peoples (סֹחֲרִים) who conduct their trade via the overland routes across the Arabian Desert to the east of Israel, and Tarshish represents the maritime traders who control the Mediterranean route to the west. These traders' reaction to Gog's designs is expressed in the form of a series of rhetorical questions, but their motive is not entirely clear. Are they decent nations challenging Gog's greed, or are they wishing to capitalize on the opportunity themselves? Since their questions echo many of the expressions found in the previous verse, it seems Gog's greed is mirrored in their own covetousness. They too have their eyes on spoil, booty, silver, gold, livestock, and other movable property. These merchants are vultures, hoping to take advantage of the spoils of this war.

Like the list of Gog's allies who come from the northern and southern extremes of the world known to Israel (vv. 3–6), the names in verse 13 constitute a *merismus*, representing the nations who control the trading lanes of the world, from the far east to the far west. Taken together these two groups represent all four points of the compass. The entire world conspires against the unsuspecting and tranquil nation of Israel.

Frame 3: The Advance of Gog (38:14–15)

While the formulaic opening in verse 14 signals the commencement of the third frame, the introductory particle, לָכֵן, "Therefore," intentionally draws a logical connection between this frame and the preceding: the arrogant advance of Gog is linked to the intentions of YHWH. The most striking feature of this brief scene is the manner in which Gog's target is identified. Twice YHWH refers to the people living securely as עַמִּי יִשְׂרָאֵל, "my people Israel" (vv. 14, 16), and once to the land as אַרְצִי, "my land." Since the normal deity-nation-land relationships are now operative, for Gog to attack this people and invade this land is to challenge their/its divine patron.

---

67. The interpretation of טַבּוּר as "navel" is as ancient as LXX but should be abandoned. So also Talmon, "הַר *har*," 437–38.

Verses 14b–16a highlight the opportunism of the invader. Precisely when YHWH's people are enjoying their security in his land, Gog will emerge from his homeland in the far reaches of the north country. He and his vast host will sweep down on YHWH's people on their horses and cover the land like a cloud. Employing an expanded version of the recognition formula, the prophet highlights his control over all these events. First, Gog's invasion is planned according to YHWH's timetable, "at the end of the years."[68] Second, Gog's invasion occurs at the overt instigation of YHWH; he comes not merely with YHWH's permissive will, but as his agent.[69] Third, YHWH's purpose in bringing on the hordes of Gog is to convince the nations of his presence and his person.[70] In an ironical twist, Gog's opportunism *vis-à-vis* Israel is seized as an occasion to achieve YHWH's own goals. In the meantime, this frame has also provided the answer to the first question raised by the first frame (vv. 3–9): why would YHWH bring Gog against his own people after the covenant relationships had been fully restored? Because an element in the divine agenda, the universal recognition of his person, remains unfulfilled.

68. The expression assumes knowledge of verse 8, and reaffirms that the invasion of the land of Israel is not imminent, but pushed off into the distant future, after YHWH's people have been regathered from the diaspora, have settled in the land, the signs of his blessing have become evident, and they have begun to enjoy their peaceful and tranquil state.

69. The formulaic declaration suggests to Ezekiel's audience that YHWH is again carrying out his covenant threats against his people. The pronouncement וַהֲבִאוֹתִיךָ עַל־אַרְצִי, follows a conventional prophetic form, "I will bring A against B." Seven times in Kings the divine threat is announced by the prophets with הִנְנִי מֵבִיא רָעָה עַל, "I will bring disaster upon B": 1 Kgs 9:9 (upon Israel); 14:10 (upon Jeroboam); 21:21 (upon Ahab), 29 (upon Ahab's house); 2 Kgs 21:12 (upon Jerusalem and Judah); 22:16, 20 (upon this place, *viz.*, Jerusalem). The formula occurs fourteen times in Ezekiel. However, the influence of the covenantal threat (Lev 26:25) is evident in the six-fold replacement of the general term for disaster (רָעָה) with חֶרֶב, "sword" (5:17; 6:3; 11:8; 14:17; 29:8; 33:2), which also accounts for the use of חֶרֶב in verse 8 above. 14:21 lists "my four severe judgments: sword, famine, wild animals, plague." 14:22 has הָרָעָה. Ezekiel's historicizing tendency is evident in his substitution of real agents for "sword" (7:24 [the most barbaric of nations]; 23:22 [Jerusalem's lovers]; 26:7 [Nebuchadnezzar upon Tyre]; 28:7 [strangers upon Tyre]), a rhetorical device to demonstrate that current events do in fact represent the fulfillment of YHWH's covenant threats. See also Odell, "Are You He of Whom the Prophets Spoke?," 116–21.

70. That the unique form of the statement intentionally draws attention to the fact that Gog is not actually the agent through whom his holiness is manifested, but the locus of the revelation, is confirmed by the observation that wherever the concern is the revelation of YHWH's holiness, it occurs in the midst of a people. So also Odell, "Are You He of Whom the Prophets Spoke?," 132.

Frame 4: The Judgment of Gog (38:17–22)

The fourth literary frame consists of two unequal parts, clearly distinguished in style and purpose (v. 17; vv. 18–22). Reminiscent to the reader of John the Baptizer's query of Jesus, "Are you the Coming One or are we to wait for someone else?"[71] YHWH opens by posing a question to Gog whether or not he considers himself the fulfillment of earlier prophecies. Assuming this rhetorical question demanded a positive answer, in the past scholars have devoted their energies to identifying which prophecies the question has in mind.[72] But in this regard they have been as misguided as Gog himself. There can be little doubt that Ezekiel's contemporaries would have identified Jeremiah's foe "from the north," as Babylon under Nebuchadnezzar, especially since Jeremiah had explicitly made this identification himself (Jer 25:9). If YHWH had actually directed this question to Gog himself, and if Gog had been aware of the earlier pronouncements concerning the "foe from the north" by Israelite prophets, he would probably have answered in the affirmative. It would certainly have bolstered his ego if, apart from his personal greed, he could have claimed the role of YHWH's agent, sent in to punish the Israelites, like Nebuchadnezzar before him. The question then feeds right in to Gog's ego-maniacal ambitions.

However, as the earlier frames have already demonstrated, Gog's self-understanding and YHWH's perception of him are quite different. According to the first frame (vv. 2–9), YHWH alone brings Gog and his hordes on. Like a conqueror himself, YHWH will lead Gog on, dragging in his captives with hooks in their jaws. But according to the second frame (vv. 10–13), Gog is totally oblivious of the fact that he is but a puppet on YHWH's strings. He thinks he is campaigning against Israel of his own free will. Correspondingly, even if Gog would have answered this question positively, the correct answer is negative.[73] Gog is in fact not "the foe from the north" of whom Jeremiah had spoken. His role is entirely different. He is not commissioned by YHWH to serve as his agent of judgment. He and his troops are brought down from the mountains for a single purpose:

71. Matt 11:3 (cf. Luke 7:19, 20).

72. For a detailed discussion of this text see Block, "Gog in Prophetic Tradition," 152–72; reproduced below, 124–41.

73. So also Odell, "Are You He of Whom the Prophets Spoke?," 122. There is no syntactic reason why this could not be the case. For a precise parallel to the present question see 2 Sam 7:5, with which compare its unequivocal declarative counterpart in 1 Chr 17:4.

that the holiness of YHWH might be displayed in the sight of the nations.[74] Whatever havoc they hope to wreak on YHWH's people they do of their own volition, and not at the command of God. This oracle, therefore, is not about unfulfilled prophecy, but about earlier prophecies illegitimately appropriated. Otherwise verses 18–23 become nonsensical. How could YHWH announce in one breath that Gog is his agent, and in the next vent his wrath upon him with such fury?

In verses 18–23 the literary style and tone change dramatically, and the second person of direct address, used throughout the preceding frames, gives way to the third person. For the first time the intensity of the opposition between YHWH and Gog, announced in the opening challenge formula (v. 3), becomes apparent as YHWH vents his fury toward Gog without restraint. The cause of the provocation is declared to be Gog's invasion of the land of Israel, an action that is now portrayed as his very own (cf. 39:2). But with the covenant relationship between YHWH and his people fully restored, YHWH cannot stand by idly. The divine patron of Israel must act.

YHWH's emotional reaction to Gog's invasion is obvious as he explodes, heaping up expressions for anger unparalleled in the book, if not in the entire Old Testament. Fortunately for Israel, the wrath previously poured out on them will now fall upon their enemy. The firmness of YHWH's resolve is reflected not only in the signatory formula, which interrupts the outburst, but the expressed motive for his utterance: "I have spoken in my passion," in verse 19a also leaves no doubt that the following threats arise out of his anger. The effects of YHWH's fury are described in verses 19b–20: a massive earthquake will rock the land on which Gog has his sights, and reverberate throughout the earth, causing all living things to quake and leveling the landscape. With its epicenter in the land of Israel, the quake will bring down mountains and cliffs, symbols of divinely grounded stability, and crumble walls, symbols of strength fabricated by human hands. The force behind this cosmic upheaval is obliquely hinted at in the divine passive, "they will be hurled down," and the addition of "before me" at the beginning of the verse. The latter enhances the theophanic flavor of this frame, reminiscent of the quaking of the earth beneath the feet of the Israelites when YHWH stepped down on Mount Sinai.[75]

Ezekiel's imagery in verses 19–20 is generally associated with Hebrew apocalyptic, and treated as a sign of the relative lateness of this

74. Cf. vv. 16, 23; 39:6–7; also vv. 22, 28.
75. Exod 19. See also Judg 5:4–5; Isa 30:27–28; Hab 3:3–7; Pss 68:8–9[7–8]; 114.

composition.[76] However, the correlation between divine anger and cosmic collapse was widely recognized in Mesopotamia long before the exile of Judah. After listing a series of evils committed by the Babylonians, the annals of Esarhaddon describe the result:[77]

> Enlil [i.e., Marduk] observed these. His heart fumed; his liver raged. The Enlil of the gods, the lord of the lands plotted evil in order to annihilate land and people. In the fury of his heart he determined to destroy the land and to bring the people to ruin. An evil curse was found upon his mouth. In the heavens and on the earth evil "forces" persisted. The symmetry (*mit-ḫur-tim*) [of the universe] collapsed. The courses of the stars of Enlil, Anu, and Ea were disrupted and augured evil. Their "forces" were constantly changing. The Araḫtu canal, a raging torrent, an angry stream, a swollen high tide like the deluge itself, flooded the city, its residences, and its temples, and transformed it into a wasteland.

Whereas in verses 19–20 YHWH's involvement in the earthquake is only obliquely alluded to, and the effects of his fury appear to fall indiscriminately on all inhabitants of the globe, the impression changes in verse 21 as YHWH announces specifically the summoning of the sword against Gog. In sharp contrast to the pre-586 BCE situation in the future, when Israel, YHWH's people, is established in his land, alien invasion will excite his passions and move him to act in defense of both the land of Israel and its people. Reminiscent of Gideon's war against the Midianites (Judg 7:22), when YHWH calls for the sword, the troops in the armies of Gog and his allies will turn their weapons against each other.[78] But the sword is not the only agent of death which YHWH sends against Gog. Verse 22 catalogues three pairs of calamities: plague and bloodshed, torrents of rain and hailstones, fire and burning sulfur.

According to verse 22, these calamities represent the execution of a divine sentence upon Gog and his hordes.[79] However, verse 23, which

76. Zimmerli (*Ezekiel* 2, 313) comments, "In comparison with the original Ezekiel oracle, the later apocalyptic style of verses 18–23 is unmistakable." Similarly Fuhs, *Ezechiel II*, 219.

77. The various recensions of the account are gathered by Borger, *Asarhaddon* 13–14, episodes 5–6. Cf. also *ARAB* 2.250, §658.

78. Compare the adaptation of the motif of the enemies of God's people destroying themselves in Zechariah's eschatological battle (14:13).

79. The niphal of שָׁפַט normally denotes "to enter into judgment," or "to commit to trial" (17:20; 20:35–36), but in this case the guilt has already been established.

offers an interpretative conclusion to the first panel, also announces a three-fold revelatory purpose: to display YHWH's greatness (וְהִתְגַּדִּלְתִּי), his holiness (וְהִתְקַדִּשְׁתִּי), and his person (וְנוֹדַעְתִּי) in the sight of many nations.[80] While this declaration relates most directly to the fourth frame, it summarizes YHWH's intentions for all the events of "that day" (cf. v. 18), beginning with YHWH's conscription of Gog and ending with his annihilation. By rocking the earth and bringing down this far-flung military alliance in the full view of the nations, they will all acknowledge the truth that Israel had gained from her own judgment and subsequent restoration.

Frame 5: The Slaughter of Gog (39:1–8)

The introductory formulae in 39:1 echo 38:2, signaling the shift to the second panel of this complex oracle against Gog. The first frame of the second panel (the fifth overall) recapitulates some of the action of 38:19–23. However, the tone changes as the emphasis shifts from YHWH's emotion to his actions against Gog. Except for two references to Gog's forces falling (vv. 4, 5), and two recognition formulae (vv. 6, 7), YHWH is the subject of every verb in the frame.

As in 38:2, the challenge formula in 39:1b draws the lines in the conflict: YHWH has set himself in opposition to Gog. By a series of eight sharp, hard-hitting declarations, YHWH outlines his strategy against the foe: he will turn Gog around, drive him on, lead him up from the remotest part of the north,[81] bring him to the mountains of Israel, knock his bow out of his left hand, force him to drop his arrows from his right hand, deliver his corpse as food for all the beasts and birds of prey, and torch the lands from which Gog and his allies have come.

While the effect of YHWH's action is to neutralize Gog's offensive power completely, YHWH will perform the ultimate indignity upon the corpses of Gog and his forces by leaving them on the, mountains and in open fields for scavenging birds and mammals to devour. Not satisfied with the destruction of the armies of Gog, YHWH will send fire against the lands from which Gog and his allies have come. The description of the

---

80. The first two involve the only occurrences of these roots in the *hithpael* stem in the book. These are examples par excellence of the estimative-declarative reflexive use of the *hithpael* stem. Cf. *IBHS* §26.2f. The niphal of יָדַע, "to make oneself known," has occurred in earlier affirmations of YHWH's self-disclosure in 20:5, 9 and 35:11.

81. As elsewhere in the book (1:4; 26:7; 32:30) צָפוֹן, "north," is used in its normal directional sense, without mythological overtones.

inhabitants as "secure" (לָבֶטַח) highlights the irony of the situation. Those who sought to take advantage of Israel's innocent and unsuspecting state now find that the long arm of YHWH extends far beyond the borders of his own land to ends of the earth.

The last line of verse 6 and verses 7–8 reiterate YHWH's revelatory aims: the international recognition of his person and his character as the Holy One[82] in Israel. This revelation was necessary because it was precisely "in Israel" that his reputation had previously been defiled, leading to the nation's exile and creating misimpressions in the foreigners' minds concerning his character (cf. 36:16–32). But those days are long past. The Gog debacle will demonstrate once and for all the hotness of YHWH, not as a theological abstraction, but in action, as he stands to defend his people against the universal conspiracy of evil. The frame concludes with an emotional declaration of the inevitability of the coming event and irrevocability of the divine determination.

Frame 6: The Spoiling of Gog (39:9–10)

In verses 9–10 the attention shifts from Ezekiel's radically theocentric portrayal of Gog's demise to a graphic and earthy picture of human survivors mopping up after an enormous battle. Gog and God have had their day; for the first time the Israelites enter the picture. This frame may be the shortest of the series, but the imagery is vivid. The scene opens with the sight of the inhabitants of the cities of Israel, untouched by Gog's invading forces, emerging from their homes to dispose of the weapons of the annihilated foe. Ezekiel highlights the magnitude and intensity of the mopping-up operations with four special rhetorical elements: (1) the hendiadyc construction, "they will burn and set on fire"; (2) cataloging seven kinds of weapons—to be burned; (3) citing the practical benefit the pile of weapons offered the Israelites—they provide firewood in a fuel-poor region; (4) recognizing the irony of the situation: the plunderers (cf. 38:12–13) have become the plundered, and vice versa. Those who had not raised a finger in their own defense may now divide the booty that has been delivered to their doorstep. The combination of these four elements creates a picture of utter and total destruction of the enemies' military

---

82. The strength of the latter determination is reflected in the threefold occurrence of the root קדש, referring twice to his holy name, which recalls 20:39 and 26:20–23. See also the end of this oracle (v. 29), and 43:7–8.

hardware. Never again would these foes from the distant regions of the earth threaten God's people.

Frame 7: The Burial of Gog (39:11–16)

The opening date notice marks the beginning of a new frame and reminds the prophet's audience of the chronological distance between the present and the events of the Gog oracle. Verses 11–13 focus on the activity of the Israelites, who go out en masse to bury the remains of Gog's armies. The corpses of the enemy strewn about "the mountains of Israel" present the Israelites with a series of problems. First, since these are the bodies of YHWH's enemies and the foes of his people, shall they be dignified with a proper burial, or left out in the open, exposed to scavenging animals and the elements? Second, given the massive numbers of the slain, which burial ground has room for all these bodies? Third, since the victims are all foreigners, shall they be buried within the land of Israel or deposited outside its borders to preserve the sanctity of the land? The aim of verses 11–13 is to answer these questions. Formally these verses resemble an edict, issued by a superior to his servants, containing precise instructions for carrying out a mission. Each verse deals with a different aspect of the enterprise.

The answer to the first question is immediately obvious: yes, the remains of YHWH's enemies must be buried in a mass burial site appointed by YHWH "in Israel," east of the sea, presumably the Mediterranean. The place is specifically identified as גֵּי הָעֹבְרִים, which is best treated as "the valley of those who have passed on," that is deceased heroes,[83] referred to elsewhere as רְפָאִים.[84] When the corpses of Gog and his horde are gathered, the site will be renamed גֵּיא הֲמוֹן גּוֹג, "the Valley of Hamon-Gog." The name appears to play on גֵּי־הִנֹּם, "the valley of Hinnom," where the bodies of animals and criminals used to be burned.[85] From now on this place

---

83. Pope (Review of *Beatific Afterlife*, 462) describes the עֹבְרִים as "those who cross over the boundary separating them from the living so that from the viewpoint of the living they 'go over' rather than 'come over.'"

84. So Ribichini and Xella, "La valle dei passanti," 434–47; Spronk, *Beatific Afterlife*, 229–90; Pope, "Notes on the Rephaim Texts," 173–75. Though Ezekiel is not averse to speaking about the residents of the netherworld (cf. הַגִּבּוֹרִים, "the mighty men," 32:27), for reasons unknown he avoids the term רְפָאִים, "shades." Perhaps it bore too many pagan associations, or was too closely tied to the cult of the dead.

85. Cf. Zimmerli, *Ezekiel 2*, 316–17.

will serve as a permanent memorial to the destruction of the enemies of YHWH and Israel.

Verses 12–13 describe the effects of the burial of Gog's remains. First, the land will be cultically purified. The observation that the process will take a full week of months, rather than the week of days prescribed in Num 19, speaks not only of the magnitude of the task, but also of the concern to render the land absolutely holy. Second, the enthusiasm of the people for the task, and the scrupulosity with which they bury the enemy will testify to their passion for the purity of the land and to their new-found security in YHWH. Third, and most importantly, their actions will result in the public glorification of YHWH. After all, the day of Gog is YHWH's day.

Verses 14–16 expand on the theme raised in verse 12, highlighting how the absolute purification of the land is achieved. A standing commission shall be appointed to supervise the burial of Gog's remains. These men shall pass up and down the length of the land for seven months, inspecting every corner for remnants of the vanquished warriors. Whenever the inspectors discover so much as a bone of the enemy on the surface of the ground, they are to mark the spot with a sign-post. Finally sextons shall follow the supervisors, and transport the bones to the Valley of Hamon-Gog to be buried.

The reiteration of the name of the site as Hamonah in verse 16 constitutes the punch line of the frame.[86] Although critical scholars in the past have tended to delete וְגַם שֶׁם־עִיר הֲמוֹנָה, "actually Hamonah is a city name," as a gloss,[87] or emended it to yield a better sense,[88] the statement performs an emphatic function. Whether the clause was added at the oral stage, or at the time of transcription, it offers an additional clue to the riddle: where are all these bodies to be buried? The answer, in a city called Hamonah.[89]

86. See Odell, "City of Hamonah," 479–89.

87. *BHS*; Zimmerli, *Ezekiel 2*, 293; even generally conservative Barthélemy, et al. (eds.), *Preliminary and Interim Report*, 5:130. For an explanation of how the gloss might have appeared in the text see Allen, *Ezekiel 20–48*, 202.

88. *REB*, "no more will be heard of that great horde," is based on Driver's proposed emendation ("Linguistic and Textual Problems," 184): וְנָמַר שֵׁמַע הֲמוֹנוֹ, "and the fame of his multitude/mob shall come to an end."

89. Syntactically the P-S structure, with P indefinite relative to S, signals a non-circumstantial verbless clause of classification (cf. Andersen, *Hebrew Verbless Clause*, 42–46). Genesis 28:19 reverses the sequence of common and proper nouns: וְאוּלָם לוּז שֵׁם־הָעִיר לָרִאשֹׁנָה, "but actually the name of the city was previously Luz." The absence of the adverbial modifier, מִיוֹם, "from [that] day," the addition of גַּם, "also," and the absence of the article on עִיר, "city," distinguish this statement from the final declaration of this book (48:35), call for a different interpretation.

Based on Ezekiel's use of הֲמוֹנָה elsewhere, the "Valley of Hamon-Gog" speaks of the tumultuous pomp of Gog and his hordes, and recalls the usage of the term in previous oracles against foreign nations, especially the final oracle against Egypt.[90] But the association of the term with Jerusalem in three earlier judgment oracles is especially instructive. The present form is linked assonantly with 7:12–14, where הֲמוֹנָה had functioned as a shorthand expression for all of Jerusalem's riotous and rebellious behavior.[91] According to 5:7, Jerusalem's הֲמוֹן, expressed in a refusal to follow the covenant demands and all kinds of abominations, had exceeded the tumult of all the surrounding nations. Some of these nations appear in 23:40–42, bringing their own base and boisterous ways right into the city of Jerusalem, at her invitation. Here too Hamonah stands for Jerusalem. But as in 23:4 and 48:35, Ezekiel uses a symbolic name, highlighting a particular characteristic of the place. In the present context Hamonah's primary function is to memorialize the demise of Israel's last and greatest enemy. However, by association it also memorializes the transformation of the city, and with it the nation. The people who had once superseded the pagan nations with their tumultuous arrogance and rebellion now impress the world with their scrupulous adherence to the will of YHWH. Once the city (and the entire land) has been purged of every vestige of defilement, the stage is set for YHWH to return (43:1–7) and replace the retrospective name for a new forward looking one (מִיּוֹם). Hamonah is gone; "YHWH is there!" (48:35).

The seventh frame concludes by reiterating that the primary concern in all this human activity is the cleansing of the land. YHWH is not satisfied with having defeated Gog and his allies; so long as their corpses are visible, the land remains unclean. A totally restored covenant relationship demands a God with a holy name, a holy people, and a holy land.

Frame 8: The Devouring of Gog (39:17–20)

The placement of the scene described in the final frame in this sequence of literary caricatures after the burial of Gog creates certain logical and logistical problems, but the reader is reminded that this is a literary cartoon,

90. Cf. Hossfeld, *Untersuchungen zu Komposition und Theologie*, 472–73; Bodi, *Ezekiel and the Poem of Erra*, 119–20.

91. While the oracle is directed against the land as a whole, the activities described in the text are basically urban, and the city is specifically mentioned in verses 15 and 23.

and realism has been sacrificed for rhetorical effect. Indeed, as the oracle has progressed the scenes have become increasingly bizarre, climaxing here in a spectacle more fantastic than all. Like political caricatures, this frame is not to be interpreted as prophetic literary photography, but as an impressionistic literary sketch.

The entire frame is cast in the form of an official invitation to special guests to attend a grand banquet hosted by YHWH. The style may be formal, almost poetic, but the imagery is grotesque, as the prophet invites all kinds of carnivorous and scavenging creatures to an enormous banquet that he has prepared for them. His picture recalls other prophetic texts, in which an overwhelming victory is followed by a *zebaḥ* meal.[92] Ezekiel's designation of this banquet as a *zebaḥ* classifies it as a ritual event,[93] but the normal image of a *zebaḥ* is caricatured by altering all the roles. In place of a human worshipper slaughtering animals in the presence of YHWH, YHWH slaughters humans for the sake of animals, who gather from all over the world for this gigantic celebration (זֶבַח גָּדוֹל) on the mountains of Israel. The battlefield has been transformed into a huge sacrificial table. In place of the flesh of rams, male goats, bulls, and fatlings of Bashan, this table is spread with an abundance of flesh, fat, and blood of "heroic figures" and princes of the earth. Verses 19–20 paint a picture of unrestrained gluttony at YHWH's table, concluding with a reminder of the true sacrificial victims: all the participants in the previous battle against YHWH including the horses. The literary image sketched here must have been shocking

---

92. Cf. Isa 34:6–8 and especially Zeph 1:7 with which this banquet displays remarkable affinities. These banquets are reminiscent of two divinely hosted *dbḥ* meals referred to in Ugaritic texts:

(UT 51 iii:77–22; ANET, 132)	For two kinds of banquets (*dbḥ*) Baal hates, Three the Rider of the clouds: A banquet (*dbḥ*) of shamefulness, A banquet (*dbḥ*) of baseness, And a banquet (*dbḥ*) of a handmaid's lewdness.
(Krt A:73–79; ANET, 143)	Go up to the top of the tower; Climb to the top of the wall; Lift up your hands to heaven, Sacrifice (*dbḥ*) to Bull, your father El; Cause Baal to come down with your sacrifice (*dbḥ*); The son of Dagan with your game.

93. The word could apply to burnt (עוֹלָה), peace (שְׁלָמִים), grain (מִנְחָה), purification (חַטָּאת), and reparation (אָשָׁם) offerings.

for a person as sensitive to cultic matters as Ezekiel, but how the priestly prophet reacted to this horrifying image we may only speculate.

The Final Word (vv. 21–29)

Although scholars tend to dismiss verses 21–29 as a series of late editorial additions,[94] verses 21–24 and 25–29 are best viewed as two halves of a whole, displaying remarkable structural balance and symmetry, as the following synopsis illustrates:

	Topic	39:21–14	39:25–29
A	The Actions of YHWH	21a	25
B	The Response of the Objects of his Action	21b	26–27
B'	The Recognition Formula (tied to Israel's exile)	22–23a	28
A'	The Hiding of YHWH's Face	23b–24	29

In addition to their parallel structures, each segment is organized internally on a chiastic pattern. Both begin and end with descriptions of the divine action, between which are sandwiched the humans' responses.[95] Each ends with a reference to YHWH hiding his face, a notion that is otherwise foreign to the book. But in content the two parts diverge, exhibiting a relationship to each other as that of "a dialectic of action and response."[96] The first describes YHWH's action of judgment in response to Israel's rebellion; the second his salvific activity on her behalf, and the response this evokes in the nation. In the first recognition formula, the nations primarily recognize YHWH; in the second Israel does so. In effect, even if not in style, verses 20–29 perform the same function in relation to chapter 39 as 38:23 had served in relation to chapter 38. Each represents a summary statement of YHWH's designs in handling his people.

In verses 21–24 the prophet describes the impact of YHWH's judgmental activity: the nations will experience the justice and power of YHWH. However, recognizing that Ezekiel's primary audience consists of fellow exiles, and it is their transformation that he seeks, the prophet

94. For a summary of recent approaches and a more detailed analysis of this text see Block, "Gog and the Pouring Out of the Spirit," 257–61 (see below, 142–55).

95. Van Dyke Parunak (*Structural Studies*, 506) recognizes the following pattern: A (vv. 22–24), B (vv. 25–27), A' (vv. 28–29).

96. Thus Odell, "Are You He of Whom the Prophets Spoke?," 151.

interrupts his observation concerning the nations with a modified version of the recognition formula to announce the implications for Israel of the victory over the military hordes: from that day and onwards they will acknowledge YHWH. The defeat of Gog would mark a turning point in the nation's history. Although the statement considers the Gog debacle an event in the distant future (cf. 38:8, 16), it apparently does not occur at the end of time. Rather it signals the beginning of a new era, which will be characterized by Israel's recognition of YHWH and the full realization of covenant relationship.

From the perspective of the battle of Gog, the events described in verses 23–24 are in the distant past. The people of Israel have returned to their land and have lived securely in it for many years. Now, after the defeat of Gog, the nations will realize that all the events preceding this restoration had in fact fulfilled the laws of divine justice. Because of the nation's perversion (עָוֹן), covenantal infidelity (מַעַל), defiling sacrilege (טֻמְאָה), and covenant betrayal (פֶּשַׁע), the Israelites had been exiled from their land. Witnessing YHWH's harsh treatment of his people, the nations had concluded that YHWH was either incompetent to defend his people against Nebuchadnezzar, or he had gone back on his own covenant commitment to them. Because neither of these explanations was true, his reputation had been profaned. Now they realize that Israel had brought this fate on herself. Their wickedness had provoked him to hide his face and deliver them into the hands of their enemies. As it turns out, the devastation of Jerusalem and the exile of Judah's population was neither a function of the superior military strength of the Babylonian forces, nor a reflection of Marduk's superiority over YHWH. This was the result of YHWH's own deliberate action against his own people. Accordingly, the glory of YHWH will be established when the nations recognize the justice of YHWH's dealings with his own people in the past and his dealings with them in the present.

Having highlighted the justice of YHWH in his judgmental actions, in verses 25–29 Ezekiel's focus turns to the impact of YHWH's saving activity. Fortunately for Israel, the judgment could not be the last word. The same covenant that had warned the nation of the consequences of persistent apostasy also declared that YHWH would not abandon his people forever. He had promised he would not forget his covenant with his people.[97] By now the connection with Gog has disappeared completely. This is a message for Israel—the Israel of Ezekiel's own day. The divine speech opens abruptly with וְעַתָּה, "And now," snatching the hearers' attention

97. Lev 26:44–46; cf. Deut 4:30–31.

away from the distant utopian future, and bringing them to the very real needs of the present. The interest is no longer in "the latter years" (38:7), or "the latter days" (38:16), but on today; not in "that day" (38:10, 14, 18, 19; 39:8, 11), or "from that day and onward" (39:22), but now. Ezekiel ends this remarkable oracle with a glorious word of grace for a despairing people, wondering how and when all the events described in the previous six chapters might be fulfilled.

Verse 25 is thematic, announcing that YHWH's mercy[98] and passion (קִנְאָה) will win out over his wrath as he restores the fortunes of Jacob. In verses 26–27 Ezekiel expands on these two ideas. Far from being a source of pride at having been selected as the objects of divine compassion, Israel's experience of grace will lead to a recognition of their own unworthiness. The prophet, speaking for YHWH, then elaborates on the notion of publicly vindicating YHWH's holy reputation. YHWH's actions toward his people, both punitive and salvific, are played out before the worldwide audience. Verse 28 describes the effect of this action on the nations in one final recognition formula, greatly elaborated to highlight the covenantal aspect of this new day of grace. At the heart of the international awareness this time is not only the knowledge of YHWH but also the recognition of Israel as his covenant people. They will realize that it was as their covenant Lord that he had sent them off into exile among them. And it is as covenant Lord that YHWH brings them back to their own land—every one of them!

The oracle concludes with one more surprising twist, as Ezekiel transforms what had been for him a stereo typical threat of judgment, "I will pour out my wrath," into a glorious gospel message, "I will pour out my Spirit." While the idiom וְנָתַתִּי רוּחִי בְ, "I will put my spirit in . . . ," in 36:27 had associated the divine action with the rebirth/revitalization of Israel,[99] the divine Spirit poured out upon the nation serves as a sign and seal of the covenant, YHWH's mark of ownership.[100] This accounts for his intervention on behalf of his people against Gog before the latter may so much as touch them.

---

98. The verb רָחַם (piel here) occurs only here in the book.

99. Cf. Ezekiel's fuller exposition of this notion in 37:1–14. For discussion of the Spirit as divine animating agency, see Block, "Prophet of the Spirit," 34–41 (see Block, *By the River Chebar*, 150–58).

100. Cf. Block, "Prophet of the Spirit," 46–48 (see Block, *By the River Chebar*, 165–66).

CONCLUSION

By way of summary, Ezekiel's aim in proclaiming this remarkable oracle of Gog and his hordes has been to provide his audience with specific and concrete proof that YHWH meant exactly what he said. The oracle looks forward to a time when the promises of restoration found in chapters 34–37 have been realized and Israel is prospering and secure in her land in the latter days (38:6, 16). Into this pacific and tranquil land YHWH deliberately brings these hordes from the north (38:4–9), who imagine themselves to be operating of their own free will (38:10–13). However, like Pharaoh of Egypt in Exod 7–14, Gog is an agent called to fulfill the revelatory purposes of YHWH. That purpose has two dimensions: to declare the greatness, holiness, and glory of YHWH's person, on the one hand,[101] and the firmness of his commitment to his people, on the other.[102] The defense of this people, who did not need so much as to lift a sword, vindicates his great name while at the same time confirming his word. The presence of the Spirit of YHWH poured out upon the returned exiles guarantees that he would never leave any of the house of Israel at the mercy of her enemies, and that he would never hide his face from them, as the contemporaries of Ezekiel had just witnessed. In short, Gog becomes the agent through whom YHWH declares concretely that the tragedy of 586 BCE will never be repeated.

In declaring this word concerning Gog, Ezekiel calls upon all who read it to recognize five themes: First, YHWH is the unrivalled Lord of human history. He raises up nations; he puts them down. Their activities are always subservient to his agenda. Second, YHWH's reputation is linked to the status and well-being of his people. So long as they are mired in bondage and subservience to alien powers his holiness and glory stand in question. Third, YHWH keeps his covenant. He does not forget the commitments he has made to his people and will not abandon the faithful in their hour of need. As a seal of his commitment he pours out his Spirit upon them. Fourth, above all else, YHWH is a God of grace and mercy, who reaches out to those who have rebelled against him and offers not only forgiveness, but the full benefits of covenant relationship. Finally, this oracle reminds us that for the believer the experience of divine grace is a humbling experience. Far from feeding egotistical ambitions and a misguided thirst for self-esteem, or from blinding one to one's sinful past, it evokes in the recipient intense feelings of unworthiness.

101. Ezek 38:16, 23; 39:7, 13, 21, 25, 27.
102. Ezek 38:14–16; 39:7, 22–29.

6

Gog in Prophetic Tradition

A New Look at Ezekiel 38:17[1]

INTRODUCTION

FEW TEXTS IN EZEKIEL have engaged the imagination of lay and professional interpreters like the Gog oracle in chapters 38–39. Few present as many problems.

1. What is the genre of the oracle? Is it to be interpreted as apocalyptic, or along the lines of the oracles against the foreign nations in chapters 25–32, or like the salvation oracles in chapters 34–37?

2. What is the relationship of this oracle to the preceding salvation oracles? To the following vision?

3. Who is responsible for this prophecy? Is it Ezekiel? Or a disciple of his?

4. How are the numerous disjunctive formulae to be accounted for?

5. How do the fragments that make up the oracle relate to one another?

6. What situation in the history of Israel was the oracle intended to address?

7. From where does the author derive his ideas?

1. This essay was originally published in *Vetus Testamentum* 42 (1988) 154–72.

8. Who is this enigmatic figure referred to as Gog of the land of Magog?

9. When and how will the events here described be fulfilled?

The disagreement among scholars on the answers to all these questions does not bode well for a clear understanding of the oracle. However, if we do not continue to explore new possibilities, progress on its interpretation will never be made. This study is offered as a small contribution to the continuing discussion of this difficult text.

NATURE AND DESIGN OF THE GOG ORACLE

The Gog oracle consists of a series of fragmentary proof sayings that, when brought together in the present creative fashion, result in a powerful proof oracle. Above all else, the oracle, cast in the form of a complex divine speech, expresses YHWH's determination once and for all to reveal his holiness to the nations, and to his own people, Israel, his covenant loyalty. Both notions had appeared earlier in a brief moment of theological reflection at the end of the oracle against Tyre (37:25–26). In fact, many of the ideas expressed only in passing in that context are picked up in this oracle and given fuller treatment:

1. The regathering of the nation (קָבַץ, cf. 38:8);

2. The manifestation of YHWH's holiness (נִקְדַּשׁ, cf. 38:16; 39:7, 25, 27);

3. In the sight of the nations (cf. 38:16);

4. Israel living securely in the land (יָשְׁבוּ לָבֶטַח, cf. 38:8, 11; 39:26);

5. YHWH executing judgments (עָשָׂה שְׁפָטִים, 27:26; cf. עָשָׂה מִשְׁפָּטִים, 39:21);

6. Israel recognizing YHWH as their God (cf. 39:21, 28).

In fact, the Gog pericope may be interpreted as a full-blown commentary on 28:25–26. This pattern of raising an idea briefly, only to drop it and then return to it with a full treatment in a later prophecy, may be observed repeatedly in the book of Ezekiel.[2] Whereas the expression "all who scorn them [i.e., Israel] round about" in the earlier text had referred to the enemies of Israel only in the vaguest of terms, they are now identified specifically as Gog and his allies. The offense, which was referred to by the verb שָׁאט, "to scorn," is now described in detail as showing contempt

---

2. Cf. 16:60–63 and 36:16–32; 36:27; 37:24–28; 36:27 and 37:1–14; etc.

for Israel dwelling at peace within her land, and taking advantage of her defenseless state to satisfy the enemies' greed (38:10–14).

The genre of the oracle is disputed.[3] Ever since F. Hitzig first applied the term "apocalyptic" to the Gog prophecy,[4] it has been fashionable to view it as an example of this genre.[5] However, in view of the recent careful analysis of apocalyptic texts by J. J. Collins,[6] this classification for Ezekiel 38–39 is best abandoned. Others have interpreted this text along the lines of Ezekiel's oracles against the foreign nations.[7] But this approach can be maintained only if the final form is adjudged irrelevant and after radical surgery has been performed on the text.

The vividness, the imagery, and the hyperbolic nature of the oracle all caution against too literal an interpretation. The intention of this text may perhaps be best appreciated if it is approached as a kind of literary cartoon strip. The images portrayed become increasingly caricatured, reaching a climax in a bizarre picture of predatory birds and wild animals seated around a table gorging themselves on human flesh (39:17–20). While each of the small sub-units has an identity and a character of its own, they are all thoroughly integrated to create a sequence of events whose total impact is much greater than the sum of its parts.

The symmetry of the final product is remarkable. Obviously, 38:1 represents a general heading for the entire oracle. Elsewhere we have also argued on grounds of style and content that 39:25–29 functions as a general conclusion to both chapters.[8] Not only is a new sub-section signaled

3. For a survey of the history of the interpretation of the Gog oracle see Odell, "Are You He of Whom I Spoke?" 1–42.

4. Hitzig, *Prophet Ezechiel*, xiv–xv.

5. Ahroni, "Gog Prophecy," 11–13. Ahroni argues that the entire text is a late, post-exilic insertion into the book.

6. Collins ("Toward the Morphology of a Genre," 9) provides the following definition:

> "Apocalypse" is a genre of revelatory literature with a narrative framework, in which a revelation is mediated by an otherworldly being to a human recipient, disclosing a transcendent reality which is both temporal, insofar as it envisages eschatological salvation, and spatial insofar as it involves another, supernatural world.

Cf. Collins' fuller discussion of apocalyptic texts in "Jewish Apocalypses," 21–59.

7. Hossfeld, *Untersuchungen zu Komposition und Theologie*, 494–96. Cf. also Nobile, "Beziehung," 255–59.

8. Block, "Gog and the Pouring Out of the Spirit," 257–70; reproduced below, 142–55.

by the introductory לָכֵ֗ן, "Therefore"; this segment deals entirely with the implications of the oracle for Israel. Gog and the nations have disappeared from view completely. This breakdown, therefore, yields the following broad structure:

The announcement of a new oracle	(38:1)
The first Gog panel	(38:2–23)
The second Gog panel	(39:1–24)
The conclusion	(39:25–29)

The balance between the two Gog panels now becomes apparent. Panel A (38:2–23) consists of 365 words; panel B (39:1–29) of 357 words, suggesting one of the most impressive examples of the "halving pattern" recognized by M. Greenberg.[9] Each of the panels may be dissected into a sequence of four separate frames as follows:

Panel A: The Defeat of Gog	(38:2–23)
Frame 1: The Conscription of Gog	(38:2–9)
Frame 2: The Motives of Gog	(38:10–13)
Frame 3: The Advance of Gog	(38:14–16)
Frame 4: The Judgment of Gog	(38:17–22)
Interpretative Conclusion	(38:23)
Panel B: The Disposal of Gog	(39:1–24)
Frame 1: The Slaughter of Gog	(39:1–8)
Frame 2: The Spoiling of Gog	(39 9–10)
Frame 3: The Burial of Gog	(39:11–16)
Frame 4: The Devouring of Gog	(39:17–20)
Interpretative Conclusion	(39:21–24)

Nature and Design of 38:17

For the interpretation of the Gog oracle Ezek 38:17 represents a crux. The text itself presents several difficulties. First, what are the boundaries of the sub-unit of which verse 17 is a part? In the context of the Gog oracle, the messenger formula at the beginning of verse 17 signals a new movement in the drama that is being played out in the prophet's mind. Since there is no comparable formula from here to the end of the chapter one concludes that verses 17–23 represent a single sub-unit, the fourth frame in the first panel of the oracle. However, in style and content verse 17 is distinct from verses 18–23. Here the prophet raises a question concerning Gog that

9. Greenberg, *Ezekiel 1–20*, 25–26.

not only catches the reader off guard after verses 14–16; it also seems to have little bearing on the furious attack upon Gog by YHWH described in verses 18–23. It must be concluded minimally, therefore, that verse 17 enjoys relative independence from the verses that follow.

Scholars have wrestled with this fact for more than a century. Von Ewald judged the verse mildly as a "parenthetical remark."[10] Later interpreters have not been so kind. A. Bertholet unraveled the entire oracle into two strands. The first recension, consisting of 38:1–9, 16b–17; 39:1–7, 17–22, begins with YHWH stirring up Gog and ends with the wild creatures devouring the remains of his hordes. The second, consisting of 38:10–16a, 18–23; 39:8–16, presents Gog as taking the initiative. He devises his own plan of attack, is destroyed supernaturally, and is finally buried by Israel.[11] According to the way verse 17 has been traditionally interpreted, it obviously belongs to the first strand.

More recently, it has been fashionable to attribute the disjunctive and incongruent features of the oracle to different layers of tradition added by successive editorial hands. According to Zimmerli, the authentic Ezekielian core is made up of 38:1–9 (with minor exceptions), 39:1–5, and 17–20. The style and theological stance of verse 17 distinguish it sharply from "the descriptive and dramatic nature of the basic text."[12] Although he does not identify the person responsible for the addition, the distinctive phraseology makes it unlikely that it is to be credited to Ezekiel.[13] Hossfeld asserts that the verse is cast in a style of speech characteristic of a theological systematician, similar to that reflected in Zech 1:1–6. He combines the preoccupation with the problem of prophetic promise and fulfillment and the systematizing attitude with the Deuteronomistic literary style, and arrives at the conclusion that the verse was included in the second reworking of the oracle[14] and the fourth of six re-editings of the book of Ezekiel.[15]

Since these reconstructions are based upon specific assumptions concerning the nature of exilic and post-exilic prophecy, we shall delay a direct response until later. Suffice it to say for the moment that the bases

10. "Einschaltung." Von Ewald, *Prophets of the Old Testament*, 188.

11. Bertholet, *Hesekiel*, 130–31. This interpretation has been followed more recently by Lindblom, *Prophecy in Ancient Israel*, 233.

12. Zimmerli, *Ezechiel* 2, 297–98.

13. Ibid., 312. Cf. Garscha (*Studien zum Ezechielbuch*, 233) who tentatively attributes verse 17 to the same person as 38:10–13.

14. Hossfeld, *Untersuchungen zu Komposition und Theologie*, 506.

15. Ibid., 526.

upon which authentic and inauthentic material are distinguished are subjective, dependent entirely upon the interpreter's own standards of literary propriety. In any case, none of the problems posed by verse 17 meets the criteria for inauthentic material established by Greenberg.[16] We shall propose below that a new approach to the interpretation of this verse will go a long way toward its rehabilitation in its present context.

Formally, verse 17 consists of the messenger formula, כֹּה־אָמַר אֲדֹנָי יְהוִה, followed by a divine speech. The latter is made up of a single principal clause, modified by a series of subordinate clauses.[17] Although verses 18–23 are also cast as divine speech at the beginning of verse 18, the style changes from YHWH's direct address of the prophet in the second person to the third person of indirect address.

In the MT (followed by the Targum) the principal clause is cast in the form of a rhetorical question: "Are you the one of whom the prophets spoke?" However, many recent translations and most scholars follow the LXX, the Vulgate, and the Peshitta in rendering this clause affirmatively.[18] The interrogative particle is explained as a dittographic error following the final *hē* on the preceding tetragrammaton. However, some have restored an affirmative sense by emending the text to read הֲלוֹא אַתָּה־הוּא, "Are you not the one . . . ?"[19] But, as we shall see, neither of these emendations is necessary if the text is interpreted differently.

16. Greenberg, "What are Valid Criteria," 123–35. The criteria he suggests are:

1. Historical—anachronism: reflection of a manifestly different situation, language or ideas belonging demonstrably to a later time.

2. Syntactical—elements causing incoherence that cannot be explained by ancient literary habit or mere textual corruption.

3. Contradiction—a weak ground unless the contradictory elements are close to each other and the contradiction cannot be accounted for on rhetorical grounds.

17. The speech may be diagrammed syntactically as follows:

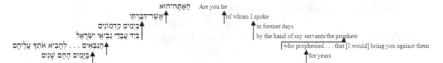

18. So the NEB, NJPS, JB, as well as BHS, contra AV, NRSV, NASB, which retain the question form.

19. Cf. Cooke, *Ezekiel*, 417. This reading is followed by the NIV.

The question posed by YHWH to Gog is reminiscent of John the Baptist's query of Jesus in Matt 11:3 (cf. Luke 7:19, 20), "Are you the Coming One or are we to wait for someone else?" In the present instance, most agree that the issue is whether or not the arrival of Gog is to be interpreted as the fulfillment of earlier prophecies. But this in turn raises the broader issue of Ezekiel's own position within the prophetic tradition of Israel.[20]

Several clues to his perception of the prophetic tradition are found in the manner in which he refers to these prophets. First, YHWH claims them as his own servants. The designation of Ezekiel's predecessors as עֲבָדַי נְבִיאֵי יִשְׂרָאֵל, "my servants the prophets of Israel," has a pronounced Deuteronomistic or Jeremianic flavor.[21] Although this was one of the reasons why Zimmerli isolated the verse as secondary, and why most scholars delete it is a later non-Ezekielian interpolation, the reasoning is flawed. In the first place, both Jeremianic and Deuteronomic influences are evident throughout the prophecy of Ezekiel. In fact, Zimmerli finds the basic text of this oracle to draw heavily on Jer 3–4. Furthermore, as Amos 3:7 indicates, the expression has been current at least since the eighth century and should not be taken as a sign of lateness.[22] Odell observes that much of 38–39 has a strong literary character.[23] We should not be surprised, therefore, to find this prophet employing traditional literary conventions. By using the phrase, YHWH is distinguishing the prophets in question from the false prophets, which often appeared in Israel and claimed to speak for him, but which he himself disowned (cf. Ezek 12:21–13:23).

YHWH affirms the authenticity and authority of the prophets' messages by referring to them as agents through whom he has spoken. The clause, אֲשֶׁר־דִּבַּרְתִּי . . . בְּיַד עֲבָדַי, "of whom I spoke by the hand of my

20. For some reason both this text and 30:8 are overlooked by Carley's otherwise helpful study, *Ezekiel among the Prophets*.

21. Kraetzschmar (*Ezechiel*, 257) speaks of an "epigonic" style. On the Deuteronomic connection see Weinfeld, *Deuteronomy and the Deuteronomic School*, 352. Variations of the phrase occur in 2 Kgs 9:7; 17:13, 23; 21:10; 24:2; Jer 7:25; 24:4; 26:5; 29:19; 35:15; 44:4; Amos 3:7; Zech 1:6; Ezra 9:11; Dan 9:6, 10. Following the designations of Dietrich, *Prophetie und Geschichte*, 41, 111, 139ff. Hossfeld (*Untersuchungen zu Komposition und Theologie*, 450) attributes all the Kings texts to Dtr P, except for 1 Kgs 17:13, which is credited to Dtr N.

22. Hossfeld (*Untersuchungen zu Komposition und Theologie*, 450) attributes Amos 3:7 to a Deuteronomistic redaction of the book.

23. Odell, "Are You He of Whom I Spoke," 228, n. 78. On the literary character of Ezekiel's prophecies see Davis, *Swallowing the Scroll*.

prophets," seems odd,[24] but this is a common Hebrew[25] and extra-Israelite[26] idiom for "by the agency of."[27] Presumably, the expression derives from the practice of an officially authorized messenger recording his superior's message or delivering by hand the written copy of the message.[28]

Second, these have been Israelite prophets. By referring to נְבִיאֵי יִשְׂרָאֵל, "the prophets of Israel," YHWH is distinguishing his spokesmen from extra-Israelite prophets. It is well known that the phenomenon of prophecy was widespread in the ancient Near East.[29] Rulers would appeal to prophets for a divine determination especially prior to battles such as the one envisioned here.[30] But the question makes it clear that YHWH is not referring to any prophecy that might have been given in Gog's homeland or at his favorite oracle site. The issue here is that YHWH's prophets have made pronouncements, ostensibly about Gog.

Third, they are former prophets. Two temporal modifiers express this notion, בְּיָמִים קַדְמוֹנִים, "in former days," answers to בְּאַחֲרִית הַיָּמִים, "in the latter days," in verse 16. The expression reflects a certain antiquity of the prophecies, which would seem on the surface to rule out any of Ezekiel's contemporaries.[31] As Zimmerli notes, like the phrase הַנְּבִיאִים הָרִאשֹׁנִים,

24. For a similar use of אֲשֶׁר, "of whom," before a verb of speech see Gen 3:17.

25. Cf. 2 Kgs 17:13, 23, etc. For references, see BDB, 391; Even-Shoshan, *New Concordance*, 424–25. It is perhaps surprising that דִּבֶּר פִּי, "to speak by the mouth of," never occurs.

26. An almost exact parallel to the present usage is found in the Zakkur Inscription A 12,

ויענני בעלשמי[ן] וימל (ל) בעלשמין אלי [ב]יד חזין וביד עדדן

"And Baalshamayn answered me, and Baalshamayn [spoke] to me by the hand of seers and messengers" (KAI 202:11–12).

27. For a brief discussion of this use of בְּיַד, see Ackroyd, "יָד *yāḏ*," 410. Further work on the idiom is required.

28. Cf. Saul's non-verbal gesture of sending pieces of the dismembered ox throughout the country by the agency of messengers (בְּיַד הַמַּלְאָכִים), along with the oral interpretation of the significance of the gesture in 1 Sam 11:7.

29. Cf. Nebuchadnezzar's use of divination to determine the direction of his Palestinian campaign in Ezek 21:26–29[21–13]. The literature on prophecy outside Israel is vast. For an overview see G. V. Smith, "Prophet, Prophecy," 989–92. For a recent discussion and bibliography of prophecy in Mari, see Malamat, "Forerunner of Biblical Prophecy," 33–52.

30. For a discussion of the role of prophetic and oracular revelation in the waging of war in the ancient Near East see Weippert, "Heiliger Krieg," 460–93.

31. May ("Ezekiel," 276) admits that the expression "in old time" indicates that the author lived a considerable time after Jeremiah, but he attributes the verse to a late editor.

"the former prophets," in Zech 1:4, this expression appears to represent "a stage of distanced reflection on past prophecy," which he does not expect in Ezekiel. Even when Ezekiel falls back on older prophecies, as in chapters 16, 23, and 34, he is still dependent upon the direct experience of the prophetic word.[32] Hossfeld speaks of the style of "einer theologischen Systematik," which is able to skim off present prophecy from earlier prophets whose pronouncements have already found historical fulfillment.[33] We shall return to the problem of the fulfillment and non-fulfillment of prophecy in a moment.

A second, textually problematic modifier contributes to the sense of antiquity of the prophecies to which reference is made. The MT adds הַנִּבְּאִים בַּיָּמִים הָהֵם שָׁנִים, literally, "who prophesied in those days years." The LXX omits הַנִּבְּאִים, but this looks like a haplographic error. More serious is the presence of שָׁנִים, "years," which is grammatically difficult in the context. The LXX and Peshitta try to smooth out the problem by adding the copula before "years." The Targum eliminates it entirely by means of explanatory additions: [ביומיא האנון [מלקדמת דנא] שנין סגיאן], "in those days, many years before this." BHS recommends either deleting שנין or emending it to הָרִאשֹׁנִים. Hossfeld is impressed with the latter suggestion, noting that the rare temporal lexeme קַדְמֹן[34] occurs in a chiastic relationship to ראשֹׁן in Isa 40:18:

> Do not recall what happened of old;
> Or ponder what happened of yore (NJPS).

Nevertheless, in the end he opts for deleting the expression. A plausible explanation for the awkward construction has been proposed by S. Talmon. He sees here a conflation of two synonymous readings, בַּיָּמִים הָהֵם and בַּשָּׁנִים הָהֵם.[35] In any case, its presence in the MT reinforces the impression that the author of this verse, whether Ezekiel himself or one of his school, had in mind the continuous or repeated delivery of the same message.[36]

This raises several issues. In the first place, it suggests that at the time this verse was written an authoritative prophetic tradition had already been established alongside the Mosaic Torah. Though most recent

---

32. Zimmerli, *Ezekiel 2*, 312.

33. Hossfeld, *Untersuchungen zu Komposition und Theologie*, 450.

34. Cf. 1 Sam 24:14; Isa 43:18; Mal 3:4.

35. Talmon, "Double Readings," 171.

36. So also Odell, "Are You He of Whom I Spoke," 121. Davidson, *Ezekiel*, 280, opines that Gog had been "the subject of repeated predictions by many prophets." Cf. Dan 9:1–2; Zech 1:1–6.

scholars appear hesitant to grant this, A. Cody at least opens the door to the possibility with his assertion,

> There existed already a *corpus* [emphasis his] of prophecy on invaders from the north, and the inspired compilers of the book—if not Ezekiel himself, as far as the nucleus of this section goes—found it good to take up that tradition, projecting it into the age that would follow the restoration of the exiles in the promised land.[37]

But this raises a second question: did such a corpus of prophetic writings exist during the time of Ezekiel's own ministry, and if it did, would Ezekiel have had access to it? Though Cody leaves the door open to this possibility, recent scholars have been reluctant to affirm it. In principle, if one takes the prophetic experience seriously, there is no need even to discuss the matter. Since in our text it is YHWH himself who speaks about the messages of the former prophets, the only conclusion that is demanded is that YHWH was aware of this stream of prophetic tradition with which Gog now is associated.

This answer will satisfy few. The question remains: Could Ezekiel have been this self-conscious about the relationship of his utterances to former prophecies? A closer examination of the evidence suggests that this was a real possibility.

First, as J. Blenkinsopp admits, "It is reasonable to suppose, and in fact explicitly attested, that collections of sayings were made during the prophet's lifetime or shortly after his death."[38] In fact, this accords well with extra-biblical evidence. To cite just one example, according to "Edition B" of Ashurbanipal's annals, prior to his campaign against the Elamites in 653 BCE, a *šabrû*-priest of Ishtar of Arbela received a dream revelation assuring the king of the success of his venture.[39] Since this edition was written in 649 BCE, the prophecy had to be recorded within four years of its reception. In fact, in the words of A. R. Millard, "It would not be rash to conclude that these oracles were to be found in writing within a few months of the days when they were supposedly or actually uttered."[40] Even if a prophet's oracles were not being recorded, where his work came

---

37. Cody, *Ezekiel*, 186.

38. Blenkinsopp, *History of Prophecy*, 23. As evidence he cites Jer 36:1–4; 45:12; and perhaps also Isa 8:16 (47, n. 10).

39. Luckenbill, *ARAB* 2 §861.

40. Millard, "La prophétie et l'écriture," 137.

to the attention of the political and religious authorities, reports of such utterances would spread widely.[41]

Second, there is strong evidence that the prophets themselves were aware of their place in the history of the Israelite prophetic movement and the prophetic tradition. Already in the eighth century Amos had placed himself firmly within that tradition:

> Surely my Lord YHWH does nothing
> Without having revealed his purpose (סוֹדוֹ)
> To his servants the prophets. (3:7; cf. NJPS)

On this basis he calls upon his audience to take him seriously. According to 2 Kgs 17:13, 23 the fall of Samaria to the Assyrians was the fulfillment of the prophecies of "his servants the prophets." In fact, the presence in both verses of כָּל, "all," before "his servants," suggests that this had been a consistent and a continuous message. Even if this text is the product of exilic reflection,[42] it affirms that within decades of Ezekiel's death, if not contemporaneously with his later years, such a prophetic tradition was being recognized. On the other hand, if verse 13 is a part of the post-Josianic redaction (Dtr2) of Kings, and verse 23 of the first Deuteronomistic edition (Dtr1), as is commonly held,[43] the possibility of Ezekiel's own consideration of himself within this tradition is strengthened. Zechariah 1:4–6 is often cited as evidence for "a distanced reflection on past prophecy that one does not expect in Ezekiel."[44] But why is it not to be expected in Ezekiel? If this text is to be attributed to the original Zechariah,[45] such reflection was current within a half century of Ezekiel. There is nothing in this passage to suggest that he was the first to think in these terms. Finally, we note Dan 9:2. To be sure, most would date this text much later, but if the events described have any basis in history at all, then within Ezekiel's and Jeremiah's lifetimes the issue of the fulfillment or non-fulfillment of prophecy was a serious matter.

Third, both Jeremiah and Ezekiel were reflective about the nature of prophecy and their own standing within the tradition. As Odell has observed, they wrestled vigorously with the issue of true versus false

41. So also Blenkinsopp, *History of Prophecy*, 23.

42. So Noth, *Überlieferungsgeschichtliche Studien*.

43. So Cogan and Tadmor, *II Kings*, 207. For a detailed investigation of the issue see Nelson, *Double Redaction*, 55–63.

44. Zimmerli, *Ezekiel 2*, 312.

45. If the opening date notice is to be taken at face value a date of ca. 520 BCE for the prologue is reasonable. Cf. Petersen, *Haggai and Zechariah*, 127–35.

prophecy.[46] Ezekiel himself had asserted that in contrast to the vain words of self-inspired prophets (13:1–16), every prediction uttered by YHWH would be fulfilled (12:21–28). There is no suggestion in the latter context that he is thinking only of his own pronouncements. In fact, his inclusive reference to the דְּבַר כָּל־חָזוֹן, "the fulfillment of every vision," in 12:23 certainly allows for a recognition of his own place in the history of the prophetic tradition.

Fourth, in the collection of Ezekiel's prophecies there are many indications of Jeremianic influence.[47] It is not at all unlikely, therefore, that the prophet himself could or would have reflected on Jeremiah's utterances concerning the foe from the north.

It is clear that Ezek 38:17 portrays a sophisticated and self-conscious reflection on the history of Israelite prophetic tradition. However, in view of the evidence cited, the supposition that such reflection could not have occurred within Ezekiel's own mind rests upon weak and subjective grounds.[48]

The Significance of 38:17 within the Gog Oracle

With this we come to a final and undoubtedly the most important interpretative question posed by this text: what is the significance of this reference to former prophets and Gog's role in relationship to their pronouncements? Scholars are generally agreed that the issue here is the fulfillment of previously unfulfilled prophecy. Zimmerli's comment is typical: "It is a question of the central problem of the historical resolution of those old prophetic pronouncements that still lay unresolved in the presence of the prophet."[49] However, the present emphasis on an apparently continuous tradition of prophecy combined with the absence of any reference to Gog elsewhere in the Old Testament raises the question of which prophecies those might have been.

46. Odell, "Are You He of Whom I Spoke," 228, n. 78.

47. Cf. the relationships between Ezek 23 and Jer 3:6–11 (Israel's harlotry), Ezek 34 and Jer 23:1–6 (good and bad shepherds), Ezek 36:24–28 and Jer 31:31–34 (new covenant), etc. For discussion, see Carley, *Ezekiel among the Prophets*, 51–7.

48. Smend (*Ezechiel*, 300) maintained that earlier prophecies had in general stood on their own as independent pronouncements, such reflection upon the meaning of earlier prophecy points to the demise of the prophetic spirit, a tendency evident also in Deutero-Isaiah and Zechariah.

49. Zimmerli, *Ezekiel 2*, 303: Cf. Hossfeld, *Untersuchungen zu Komposition und Theologie*, 506.

Three possibilities have been suggested. First, one older interpretation held that Ezekiel had some lost oracles in mind. Hitzig suggested that these oracles must have existed at one time, even though no trace of them is left.[50] This would be remarkable. It would mean that Ezekiel is heir, not only to the prophetic tradition as recorded in the Old Testament, but also to an unattested wing of the movement. But since this case rests entirely upon the absence of evidence, it can neither be proved nor disproved.

A second older view understood the reference to be, not to any specific oracle(s), but to previous general announcements of the destruction of the enemies of God's people. Thus J. Skinner comments,

> It is possible . . . that the allusion is not to any particular group of prophecies, but to a general idea that pervades prophecy—the expectation of a great conflict in which the power of the world shall be arrayed against Jehovah and Israel, and the issue of which shall exhibit the sole sovereignty of the true God to all mankind. It is of course unnecessary to suppose that any prophet had mentioned Gog by name in a prediction of the future. All that is meant is that Gog is the person in whom the substance of previous oracles is to be accomplished.[51]

However, both of these views have been abandoned by most recent scholars in favor of the fulfillment of specific extant Old Testament prophecies. Which those might have been remains a matter of debate. The Gog oracle displays the closest resemblance to Joel 4:9–21[3:9–21] and Zech 12:3–9 and 14:1–8. But the Zechariah texts are certainly younger than our passage, and the same may be true of the Joel text.[52] Zephaniah 1:14–18 and 3:8 have also been proposed as antecedents,[53] but these prophecies are too general to be firmly connected with the present oracle. Zimmerli finds clues to the antecedent in two expressions in the basic text.[54] On the one hand, the announcement of the foe being destroyed עַל הָרֵי יִשְׂרָאֵל, "on the mountains of Israel" (38:8; 39:2, 4, 17), points to Isa 14:24–25. On the

50. Hitzig, *Ezechiel*, 294. Cf. Herrmann, *Ezechiel*, 248.

51. Skinner, *Ezekiel*, 372 (new edition: 4:316). Cf. Starck, as cited by Keil, *Ezekiel II*, 169. For recent proponents of this view see Feinberg, *Prophecy of Ezekiel*, 225; Alexander, "Ezekiel," 933, who cites Deut 30:7; Isa 26:20–21; Jer 30:18–24.

52. Though this was the antecedent favored by Greenhill, *Ezekiel*, 760.

53. Cf. Wevers, *Ezekiel*, 289; Smend, *Ezechiel*, 300; Bertholet, *Hesekiel*, 190; Van den Born, *Ezechiël*, 226.

54. Zimmerli, *Ezekiel 2*, 299–304; Becker, *Der priesterliche Prophet*, 2:89, cites Isa 5:26–30; 8:5–10; 10:27b–34; 14:24–27; 17:12–14.

other, the reference to "the foe from the north" (מִיַּרְכְּתֵי צָפוֹן, 39:2) derives from Jer 4–6. Especially striking is 6:22:

> See, a people is coming from the north land (מֵאֶרֶץ צָפוֹן),
> And a great nation is roused[55] from the remotest parts of the
> earth (מִיַּרְכְּתֵי־אָרֶץ).[56]

The only problem with this interpretation is that Isaiah's prophecy was originally concerned with the Assyrians (cf. Jer 14:25), and Jeremiah himself understood his oracle to have been fulfilled in Nebuchadnezzar and the Babylonians (cf. Jer 19–20; 30:9), a fact admitted by those who hold to this interpretation.

The only way out of this dilemma is to propose a reinterpretation of an old oracle on the basis of new realities. Thus Zimmerli writes,

> In the Gog pronouncement we see the prophet of the exile, in
> the completely new exposition of older prophetic word, busy at
> this very task. Into the announcement of the foe from the north
> (Jeremiah) and of YHWH's victory over his enemy in the holy
> land itself (Isaiah) which has come to him from older prophecy,
> he introduces the concrete details about the northern king Gog
> and his hordes which were completely absent from the older
> Jeremiah preaching and actualizes them by means of the pres-
> ent references.[57]

In the process of finding a second stage of divine fulfillment, above and beyond the immediate (the return of the exiles), the first step on the way to apocalyptic has been taken; future events are arranged in a sequential order.[58] All this derives from the basic text. The addition of verse 17, however, reflects one of the great issues in the minds of the exiles: will YHWH keep his word, his promises of Israel's salvation (cf. 29:17–20). With this comment, a reassuring affirmative answer is given.

A similar stance is adopted by Michael Fishbane. He observes that the impression of Jeremianic influence on this oracle is confirmed by the description of Gog as "arising like a cloud" (עָנָן, 38:9, 16), which recalls Jer 4:6, 13. Even though "the deuteronomistic glossator" of Jer 25:9 interpreted Jeremiah's oracle as a reference to Babylon,

---

55. יֵעוֹר is reminiscent of תער in Ezek 38:14, which Zimmerli (*Ezekiel* 2, 288), following the LXX, accepts as the original reading in place of the MT תדע.

56. Cf. also Jer 1:13–15 and in Jeremiah 4–6, specifically 4:6, 13; 6:1.

57. Zimmerli, *Ezekiel* 2, 303.

58. Ibid., 304.

> [P]resumably, Ezekiel (or a pseudo-Ezekiel) believed the advent of Gog to be the true fulfillment of this ancient prediction. In the process, a national oracle has been expanded and has assumed apocalyptic significance.[59]

This text, therefore, provides a clear illustration of a prophetic *traditum* (the unadulterated content of a tradition) and its *traditio* (the adapted, transformed, reinterpreted version of a tradition).[60]

On the other hand, upon closer examination, this explanation is not as convincing as it sounds. Odell has identified at least three problems with Zimmerli's treatment of the Gog oracle as a reinterpretation of unfulfilled prophecy.[61] Her criticisms also apply to Fishbane's explanation.

First, Zimmerli's procedure is self-contradictory. His argument that in the base text the prophet Ezekiel is concerned with unfulfilled prophecy is based upon allusions in 38:17 and 39:8. But both of these are identified as secondary additions to the text.

Second, his treatment of the implications involved in viewing the central issue in the Gog oracle to be the "historical resolution" of older prophecies is unsatisfactory. Normally, when a prophecy is being reinterpreted in the face of its non-fulfillment, the disconfirmation of the divine word is shielded by transferring the significance of the oracle from the historical to the eschatological sphere. However, according to Zimmerli's handling of this pericope, all the eschatological terminology occurs in secondary expansions.

Third, his dismissal of Babylon in favor of Gog as the fulfillment of Jeremiah's prophecy is incredible. As Odell asserts,

> If Jer 4–6 had been interpreted during the Babylonian period as a prophecy of the invasion of the Babylonian army, it is difficult to see how Ezekiel could have regarded these prophecies as unfulfilled. Jeremiah had proclaimed destruction from the north and it had come.[62]

As a matter of fact, from his Babylonian vantage point, Ezekiel had been a witness to the event. It is extremely difficult to imagine him reversing the roles so drastically. In the earlier prophecies the foe from the north had been YHWH's agent of YHWH's judgment upon his own people for their

59. Fishbane, *Biblical Interpretation*, 477.
60. Ibid., 514. For his explanation of these terms see Fishbane's "Introduction."
61. Odell, "Are You He of Whom I Spoke?," 36.
62. Ibid., 36.

covenantal infidelity. Now he appears as an almost diabolical figure, intent on extreme violence upon a nation not only at peace within their homeland, but spiritually reunited with their divine patron. The magnitude of the shift in prophetic perspective renders such an interpretation unlikely.

To these arguments we add a fourth consideration, which may yet turn out to be the most significant of all. Common to all three of the interpretations presented above has been the assumption that the author of 38:17 (whether Ezekiel or pseudo-Ezekiel) viewed Gog as the fulfillment of previous prophecy. This interpretation is not only ancient (cf. the LXX); it is virtually universal. Perhaps this is our problem; perhaps, as in so many other instances, we have allowed the reading in the LXX to get us all off on the wrong foot. Could it be that the exegetical gyrations that Zimmerli and Fishbane and others have performed to square Ezekiel's oracle with previous prophecies have been for naught? We think so.

How then should the verse be interpreted? The solution is embarrassingly simple. First, there is no reason to depart from the Massoretic text. The LXX reading, with its opening affirmation in place of the MT's rhetorical question, may just as well be explained as a haplographic error on the part of the translators as a dittographic mistake by the Massoretes.

Second, there is no reason to insist on a positive answer to the question, "Are you he of whom the prophets spoke?" Rhetorical questions anticipating a negative response are often introduced with the interrogative particle.[63] To cite but one unequivocal example, in 2 Sam 7:5, YHWH instructs Nathan to ask David, "Are you the one who should build me a house to dwell in?" Being introduced by the messenger formula, and consisting of an opening principal clause followed by a subordinate clause, the construction is remarkably similar to our text.[64] On first sight, in view of David's prior suggestion, we could have anticipated a positive response. However, the context leaves no doubt that the answer is negative. This is confirmed by the parallel text in 1 Chr 17:4, which transforms the questions into a declaration: כֹּה אָמַר יְהוָה לֹא אַתָּה תִּבְנֶה־לִּי הַבַּיִת לָשָׁבֶת, "Thus has YHWH declared, 'You are not the one who is to build me a house in which to dwell.'" The present text is precisely this type of question. It is remarkable that in the past this possibility appears seldom if ever to have been considered. In the meantime, however, it has been gratifying to learn that Odell has arrived at the same conclusion independently.[65]

63. Cf. BDB, 209.

64. 2 Sam 7:5   כֹּה אָמַר יְהוָה לֹא אַתָּה תִּבְנֶה־לִּי הַבַּיִת לָשָׁבֶת
    Ezek 38:17   כֹּה־אָמַר אֲדֹנָי יְהוִה הַאַתָּה־הוּא אֲשֶׁר־דִּבַּרְתִּי

65. Odell, "Are You He of Whom I Spoke?," 122.

Third, the present context highlights the tension between YHWH's and Gog's designs.[66] Now it may well be that if YHWH had actually directed this question to Gog himself, and if Gog had been aware of the earlier pronouncements concerning the "foe from the north" by Israelite prophets, he would indeed have answered in the affirmative. This appropriation of earlier prophecies concerning the foe from the north would have been in keeping with ancient Near Eastern practice, in which past predictions were often exploited to legitimize present action.[67] It would certainly have bolstered his already inflated ego if, apart from personal greed (cf. 38:10–13), he could also claim the role of YHWH's agent, like Nebuchadnezzar before him, sent in to punish the Israelites. The question then feeds right into his ego-maniacal ambitions.

However, Gog's self-understanding and YHWH's perception of him are quite different. According to the first frame (38:2–9), it is YHWH, and YHWH alone, who is bringing on Gog and his hordes. Like a conqueror he will lead Gog in, dragging in his captives with hooks in their jaws. On the other hand, according to the second frame (38:10–13), Gog appears totally oblivious to the fact that he is but a puppet on YHWH's strings. He imagines that he is campaigning against Israel of his own free will. Correspondingly, even if Gog would have answered the question in verse 17 positively, the correct answer is negative. Gog is in fact not the "foe from the north" of whom Jeremiah spoke. His role is entirely different. He is not commissioned by YHWH to serve as his agent of judgment; he and his troops are brought down from the mountains for a single purpose; that the holiness of YHWH might be manifested in the sight of all the nations (38:16, 23; 39:6–7; cf. vv. 22, 28). Whatever havoc they wreak on YHWH's people they do of their own volition, and not at the command of God.

CONCLUSION

This oracle, therefore, is not about unfulfilled prophecy. Nor is it an illustration of the transformation of a *traditum* into a *traditio*. It is about earlier prophecies illegitimately appropriated. Otherwise verses 18–23 become nonsensical. How could YHWH announce in one breath that Gog is his agent, and in the next vent his wrath on him with such fury? The heat of YHWH's emotions is obvious in these verses as he explodes with a heaping

66. So much so that some have identified the sources on the basis of YHWH's versus Gog's initiative. Cf. Lindblom, *Prophecy in Ancient Israel*, 233.
67. Cf. Ellis, "Observations on Mesopotamian Oracles," 173–78.

up of expressions for anger unparalleled in the book, if not the entire Old Testament. The problem is not resolved by ascribing verse 17 and verses 18–23 to different editorial hands. Surely this situation would have been as intolerable to later learned editors as it would have been to the prophet himself, and they would hardly have conjoined the text this way.

"Are you he of whom I spoke by my servants the prophets?" Contrary to the delusion of Gog himself, the misunderstanding of 2,300 years of interpretative tradition, and the misreading of all the modern translations, the answer is a firm "No!"[68]

68. Appreciation is expressed to my assistant Gregory L. Mathias for his proofreading of the manuscript.

7

Gog and the Pouring
Out of the Spirit
Reflections on Ezekiel 39:21–29[1]

INTRODUCTION

DURING THE PAST HUNDRED years, scholarly discussions on Ezekiel's Gog Oracle (Ezek 38–39) have focused primarily on two major problems: (1) the authenticity of the oracle in the prophecy of Ezekiel, and (2) the connection between the oracle and the context within which it is embedded. Although before the turn of the century this text was still commonly attributed to the prophet Ezekiel, and thought to derive from the period of Judah's exile,[2] after 1900 it became increasingly fashionable to look elsewhere for its origin and setting.[3] In recent years interpreters

1. This essay was originally published in *Vetus Testamentum* 37 (1987) 257–70.

2. E.g., Smend, *Prophet Ezechiel*, 293–306; Bertholet, *Hesekiel*, 187–94.

3. In 1943 William A. Irwin could write, "Recent critical opinions is practically unanimous that these chapters are spurious" (*Problem of Ezekiel*, 172). Charles C. Torrey (*Pseudo-Ezekiel*, 96) saw in רֹאשׁ (38:2; 39:1) a reference to Javan (Greece) and in Gog Alexander the Great. So also Browne, *Ezekiel and Alexander*. Van den Born ("Études sur quelques toponymes bibliques," 197–201) interprets אֶרֶץ הַמָּגוֹג (38:2) as "land of the Macedonian." Berry ("Date of Ezekiel 38:1—39:20," 224–32), understands 1 Macc 6:18–19 as the background to the Gog oracle, and equates Gog with Antiochus Eupator. The basic problems with the Ezekielian interpretation are summarized by Cooke (*Ezekiel*, 406–8).

have become more modest in their understanding of the text, generally acknowledging at least the core of the prophecy as from the prophet himself.[4]

The problems raised by this oracle are not restricted to its relationship to the broader context of the book. The text itself presents a host of difficulties. It is obvious that the prophecy against Gog consists of a series of smaller units that appear to present a collage of scenes sometimes only loosely conjoined.[5] Our concern here is restricted to the conclusion of the pericope that presents enough difficulties of its own.

The conclusion to the Gog oracle presents many questions. Where does the oracle against Gog actually end? Why does 39:21–29 contain a series of recognition formulae? How should we account for the literary features that occur only here in the book? Why do these verses appear to have so little to do with the themes of what precedes? What is the function of the conclusion in its present context? These questions are complex and to my mind have not yet been satisfactorily answered.

RECENT TREATMENTS OF THE CONCLUDING SECTION

Long before the non-Ezekielian interpretation of the Gog prophecy had become popular the anomalous character of 39:21–29 was being acknowledged. In 1880 Smend recognized that verses 25–29 presented a contrast to the bombastic (*schwülstig*) and lack-lustre (*matt*) tone of 38:1—39:24, which he regarded as the product of simple reflection.[6] Fifty years later this section had been completely amputated from its context. The principal issue remaining in the debate was the best location for the actual amputation.

4. Fohrer, *Ezechiel*, 212–29; Wevers, *Ezekiel*, 286; Zimmerli, *Ezechiel 2*, 296–305.

5. See the helpful study by Zimmerli, *Ezechiel 2*, 933–95 (English translation, 296–324). However, Zimmerli's exploitation of these differences to support his theory of the history of the text is not entirely satisfactory. The composite nature of the oracle is as problematic for his interpretation as for those who argue for basic unity of authorship. Surely the final hypothethical redactor responsible for the present canonical shape of the text would have been as sensitive to the points of apparent disjunction as would a single author. For a demonstration of an exegetical methodology based upon the canonical form of the text and assuming essential unity of composition see Greenberg, *Ezekiel 1–20*; Greenberg, "Design and Themes," 181–208. For a comparison of the methods represented by these interpreters see Levenson, in a review of Zimmerli and Greenberg, *Interpretation* 38 (1984) 210–17.

6. Smend, *Ezechiel*, 295.

Some ended the Gog oracle as early as 39:16. Following the lead of G. Hölscher,[7] Cooke argued that by the time YHWH calls the predatory birds and beasts to his sacrificial feast, Gog and his hordes have all been buried. They are not mentioned again. Instead, the fare at this banquet is made up of the flesh and blood of the mighty men, the princes of the earth (v. 18), that is, the enemies of the Jews in general. Therefore, verses 17–20 represent a new mini-apocalypse. Verses 21–29, for their part, have nothing to do with either the Gog prophecy or the immediately preceding scene. They represent a summary of Ezekiel's teaching, forming a conclusion to chapters 34–37.[8]

Wevers ends the Gog oracle at verse 20. He maintains that verses 21–22 are an expansion of the oracle, but their secondary nature is recognizable by the reference to the house of Israel as the subject of the recognition formula in verse 22. He also holds verses 25–29 to be distinct, serving as editorial insertions intended to bring chapters 37–39 to a close on the theme of restoration.[9] Zimmerli, who provides the most detailed study of this part of the text, also concludes the oracle here. He argues that the kernel of Ezekiel's prophecy against Gog is now represented by 38:1–9, 39:1–5, 17–20.[10] To him verses 21–29 are a final expansion, with verses 21–22 still looking back to the Gog oracle, but verses 23–29 leaving it entirely and bringing the reader back to the basic themes of the prophet's message. However, Hermann's interpretation of the last section (vv. 25–29) as the conclusion to chapters 13–37 is rejected. Verses 25–29 are tied to 23–24 by the expression, "to hide the face" (הִסְתִּיר פָּנִים). The entire section, verses 23–29, is treated as an extended expansion of 21–22. The repetition of the recognition formula in verse 23 resumes the combined beginnings of the latter.[11]

Although Fohrer does not deal with this text in his article, "Die Glossen im Buche Ezechiel,"[12] he deletes verses 23–29 without discussion in his commentary as a (*variierende*) gloss, apparently from several hands.[13]

---

7. Hölscher, *Hesekiel*, 178, 186–88.

8. Cooke, *Ezekiel*, 421–22. That this epilogue represented the conclusion to chapters 34–37 prior to the existence of the Gog pericope had already been proposed by Herrmann, *Ezechiel*, 251.

9. Wevers, *Ezekiel*, 285.

10. Zimmerli, *Ezekiel 2*, 289–89.

11. Ibid., 319–21.

12. In Fohrer, *Studien*, 204–17.

13. Fohrer, *Ezechiel*, 218.

By proposing that only verses 25–29 represent extraneous material to be excised from the Gog oracle, Herrmann and Eichrodt have cut away the smallest portion. The former treats verses 21–24 as an encouraging conclusion to the Gog material, fashioned in characteristic Ezekielian expression and thought. However, as already noted, verses 25–29 are tied to the preceding, neither chronologically nor with reference to content. The return to the great themes of salvation, the change in Israel's fortune, her regathering and resettlement in her own land, suggest that this section originally could have served as the conclusion to chapters 34–37 before the Gog prophecy had come into existence and had been inserted in its present position.[14] In similar vein Walther Eichrodt comments,

> Finally, in 39.25–29 we find a portion of text clearly dissimilar to all that has preceded it, which shows no acquaintance with the main concern of these chapters and differs linguistically. It is certainly directed towards a different historical situation and towards a different objective, which are on exactly the same line of thought as ch. 34–37. One may therefore feel inclined to regard it as the original transition from 37.28 to 40.1ff.[15]

Although at first sight it appears that Eichrodt is following Herrmann here, later he proposes that this conclusion was composed subsequent to the insertion of the Gog oracle to re-establish the tie with chapter 37.[16]

The apparent unanimity of scholars in recent years in deleting the last verses of chapter 39 from the actual Gog oracle is impressive. However, so is the lack of agreement on the boundaries of the segment to be excised. All seem to find convincing arguments for their positions, but the general confusion hardly encourages confidence in either the procedures or the results. Most have assumed that the primary task of the interpreter is to isolate the various units that constitute a composition on the basis of divergent linguistic and literary styles, and then to propose a reconstruction for the history of the passage.

This method is suspect for several reasons. First, it assumes that ancient writers were bound by the same rules of consistency and clarity as modern scholars. Second, it fails to recognize that isolating the separate literary fragments and proposing origins for them does not resolve the tensions created by the text as it stands. These tensions may be the result of deliberate composition, regardless of whether the account derives from

14. Herrmann, *Ezechiel*, 251.

15. Eichrodt, *Ezekiel*, 521.

16. Ibid., 529.

a single author or a final redactor (unless, of course, the entire book was produced by random arrangement of the various identifiable segments). Finally, by concentrating on the disjunctures in a pericope, the intention of the entire pericope may be lost, not to mention its function in the broader context. Wherever one may make the excision, in their present context the final verses of Ezekiel 39 do in fact represent a conclusion to the Gog oracle, which in turn concludes Ezekiel's message of hope and restoration. Should we not ask ourselves what the significance of these verses is in their present position? This procedure does not blind the student of the text to its difficulties. Rather, it provides an approach to those points of tension that is essentially positive rather than nihilistic.

A Suggested Alternative Interpretation

The Characteristics of Ezekiel 39:21–29

Even if they do not agree in the fine points, it is not surprising that scholars have isolated the last part of Ezekiel 39 from the Gog oracle. In the first place, in verse 23 the chronological perspective changes, reverting from the eschatological conflicts between YHWH and Gog back to the exile of Israel, circumstances that had last been dealt with in chapter 37. Second, the center of attention shifts from the fate of Gog and his hordes to the prospects for Israel following the exile. In fact, Gog is never mentioned after verse 16. Third, verses 21–29 introduce the reader to several stylistic forms that are unique, not only to the Gog oracle, but to the book as a whole: "from that day and onwards" (מִן־הַיּוֹם הַהוּא וָהָלְאָה, v. 22);[17] "I will hide my face from them" (וַאַסְתִּר פָּנַי מֵהֶם, vv. 23, 24, 29).[18] "Their adversaries" (צָרֵיהֶם, v. 23) as a reference to Israel's enemies;[19] YHWH's exercise of "mercy" (וְרִחַמְתִּי, v. 25).[20] Beyond these we should note the only occur-

17. The expression occurs elsewhere only in Num 15:23 and 1 Sam 8:9. But cf. the phrase בַּיּוֹם הַשְּׁמִינִי וָהָלְאָה in Ezek 48:27; Lev 22:27.

18. The expression is common elsewhere: Deut 31:17–18; 32:20; Isa 8:17; 54:8; 64:6[7]; Jer 33:5; Mic 3:5; Pss 13:2[1]; 22:25[24]; 27:9; 30:8[7]; 69:18[17]; 88:15[14]; 102:3[2]; 143:7 (cf. also 44:25[24]; 104:29); Job 13:24; 34:29. For a full-length study of the concept see Balentine, *The Hidden God*.

19. The expression occurs elsewhere in 30:16, but the text is doubtful. Cf. *BHS*. Its usage resembles Neh 9:27. Cf. the use of אֹיְבֵיהֶם, in verse 27.

20. The root is used in its literal sense, "womb" in 20:26. רחם as a designation of YHWH's mercy is common in other prophets (cf. BDB, 933), but Ezekiel seems to prefer חָמַל. Cf. v. 11; 7:4, 9; 8:18; 9:5; 16:5; 36:21.

rence of Israel as the subject of the recognition formula in verse 22, and the rare absolute use of Jacob for Israel in verse 25.[21]

In spite of the novel features in verses 21–29 caution against haste in eliminating the text as non-Ezekielian or inauthentic or misplaced on these bases is advised. The apparent concentration of unique forms does not need to indicate a change in authorship any more than do *hapax legomena* in other contexts.[22] In fact, it has been observed that many echoes of earlier prophecies of Ezekiel are to be found here: the revelation of YHWH's glory (cf. 28:22); the recognition of YHWH's patron divinity status for Israel (cf. 28:26; 34:30); Israel's return, that is the recovery of the nation from the diaspora, still viewed in anticipation (cf. 20:42–43; 36:24, 28); YHWH's execution of justice (עָשָׂה מִשְׁפָּט, 18:5; cf. vv. 8, 10); the falling of the people by the sword (cf. 23:25; 24:21); the reference to Israel's uncleanness (36:25, 29); jealousy as the motive of YHWH (cf. 36:5).[23] All these features argue strongly for at least some connection of verses 21–29 with Ezekiel.

It remains to be seen whether this can be extended to a direct and intentional connection with the Gog prophecy. It is to this question that we now turn. What evidence is there for interpreting the last verses of chapter 39 as an intentional part of and conclusion to the Gog oracle?

The *terminus a quo* of the Concluding Unit

Concerning the *terminus ad quem* of the final unit of Ezekiel 39 there is no dispute. The concluding signatory formula, נְאֻם אֲדֹנָי יְהוִה[24] followed by the date formula in 40:1 fixes it at the end of verse 29. However, the beginning of the unit is not so easily determined.

It is doubtful whether we should find the beginning of the epilogue in verse 17, as did Hölscher and Cooke, who were offended by the invitation of the birds and beasts of prey to a banquet, the fare of which consisted of the corpses of Gog and his hordes after their bones had already been buried.[25] But this is a visionary oracle, played out in

---

21. Cf. the reference to "my servant Jacob" in 18:25; 37:25.

22. For a discussion of the vocabulary of Ezekiel, see Zimmerli, *Ezekiel 1*, 21–24.

23. Cf. Cooke, *Ezekiel*, 422–23.

24. The signatory formula in this full form occurs some eighty times in the book. It has already served to punctuate the Gog prophecy at 38:18, 21, 39:5, 8, 10, 13, 20. The abbreviated form נְאֻם יְהוִה appears an additional four times.

25. Hölscher, *Hesekiel*, 178, 186–88; Cooke, *Ezekiel*, 421–22.

several different scenes, whose connections need not always conform to our standards of logic and progression. Verses 17–20 seem to have been understood by Henry Van Dyke Parunak as happening simultaneously with, if not prior to, 39:11–16. As he observes, "the earlier paragraph describes the burial of bones, which is all that one would expect the beasts to leave after a period of exposure that persists as long as seven months."[26] In any case, verses 17–20 appear to be an expansion of the brief reference to YHWH's giving the troops of this enemy host up to the predatory creatures in verse 4.

The correctness of the opinion of Zimmerli and Wevers that the Gog oracle proper ends with verse 20 is confirmed by the dramatic change in subject matter as the text moves from verse 20 to 21. In the former the concern is still the banquet of YHWH at which the beasts gorge themselves. Verse 21 introduces an entirely new idea, the implications of the Gog episode for the honor of YHWH. The feast is never mentioned again. Thus the outer limits of the final unit are defined by the concluding signatory formula, נְאֻם אֲדֹנָי יְהוִה, which occurs at the ends of verses 20 and 29.[27]

Coherence and Structure of the Concluding Unit

The epilogue to the Gog oracle as delimited contains no sharp formal divisions. The "therefore" (לָכֵן) in verse 25 serves both as a weak divider as well as a sign of coherence in that the succeeding material is connected logically to the preceding.[28] Beyond this the text contains three occurrences of modified forms of the recognition formula (vv. 22, 23, 28).[29] However, although elsewhere these may indicate conclusions to separate sections, here they highlight the central thesis of the message, rather than breaking it up into neat sections. In fact, the verbatim parallelism of the beginnings of verses 22 and 23 immediately juxtaposed argues against dividing them too sharply. Furthermore, verse 23 is not in the shape of the usual

---

26. Van Dyke Parunak, *Structural Studies* 505, n. 11.

27. Van Dyke Parunak's division after verse 21 is not convincing.

28. So also Wevers, *Ezekiel*, 294.

29. Zimmerli, *Ezekiel 2*, 319, also sees the recognition formula in verse 21. But this is doubtful. As in 21:4[20:48], רָאָה should be interpreted in its unusual sense "to see." The text is not yet dealing with the nation's recognition of the intended implications from YHWH's actions, only with their status as witnesses to that action. This applies to "all flesh" in 21:4 as well.

recognition formula, since it is not the person of YHWH that is being acknowledged, but the reason for his treatment of his people.

It seems better to divide the text logically into two parts, verses 21–24 and 25–29. Although in many respects each section goes its own way, still this results in a remarkable balance and symmetry. Both sections may be divided into four parts:

A	the actions of YHWH	21a	25
B	the response of the objects of his action	21b	26–27
B'	the recognition formula (tied to Israel's exile)	22–23a	28
A'	a reference to YHWH hiding his face	23b–24	29

As the letters to the left suggest, in addition to this parallel structure, a chiastic pattern is also discernible in each. Both sections begin and end with descriptions of the divine action, between which are sandwiched the human responses.[30] This suggests a certain deliberateness in the arrangement of the material. This conclusion is supported by the fact that each ends with a reference to YHWH's hiding his face, a concept that is otherwise foreign to the book. In content, however, the two parts are not identical, but represent two different sides to YHWH's treatment of Israel: the first dealing with his judgment, the second with the permanence of his restoration.

The Relationship of the Epilogue to the Gog Oracle

If these two sections do indeed represent a deliberately composed unit, their relationship to the Gog oracle after which they appear remains to be accounted for.

It has already been observed that marked differences in style exist between this section and the preceding. This could just as well be attributed to the nature of the material as to different hands. But the links between the epilogue and the Gog oracle proper should not be overlooked. On the one hand, the motive for YHWH's setting his glory (כָּבוֹד, v. 21) among the

---

30. I am not the first to recognize a chiastic structure in this passage. Van Dyke Parunak (*Structural Studies*, 506) sees a simpler ABA' pattern in 39:22–24. The A and A' segments consist of verses 22–24 and 28–29 respectively, showing correspondence through the repetition of וְיָדְעוּ בֵּית יִשְׂרָאֵל כִּי אֲנִי יְהוָה אֱלֹהֵיהֶם "And the house of Israel will know that I am YHWH their God" (both verses, 22 and 28, using the unusual form אֱלֹהֵיהֶם) and אַסְתִּיר פָּנַי מֵהֶם, "I will hide my face from them." The latter is affirmed and converted in both verses 23 and 24, whereas verse 29 using a future sense denies the action of YHWH.

nations, which begins the first half of the epilogue, echoes the reference to him glorifying himself (נִכְבַּד) in verse 13. On the other hand, the introduction of the second part (v. 25) with a reference to YHWH's concern for his holy name (שֵׁם קָדְשִׁי) finds its counterpart in 39:7.[31] Appropriately, the concern for his glory in both instances is expressed in the context of the nations, whereas the holiness of his name is defended within the context of Israel in both. This agreement hardly seems accidental.

A second connection is drawn between the epilogue and the oracle by the עַתָּה, "Now," with which YHWH's speech is introduced in verse 25. This presents a deliberate contrast to the eschatological מִיָמִים רַבִּים and בְּאַחֲרִית הַשָּׁנִים in 38:8, בְּאַחֲרִית הַיָמִים in 38:16, and בַּיּוֹם הַהוּא in 38:10, 14, 18, 19; 39:11, thrusting the prophet back into the world of the present. The conflicts involving Gog are still in the distant future, a period that follows on a return of peace and security for Israel in its land. The description of Israel in verse 27 appears to contain a deliberate summing up of the state of the nation at the time of Gog's invasion as described in 38:8, 11. But עַתָּה, "Now," brings the prophet back to the present crisis, the exile of Israel, a crisis that requires an equally dramatic demonstration of divine mercy and power.

These are not the only connections. Verses 21–22 are obviously transitional. The past tense of the verb in "my justice that I have executed" (מִשְׁפָּטִי אֲשֶׁר עָשִׂיתִי)[32] and "my power that I have imposed upon them" (יָדִי אֲשֶׁר־שַׂמְתִּי בָהֶם) points back to the war against Gog. Specifically, the pronominal suffix in בָּהֶם requires an antecedent, which would be missing if this marked the beginning of a totally new section. The same applies to "from that day and onward" (מִן־הַיּוֹם הַהוּא וָהָלְאָה) in verse 22. Without the preceding oracle, the reader would be left asking, "What day?" Since these first two verses are tied so closely to the prophecy, and the entire epilogue is written as a coherent unit, it may only be concluded that this section is

---

31. Cf. also the reference to YHWH sanctifying himself in 38:16 (נִקְדָּשׁ) and in verse 23 (הִתְקַדִּשׁ), which also speaks of him magnifying himself (הִתְגַּדִּל), and making himself known (נוֹדַע).

32. The interpretation of מִשְׁפָּטִי as "my justice" rather than the commonly accepted "my judgment" may be defended on several grounds: (1) in Ezek 18:8 the phrase עָשָׂה מִשְׁפָּט requires the sense "to execute justice." Zimmerli's reference to וְעָשִׂיתִי בְתוֹכֵךְ מִשְׁפָּטִים in 8:8 as a parallel (Ezekiel 2, 319) is not convincing since our text lacks the suffixed preposition and uses the singular rather than the plural of מִשְׁפָּט. (2) In the present context, "to execute judgment" (or "enter into judgment") is rendered with the niphal of שָׁפַט. Cf. וְנִשְׁפַּטְתִּי in 38:22. (3) What the greed and opportunism of Gog demands, attacking innocent unsuspecting Israel, is justice. Cf. 38:10–13.

intentionally placed where it is. Without this epilogue the Gog oracle is left hanging with no conclusion at all.[33]

THE SIGNIFICANCE OF 39:21–29 IN ITS CONTEXT

Having argued that the epilogue is structurally and thematically integral to the context in which it is embedded, one must enquire concerning its function here. What does it contribute to the Gog oracle? What contribution does it make to the message of the book as a whole? We offer several suggestions.

(1) The epilogue provides the Gog oracles with a satisfactory conclusion. In the first place, it highlights the revelatory impact of YHWH's defeat of Gog, first on the nations, and then on Israel. Recalling YHWH's goals in 38:16, 23; 39:7, 13, this text declares that when the nations witness YHWH's execution of justice and demonstration of power on Gog, his glory will be set among the nations. Second, it emphasizes the revelatory impact of the defeat of Gog for Israel. The expanded recognition formula in 39:22 emphasizes that the victory of YHWH serves as the *terminus a quo* of the house of Israel's acknowledgement of him as their God.

(2) The epilogue highlights the revelatory impact of YHWH's dealings with Israel. Although structurally connected to the previous verses, in verse 23 Gog fades from view and the implications of YHWH's more immediate dealings with Israel return into focus. This section begins with a long recognition formula for the nations, according to which they will now see the cause of Israel's exile (her covenantal treachery [מַעֲלוּ־בִי]). But more than this, they will also recognize that, far from being a symptom of YHWH's impotence (cf. 36:20), the nation's experience was the deliberate expression of his wrath. YHWH had hidden his face from them;[34] he had given them into the hand of the adversaries; he had dealt with them according to their rebellion (פֶּשַׁע), as well as their uncleanness (טֻמְאָה).

---

33. If this section had originally served as the conclusion to the salvation oracles of chapters 34–37 as Herrmann, *Ezechiel*, 251, and Cooke, *Ezekiel*, 422, suggest, critics would surely have treated it as secondary to that context as well. The transition between 37:28 and 39:21 is harsh and the material redundant.

34. Cf. verse 17 above. Also van der Woude, "פָּנִים *pānîm* Angesicht," 446–59, esp. 452–53.

(3) In returning to the needs of the present, the epilogue emphasizes the role of divine mercy (note the first occurrence of the term רחם in this sense in the book) in creating the conditions that immediately precede the Gog debacle: a nation regathered and secure in its own land (v. 27). As in 28:25, the regathering of the nation also serves as a demonstration of YHWH's holiness.

(4) With the expanded recognition formula taking up the last two verses, the text emphasizes that the covenant relationship involving deity, people, and land has been reinstituted. Its restoration is full and permanent. YHWH will never leave any of them, neither will he hide his face from them again. In so doing these verses also serve as a fitting conclusion to the salvation oracles of chapters 34–39 as a whole. The grand themes of this great section are summarized in a new announcement of renewal, return, and restoration.

(5) The last clause highlights the special role of the Spirit of YHWH in the confirmation of the covenant. The conjunction אֲשֶׁר specifically attributes the permanence of the new relationships to the pouring out of the Spirit upon the house of Israel. This conclusion applies whether the particle is interpreted temporally[35] or, as I prefer, causally.[36] Although the clause is reminiscent of the giving of the Spirit described in 36:27, a fundamental difference in significance seems to characterize the two phrases. "To put my spirit within" in the former is obviously associated with the renewal of the covenant, but it seems to relate more immediately to the rebirth of the nation, her receiving new life (cf. the fuller exposition of this notion in the vision of the valley of the dry bones, 37:1–14). In 39:29 to "pour out my Spirit upon" represents a sign and seal of the covenant. This represents the divine mark of ownership, which accounts for YHWH's intervention against Gog on Israel's behalf before the latter is even touched.

The expression "to pour out" God's "Spirit upon" occurs several times in other prophetic writings. In Joel 3:1[2:28], as in our text, the concept appears in a salvation oracle, specifically in the context of the renewal of the covenant and the restoration of prosperity and peace for Israel.[37] In

---

35. So Zimmerli, *Ezekiel 2*, 295. Cf. LXX ἀνθ᾽ οὗ; Vg. *eo quod*.

36. So Cooke, *Ezekiel*, 424, in the sense of יַעַן אֲשֶׁר. Cf. 12:12; 16:43; 21:9[4]; 26:2; 31:10; 44:12.

37. Cf. Joel 2:18—3:2[2:29], specifically 2:18. "Then YHWH will be zealous for his land, and will have pity on his people," and verse 27, which immediately precedes the reference to the pouring out of the Spirit, "thus you will know that I am in the midst of

Zech 12:10, the pouring out of the spirit of grace and supplication occurs in the context of the restoration of the dynasty of David and God's renewed activity on behalf of Jerusalem, and in the context of the renewal of the covenant.[38] Although a different verb is used in Isa 32:15 (יֵעָרֶה), once again the pouring out of the Spirit from on high represents the divine activity that immediately precedes the restoration of peace and prosperity in Israel. These are normally the consequence of the reestablishment of the covenant. The covenantal context of the pouring out of the Spirit is unmistakable in Isa 40:1–5:

> But now listen, O Jacob, my servant;
> And Israel, whom I have chosen.
> Thus says YHWH who made you,
> And formed you in the womb,
> Who will aid you,
> "Do not fear, O Jacob my servant;
> And you, O Jeshurun, whom I have chosen,
> For I will pour (יָצַק) water on the thirsty land
> And streams on the dry ground;
> I will pour (יָצַק) my Spirit on your descendants;
> And they will spring up among the grass
> Like poplars by streams of water."
> This one will say, "I belong to YHWH";
> And that one will call on the name of Jacob;
> And another will write on his hand, "Belonging to YHWH,"
> And will name Israel's name with honor.

It would appear from all these references that the pouring out of the Spirit of YHWH upon his people signified the ratification and sealing of the covenant relationship. It represented the guarantee of new life, peace, and prosperity. But it signified more than this. It served as the definitive act

---

Israel, and that I am YHWH your God, and there is no other; and my people will never be put to shame." As Wolff (*Joel and Amos*, 67) points out, the context requires that כָּל־בָּשָׂר, "all flesh" not be interpreted universally, as it is commonly understood, but for all Israel. In Peter's Pentecost sermon this sense is not changed. Acts 2:5 notes that the people gathered on the occasion in Jerusalem were Jews from all parts of the empire. Peter himself emphasizes that he is speaking to the men/house of Israel. Cf. vv. 22, 36.

38. Note the reference to the covenant formula in 13:9, "I will say, 'They are my people', and they will say, 'YHWH is my God.'" Admittedly, there is some distance between the two verses, and it may be argued that originally these were uttered as separate oracles. But the repeated references to "in that day" (12:11; 13:1, 2, 4) suggest some connection, as does the juxtaposing of these oracles.

whereby he claimed and sealed the newly gathered nation of Israel as his own.

CONCLUSION

Although some continue to argue that chapters 40–48 once followed immediately upon chapter 37,[39] with my interpretation of the epilogue and the pouring out of the Spirit we may have stumbled upon the answer to the enigma that the prophecy concerning Gog poses in its present context. Ezekiel 37:15–28 had concluded with an emphatic declaration that the covenant of peace (בְּרִית שָׁלוֹם, v. 26) that YHWH was establishing with the newly revived nation and the Davidic dynasty was to be an eternal covenant (בְּרִית עוֹלָם, v. 26). In fact, the term "eternal" (עוֹלָם), occurs five times in the last four verses. However, in the present context, the promise of the permanence of the new relationship between deity and nation remains just that, a promise, a word. The function of the Gog oracle is to provide specific and concrete proof for the prophet that YHWH meant exactly what he said.

The oracle foresees Israel as prosperous and secure in her land for a considerable period of time. In fact, in contrast to the immediacy of the prophetic utterance, the Gog episode is set in the latter days (38:8, 16), when YHWH's people will enjoy all the blessings attendant on the revival of the nation and her relationship with her deity (38:8, 11, 14). Into this pacific and tranquil land YHWH deliberately brings these hordes from the north (38:4–9), who may imagine that they are operating of their own free will (38:10–13). However, like the Pharaoh of Egypt (Exod 7–14), Gog is merely functioning as an agent serving the revelatory purposes of YHWH. That purpose has two dimensions: to declare the greatness, holiness, and glory of his person (38:16, 23; 39:7, 13, 21, 25, 27) and the firmness of his commitment to his people (38:14–16; 39:7, 22–9 [note the reference to "my people Israel" and "my land"]). The defense of this people, who did not need so much as to lift a sword, vindicated his great name while at the same time confirming his word. The causal clause, "For I shall have poured out my Spirit on the house of Israel," explains not just the events described in the immediately preceding verses, that is, the regathering of the nation,

---

39. Lemke, "Life in the Present," 180, n. 19, points out that 37:26–28 makes reference to YHWH's dwelling with his people and his sanctuary being in their midst. Appeal can be made to at least one ancient manuscript, Papyrus[967], which in fact exhibits such an arrangement. Cf. Filson, "The Omission of Ezekiel 12:26–28," 27–32.

but also YHWH's fulfillment of his covenant to his people. The presence of the Spirit of YHWH, poured out upon his people, served as the permanent witness and seal of the בְּרִית שָׁלוֹם and the בְּרִית עוֹלָם.[40] The presence of the Spirit of YHWH poured out upon the returned exiles guaranteed that he would never leave any of the house of Israel at the mercy of her enemies, and that he would never hide his face from them again, as the contemporaries of Ezekiel had just witnessed. In short, Gog becomes the agent through whom YHWH declares concretely that 587 B.C. shall never again repeat itself.

---

40. The implications this covenantal interpretation of the pouring out of the Spirit has for the progress of the Holy Spirit's activity in the book of Acts are tantalizing, but beyond the scope of this article. It should be noted, however, that with every stage in the advance of the gospel, and the incorporation of new groups of people into the church, reference is made to the manifestation of the Spirit's presence. Cf. the coming of the Spirit upon the Jews of Jerusalem (Acts 2:4, 33, 38), the Samaritans (8:14–17), the Gentile proselytes of Judaea (10:44–48, cf. 11:16), and the Gentiles of Asia Minor (19:1–6). Each account represents a new advance in the scope of the new covenant instituted in Christ. Furthermore, when Paul speaks of being sealed with or by the Holy Spirit (2 Cor 1:22; Eph 1:13; 4:30), is he not also speaking of the reception of the Holy Spirit as the divine confirmation of the covenant?

8

Envisioning the Good News

Ten Interpretive Keys to Ezekiel's Final Vision[1]

INTRODUCTION

THE BOOK OF EZEKIEL concludes on a glorious note, with a vision of YHWH returning to his temple and establishing his residence in his city in the midst of his people. The new date notice, followed by the divine arrest of the prophet, and his transportation to a new site signal the beginning of a new literary unit. But this unit is larger and more complex than any other, extending until the end of the book (48:35). An envelope structure is created by framing this entire block with an initial notice of the city near the high mountain (40:2) and a concluding reference to the city, now identified as יְהוָה שָׁמָּה, "YHWH Shammah" ("YHWH is there"). While the style and substance of the intervening materials display considerable variety, the entire unit is held together by the figure of a man, who, in tour-guide fashion, escorts the prophet around the temple complex.

Generically, this section is described as a vision report (40:1). However, few sections of the book have yielded such a wide range of

---

1. This is an adaptation of a paper presented to the Evangelical Theological Society in Lisle, Illinois, November 18, 1994.

interpretations, causing the reader to wonder whether this block of material should not be classified as a visual riddle (חִידָה)[2] or visual metaphorical speech (מָשָׁל).[3] Any solution to the riddle we might propose should be deemed provisional, but to unlock its meaning one will need to employ several different hermeneutical keys. The importance attributed to any one of these keys will determine the outcome. We offer the following as a preliminary list of factors that must be considered in solving the riddle of Ezekiel's final vision.

1. The Nature of the Text

The text of many sections of chapters 40–48, particularly chapters 41 and 42, has suffered greatly in transcription and/or transmission. Many readings are uncertain, but the way one resolves textual problems occasionally has a critical bearing on one's approach to the material as a whole.[4] Sometimes the lack of sense in MT forces the textual critic to appeal to the Septuagint and other versions for a plausible resolution, but in such cases one is left with the suspicion that like our own proposals the versional renderings represent simply educated guesses at the meaning of the Hebrew *Vorlage*.

2. The Literary History of the Text

Whereas an earlier generation of Ezekiel scholars was hesitant to recognize Ezekiel's hand anywhere in chapters 40–48,[5] recent students of the prophet have tended to be more generous. Especially influential has been the work of H. Gese, who argues for a complex multi-phased evolution for the text, but credits Ezekiel with large portions.[6] Others, following a

2. On which see 17:2.

3. On which see 17:2; 21:5[20:49]; 24:3.

4. E.g., בְּמֹתָם / בְּמוֹתָם ("their high places"/"in their death") in 43:7; תָּבְנִית / תַּבְנִית ("form"/"plan") in 43:10.

5. This includes those who denied any of the book to the exilic prophet (e.g., Torrey, *Pseudo-Ezekiel*). Cf. the recent attempt to revive the late pseudepigraphic interpretation of the book by Becker ("Erwägungen zur Ezechielischen Frage," 137–49), who insisted that the historical Ezekiel communicated his messages only in poetic form, that he was only a prophet of doom, or that he functioned in Jerusalem, rather than in Babylon. Haran ("Law-Code of Ezekiel XL–XLVI," 46, n. 2) evaluates the results as "somewhat frivolous" and the methodology "for the most part, far from sound."

6. Apart from numerous glosses, Gese (whom Zimmerli tends to follow)

holistic approach, have been even more conservative in attributing virtually all of chapters 40–48 to the exilic prophet.[7] A related problem is the
relationship of this section to the priestly material in the Pentateuch, on
which see below.

3. The Historical Context of the Vision

The opening notice dates the present visionary experience on the tenth
day of the first month, twenty-five years after the deportation of Jehoiachin, and fourteen years after the fall of Jerusalem (40:1). If the preceding salvation oracles are to be dated shortly after the fall of the city (cf.
33:21–22), more than a decade separates this prophetic experience from
the preceding oracles. What historical circumstances provoked the present vision we may only speculate, but two features of the date notice deserve consideration. First, the vision occurs in the "twenty-fifth year" of
the exile. The number is significant for its correspondence with multiples
of twenty-five that dominate the temple vision. However, as one-half of
fifty it also invites linkage with the Israelite jubilee, "the year of release."[8]
The midpoint of the jubilee cycle marked a turning of the corner, turning the sights away from the tragedy of exile in the direction of renewal.
Because YHWH is the true owner of the land, it cannot be forever out of
the possession of those to whom he had granted it; it must be returned on
schedule, despite historical realities.[9]

Second, the vision occurs on the tenth day of the first month, which
invites association with Exod 12:2, according to which the beginning of

---

recognizes as secondary the נָשִׂיא ("prince": 44:1–3; 45:21–25; 46:1–10, 12), Zadok
(44:6–16; 44:17–31 [with insertions]; 45:13–15), and land division (48:1–29) "strata."
See Gese, *Verfassungsentwurf*, 109–15, for a summary. More recently Tuell (*Law of the
Temple*) has found an Ezekielian core (with minor insertions) in 40:1—43:7; 44:1–2;
47:1–12; 48:30–35. Most of the remainder (which he calls "the Law of the Temple")
represents later (Persian period) additions.

7. See Greenberg, "Design and Themes," 81–208; Hals, *Ezekiel*, 285–89;
McConville, "Priests and Levites in Ezekiel," 3–31. Stevenson (*Vision of Transformation*, 3) follows a holistic approach, but she attributes the text to an exilic rhetor, without committing herself to the prophet Ezekiel. For a convincing rejection of Gese's
methodology and conclusions see Duguid (*Ezekiel and the Leaders*, 27–31, 87–90),
who dismisses the notion of so-called נָשִׂיא and Zadokite strata as myth.

8. Lev 25. Ezekiel's familiarity with the Jubilee is evident in 46:17.

9. See also Fager, *Land Tenure*, 76; cf. Zimmerli, *Ezekiel 2*, 346–47. Less likely is
J. Van Goudoever's suggestion that the twenty-fifth year marks the end of the jubilee
cycle ("Ezekiel sees in Exile a New Temple-City," 344–49).

the year commemorated Israel's release from Egyptian bondage. On the other hand, Ezekiel's present location in Babylon also suggests association with the annual Babylonian *akitu*, an elaborate eleven-day festival in the month of Nisan, celebrating the supremacy and enthronement of Marduk and ensuring the success of the enterprises of the coming year. The climax of the celebrations involved the king of Babylon "seizing" the hand of Marduk and conducting his image in procession to the *akitu* temple outside the city, where the *akitu* rituals were performed.[10] Like the inaugural vision, and the earlier vision of the departure of the כְּבוֹד־יְהוָה ("glory of YHWH"), this vision strikes at the heart of paganized perspectives of Ezekiel's countrymen, who interpreted their exile as a sign of Marduk's supremacy over YHWH. But just as in the earlier contexts YHWH had demonstrated his sovereign freedom to appear to Ezekiel in Babylon, the heart of "Marduk-land," and to abandon the temple in Jerusalem of his own free will, so now he proclaims in visionary form his kingship, not only in Jerusalem (the city is not named), but also over the entire world. He will not wait for any human king to lead him in procession; he comes of his own free will and in his own time (43:1–9). Accordingly, this vision serves a polemical purpose: to celebrate the kingship of YHWH, and to inspire new hope and faith in the exiles.

4. The Declared Genre of the Material

Ezekiel 40:2 identifies the genre of 40–48 as מַרְאוֹת אֱלֹהִים ("divine visions"), which links this block most directly with Ezekiel's inaugural vision (1:1) and the earlier temple vision (8:1).[11] The substantive parallels among these texts require that the same hermeneutical principles employed in the interpretation of the previous prophecies apply here, and that this block be interpreted in the light of the previous visions of God. Here Ezekiel is offered a glimpse of spiritual possibilities for Israel based upon the reality revealed in chapter 1 and answering the abuses exposed in chapters 8–11 and the inadequacy of the מִקְדָּשׁ מְעַט, "sanctuary in small measure" (11:16) of the exilic situation.

---

10. See J. Klein, "Akitu," 138–40; Black "New Year Ceremonies," 39–59; Halpern, *Constitution of the Monarchy*, 51–61.

11. The divine seizure (הָיְתָה עָלַי יַד־יְהוָה, "the hand of YHWH was upon me") and transportation of the prophet by the spirit of YHWH also link this text with 37:1.

5. Precursors to this New Temple Vision

If the links between 36:16–38 and the multi-phased judgment oracle found in chapter 20 are impressive, the links between chapter 20 and Eze-kiel's final vision are even stronger. Indeed, since the agenda there is set in historical phases VI (20:32–38) and VII (20:39–44), the present block of material represents another case of typically Ezekielian resumptive ex-position. It builds on the announcement of the renewal of the covenant and the restoration of the exiles to the land of Israel (20:37–38). Earlier YHWH had declared, אֶמְלוֹךְ עֲלֵיכֶם, "I will be king over you."[12] Although the notion of YHWH's renewed kingship over Israel had also been sug-gested by the "divine shepherd" vocabulary in 34:7–22, explicit references to him as "King" over his people have been lacking—until 43:7, where Ezekiel witnesses the "enthronement of YHWH," and hears his declara-tion of kingship over Israel. Phase VII in chapter 20, which describes Is-rael's final historical state, anticipates several other features found in the present complex: (1) The adverb אַחַר, "afterward" (20:39) points to the climax of Israel's history. The word is missing in 40–48, but the placement of the latter after the Gog oracle, which is fixed chronologically בְּאַחֲרִית הַשָּׁנִים, "in the latter years" (38:8) is suggestive. (2) While the meaning shifts slightly, the expression מַתָּנוֹת, "gifts" (20:39) is not picked up again in the book until 46:16–17. (3) הַר־קָדְשִׁי . . . הַר מְרוֹם יִשְׂרָאֵל, "my holy mountain, the high mountain of Israel," in 20:40 anticipates הַר גָּבֹהַּ מְאֹד, "an extremely high mountain" in the land of Israel (40:2). (4) The offer-ings prescribed in 46:1–15 answer to the gifts YHWH says he will receive in 20:40–42 as a sign of Israel's acceptance. (5) The spiritual geography reflected in the design of the temple complex and the strict control of access to the temple in 40–43 fulfill YHWH's stated objective in 20:41: וְנִקְדַּשְׁתִּי בָכֶם, "I will manifest my holiness among you." (6) The promise of return to the land of Israel (20:42) is fulfilled concretely in the division of the land among the twelve tribes (chs. 47–48). In the light of these con-nections, Ezek 40–48 may justifiably be interpreted as an exposition of the theme, "the restored kingship of YHWH," raised earlier in chapter 20.[13]

But this section also resumes a topic raised only for a moment in 37:26–28—the establishment of YHWH's permanent residence, his sanc-tuary, among his people. Indeed, it is not totally surprising that at least one

---

12. The fulfillment is described in 36:18–38 and 37:15–28.

13. This connection is also drawn by Stevenson, *Vision of Transformation*, 154–60.

LXX manuscript, Papyrus[967], places this vision immediately after chapter 37, which leads to a further consideration.

6. The Literary Structure of the Vision.

While some despair of finding a coherent program in Ezekiel's final vision,[14] at the macroscopic level at least, following the opening preamble (40:1–4), the text divides into three major units: 40:3—43:27; 44:1—46:24, and 47:1—48:35, which deal respectively with YHWH's establishment of his residence in the temple, Israel's response to his presence in their midst, and the apportionment of the healed land to the twelve tribes. The significance of this arrangement goes beyond its sheer logic; it displays obvious parallels to the priestly Torah. The latter also begins with the provision for YHWH's residence in the midst of Israel (Exod 25:1–40), then prescribes Israel's response to his presence (all of Leviticus and much of Numbers), and concludes with arrangements for the apportionment of the land to the twelve tribes (Num 34–35). These parallels provide an early clue that Ezekiel may be functioning as a second Moses.

7. The Literary Context of this Vision.

Since chapters 40–48 come after the Gog oracle, some have interpreted chapters 40–48 cosmologically, as the culmination of an ancient mythic pattern in which a deity overcomes a challenge from the forces of chaos in a fierce battle, which is followed by a victory procession, the enthronement of the deity, and a feast of celebration.[15] However, one also needs to consider the broader context. The parallels between Ezek 40–48 and the priestly Torah can hardly be coincidental in view of the remarkable correspondences between the broad structure of Ezekiel's restoration oracles 40–48 and the Exodus narratives as a whole, as Table 2 illustrates. These correspondences strengthen the impression that Ezekiel is perceived as a second Moses. Is he the prophet predicted in Deut 18:14–22?

---

14. Note the pessimistic evaluation of Tuell ("Temple Vision," 98): "[T]he legislation of these chapters is a crazy-quilt affixed to the core vision in a nearly random fashion. No attempt to find here a coherent 'program' can succeed, for there is no such program to be found. If we would hear Ezekiel's voice from among this babble, we need to reclaim the core vision."

15. Thus Niditch, "Ezekiel 40–48," 208–24, esp. 220–23.

Table 2: Ezekiel 40–48 and the Exodus Narratives

Feature	Exodus Narrative	Ezekiel's Restoration Oracles
YHWH commissions a human agent	Exodus 3–4	Ezekiel 33
YHWH separates Israel from the nations and delivers her from bondage.	Exodus 5–13	Ezekiel 34–37
Enemy forces challenge YHWH's salvific work on his people's behalf	Exodus 14–15	Ezekiel 38–39
YHWH appears on a high mountain.	Exodus 19	Ezekiel 40:1–4
YHWH provides for his residence among his people	Exodus 25–40	Ezekiel 40:5—43:27
YHWH prescribes the appropriate response to his grace	Leviticus 1:1—Numbers 21	Ezekiel 44:1—46:24
YHWH provides for the apportionment of his land to his people	Numbers 34–35	Ezekiel 47–48

8. THE RELATIONSHIP BETWEEN THE MOSAIC TORAH AND EZEKIEL 40–48

Perhaps the most significant issue in the interpretation of Ezekiel 40–48 is the relationship of this vision to the Mosaic Torah. Since this is the only corpus of legislation in the Old Testament that does not come from the mouth of Moses,[16] a comparison with the Mosaic Torah is in order. Numerous parallels may be cited.

a. The Torahs have virtually identical linguistic textures.[17] Both are preoccupied with priestly concerns: the sanctuary and its furnishings, the offices of the cult personnel, the sacrificial system with its sin and guilt offerings, the relationship of the tribes of Israel to the cult and its center.

b. Both recognize the Levites as religious functionaries, but restrict the office of priesthood to a specific line within the tribe.

16. A fact noted by Levenson, *Theology of the Program*, 39.
17. So also Haran, "The Law-Code of Ezekiel XL–XLVI," 59.

c. Both Torahs were directly revealed by YHWH to his mediary to be passed on to the people (cf. Exod 19:3; 24:12, *et passim*, and Ezek 40:4; 44:6).

d. Both Torahs were revealed on a high mountain, the first on Mount Sinai, referred to as "the Mountain of God" (Exod 24:12–18); the second on an initially unnamed mountain (Ezek 40:2), but later identified as "YHWH is There" (48:35).

e. In both cases, the revelation of the plans of the sanctuary follow the establishment of the covenant between YHWH and his people.[18]

f. In both the presence of YHWH is visibly demonstrated by the entrance of his *kābôd* ("Glory") into the sanctuary (Exod 40:34–38; cf. Ezek 43:1–9).

g. In both neither human mediator is permitted to enter the land he envisions. Moses is permitted to view it from Mount Abarim (Num 27:12–13; Deut 32:48–52); Ezekiel observes the land from the mountain of revelation, but when the vision is over he returns to Babylon to share it with his fellow exiles.[19]

Levenson is certainly correct in viewing Ezekiel's mountaintop prophetic experience as a programmatic revelation, and the prophet himself as a second Moses. However, these links should not blind the reader to the substantial contradictions that exist between Ezekiel's and Moses' Torahs. Some of the more obvious examples may be highlighted as Table 3:

---

18. In the former it follows immediately after the ratification of the covenant (Exod 24:1–11; cf. chapters 25–31); in the latter the two events are separated by the Gog oracle.

19. See Levenson, *Theology*, 42–44.

Table 3: The Mosaic Torah and the Ezekielian Torah

Feature	Mosaic Torah		Ezekielian Torah	
Priestly line	Aaronic	Exodus 28	Zadokite	40:46; 43:19; 44:15
Vestment Materials	Gold Dyed wool Luxury linen	Exodus 28	Plain linen	44:17–19
Sanctuary Furnishings	Ark Lamp Stand Anointing oil Table of Showbread	Exodus 25	Missing Missing Missing Missing	
New Moon Offering	Two bulls One ram Seven male lambs	Numbers 28:11	One bull Six sheep One ram	46:6–7

These and other differences challenge the fundamental prophetic law of non-contradiction; true prophecy must agree with Mosaic revelation (Deut 18:15–18).[20] Explanations for these discrepancies have varied. Does this reflect the fact that Ezekiel's Torah might antedate that of Moses (P)? Or do these sets of regulations reflect competing exilic priestly traditions, with the "Mosaic" tradition winning the day? Does Ezekiel, viewed by some as "the spiritual father of Judaism,"[21] lay the foundation for post-exilic Judaism of which P was regarded as the salient expression? Or does Ezekiel's Torah represent a deliberate departure from Moses?[22] Was the exilic prophet offering a purified liturgy to replace the priestly tradition, which he views as fundamentally and intentionally flawed from the be-

20. The herculean efforts of an otherwise obscure rabbinic scribe to answer the questions raised by these discrepancies are reflected in the following citation from *b. Shabbath* 13b: "Rabbi Judah quoted the statement of Rab: A certain man has been remembered for a blessing, and Hananiah ben Hezekiah is his name. For were it not for him the Book of Ezekiel would have been suppressed, since its words contradict those of the Torah. What did he do? He brought up three hundred barrels of oil and stayed in the upper room until he had explained away everything."

21. Haran ("The Law-Code of Ezekiel XL–XLVI," 63, n. 30) credits Duhm and Smend with this notion.

22. Haran (ibid.) observes that "P" is much more carefully crafted and displays many more signs of authenticity and originality than Ezekiel's Torah, which he characterizes as an "impoverished offshoot of the former."

ginning, and which he characterizes as "no good laws" (חֻקִּים לֹא טוֹבִים, 20:25)?[23]

The heavy influence of the Mosaic Torah on Ezekiel is evident in the judgment oracles. Indeed he attributed Israel's demise to their infidelity to the covenant, and understood the judgment of 586 BCE as the precise fulfillment of the covenant curses. To be sure, for rhetorical and polemical purposes, the prophet was not above radically revisionist reconstructions of the nation's past (cf. chapters 16, 20, 23), but never did he lose respect for the Mosaic tradition. Nor should we expect him to, since he was, after all, of the traditional priestly line himself.

9. FANTASTIC AND STYLIZED ELEMENTS IN THE VISION.

While some elements of Ezekiel's vision of the future derive from well-known physical realities, others are quite idealistic and even unimaginable. The high mountain on which he observes the new city is reminiscent of the high and holy mountain of YHWH encountered earlier in 17:22 and 20:40,[24] but also has affinities with the mythical Mount Zaphon on which dwelt Baal, the storm deity of the Canaanites, and Mount Olympus, the home of the Greek gods. The river, whose source lies within the temple complex itself flows through the Judaean desert increasing dramatically in size, and turning the wasteland into an Edenic paradise, even healing (רָפָא) the Dead Sea (47:1–12). The plan of the city is idealized as a perfect square with three gates punctuating each side to provide admittance for the twelve tribes. The emphasis on the twelve tribes itself reverses five centuries of history. The apportionment of the land of Israel among the tribes to a large extent disregards topographic and historical realities. The dimensions of the temple and the city are dominated by multiples of five, with twenty-five being a particularly common number. All in all Ezekiel's scheme appears highly contrived, casting doubt on any interpretation that expects a literal fulfillment of his plan.

23. See Levenson, *Theology*, 39.

24. Compare earlier prophets' references to Zion as the mountain of the house of YHWH, established as the highest of all the mountains and raised above the hills (Isa 2:2; Mic 4:1), a description that scarcely fits the ridge on which Jerusalem is built, a mere 2,500 feet above sea level.

10. The Influence of Ezekiel's Design on Later Writers.

Some have interpreted Ezekiel's Torah as a program for the postexilic restoration of the nation of Israel in its own homeland.[25] However, if this was the case and had he lived to see the actual return, he would have found the religious and political scene in Judah extremely disappointing. To be sure, many exiles returned to Jerusalem, a נָשִׂיא, "prince," was recognized among them (Sheshbazzar, Ezra 1:8), and the temple would be rebuilt. Nonetheless, not only were the returnees but a handful of Judaeans, the land was never divided among the tribes, no figure like Ezekiel's נָשִׂיא emerged in the community, the reconstructed temple fell far short of Ezekiel's plan, and most seriously of all, YHWH's *kābôd* failed to return (cf. Hag 2:3–9).

However, this does not mean Ezekiel's vision was forgotten. The massive Temple Scroll composed by the Dead Sea covenanters several centuries before Christ displays numerous connections with Ezekiel. But the blueprint for the temple and the city of Jerusalem envisioned there go their own ways for the most part.[26] Closer adherence to Ezekiel is evident in early Christian writings, most notably Rev 21–22, which displays a series of important links with our text:

1. A visionary transport of the prophet to a high mountain (21:10).

2. The sight of a new world with Jerusalem at the center (21:1–2, 10).

3. The dwelling of God in the midst of his people, which produces a state of perfect well-being (21:3–4).

4. The presence of the glory of God in the city (21:11).

5. A heavenly interpreter with a measuring rod with which he measures the city (21:1–15).

6. A symmetrical plan of the city complete with high walls and twelve gates, one for each of the tribes (Ezek 48:30; cf. Rev. 21:11–21).

7. An emphasis on the purity and holiness of those within (21:27).

8. The presence of the river of life (22:1).

---

25. Zimmerli (*Ezekiel* 2, 328–29) speaks of a "draft constitution," that envisions "the complete fulfillment of the future which YHWH had promised for Israel." Cf. Clements, *God and Temple*, 106.

26. For the *editio princeps*, see Yadin, ed., *The Temple Scroll*. See also Maier, *The Temple Scroll*. For a study of the influence of Ezek 40–48 on the Qumran community see Martinez, "L'interprétation de la Torah d'Ézéchiel," 441–52.

Table 4: A Comparison of the Holy City in Ezekiel and Revelation

Element	The Ezekielian Perspective	John's Perspective
Identity of the Holy City	unnamed in 40:2 renamed "YHWH Shammah" (48:35)	the new Jerusalem (21:2)
Nature of the City	square	cubical (21:16)
Construction Material	apparently constructed of ordinary stones	constructed of precious materials stones and metals
Role of the temple	at the center of everything	its existence emphatically denied (21:22)
Role of Sacrifices	at heart of the ritual	the (sacrificial) Lamb lives among the people
Nature of the Residents	continuing need to distinguish between the pure and impure	absolute purity of all (21:26–27)
Scope of the Vision	parochially Israelite	universal (21:24–27)

Although the skeletal parallels are impressive, the major divergences in detail point to two different fulfillments, as reflected in Table 4. Alexander sees in Ezekiel a portrait of the millennium and in Revelation the eternal state, the former representing a kind of "first fruits," a microcosm, a beginning, of the latter. Ezekiel's sacrifices provide the basis for dispensationalist insistence on a role for sacrifices in the millennium. In response to the New Testament rejection of any and all sacrifices after the final sacrifice of Christ, the function of sacrifices is redefined. Rather than perceiving them as efficacious, since only Christ's sacrifice actually atones for sin, the Mosaic offerings represent "picture lessons" looking forward to the Messiah's work. Since Ezekiel's millennial sacrifices look back on the same event they are regarded as memorial "picture lessons."[27] But J. C. Whitcomb rejects the memorial interpretation, preferring a ceremonial understanding. At the quasi-physical level they offer temporal cleansing and forgiveness to the one offering the sacrifices (hence guaranteed protection from physical and temporal punishment), and reminding

27. Alexander, "Ezekiel," 946–52.

the Gentiles outside of the continued presence of sin.[28] However, these interpretations interpret both Ezekiel and John too literally. John appears to have taken an earlier motif and adapted it for his own purposes.

Conclusion

Having cited ten factors to consider in interpreting Ezek 40–48, it is not surprising that scholars have arrived at such widely divergent conclusions considering the nature and meaning of Ezekiel's final vision. The shape of our work will depend on how we juggle these elements, and how we rank them. Since the post-exilic community appears not to have made any effort to implement Ezekiel's program, many interpret the vision eschatologically, in keeping with its present literary location after the Gog oracle. Accordingly, the high mountain of Ezekiel's vision is none other than Zion, the place of security and divine revelation, and the source of life and blessing, which figures so prominently in other eschatological texts.[29] But the mountain is also a new Sinai on which the Torah of YHWH is revealed to his special mediator (Ezekiel as a new Moses), and the נָשִׂיא is a messianic figure, in whom are combined monarchic and priestly functions.[30] Accordingly, chapters 40–48 present a picture of the reconstituted nation finally functioning as a genuine theocracy. Levenson speaks of "a liturgical manifesto," a constitution for "the kingdom of priests and a holy people,"[31] and the present era as an in-between period, sandwiched between two temple epochs.[32] Levenson frequently offers what is essentially

28. Whitcomb, "Christ's Atonement," 201–17. Similarly Rooker, "Evidence from Ezekiel," 132–33.

29. See Isa 2:1–4 (= Mic 4:1–5); 33:20–24; Joel 4:17–18[3:17–18]; Zech 14:4; Ps 48. See Levenson, *Theology*, 7–24.

30. A view reflected in the Rabbinic commentaries of Kimchi and Mezudat David. Cf. Levey, *Ezekiel*, 5, 119. See the discussion by Levenson (*Theology*, 57–107) and Caquot ("Le messianisme d'Ezechiel," 21–22).

31. Levenson, *Theology*, 129.

32. Ibid., 150. Cf. his comment on p. 45:

The highly specific nature of the description of the Temple, its liturgy and community bespeaks a practical program, not a vision of pure grace. For example, when the text says that eight steps led up to the vestibule of the inner court (Ezek 40:31),can this be other than a demand that the new Temple be constructed just so? Can this be only description? The fact that God has already constructed the Temple does not mean that man has no role in its construction. On the

a theological interpretation of elements of the vision, but a more literalist millenarian understanding has had a long history in Christian circles.[33] Since Israel's prophets tended not to distinguish between near and distant aspects of the great events of which they spoke, it is not always easy to distinguish between millennial and eternal realities.

While many features of chapters 40–48 commend an eschatological interpretation, this view is weakened considerably by the absence of eschatological language. Expressions like "on that day," "in the latter days," and "after many years," common in the Gog oracle, are lacking entirely. עוֹלָם, "forever, eternal," occurs three times, but in none of these does it carry a eschatological sense.[34] Nor is it clear the "prince" should be interpreted messianically. In Ezekiel's Torah he functions primarily, if not exclusively as a liturgical personage, without a hint of a Davidic connection.[35] Furthermore, contrary to popular opinion, the description of the temple is not presented as a blueprint for some future building to be constructed with human hands.[36] Nowhere is anyone commanded to build it. The man with the measuring line takes Ezekiel on a tour of an existing structure already made. Indeed, were it not for the present literary location of the temple vision, it is doubtful the eschatological interpretation would ever have arisen.

Ezekiel's salvation oracles have looked forward to the day when the twelve tribes of Israel would be regathered and returned to their hereditary homeland, the Davidic dynasty would be restored, YHWH's covenant

---

contrary, what Ezekiel was shown is the divinely constructed model, the *tabnît* like the one David showed Solomon (1 Chr. 28:11–19).

33. The history of millenarian movements in Christendom is explored by Cohn, *Pursuit of the Millennium*. Cf. the anthology of essays, *Case for Premillennialism*, Campbell and Townsend, eds. For millenarian interpretations of these chapters see Feinberg, *Prophecy of Ezekiel*, 233–39; Alexander, "Ezekiel," 942–52.

34. The language of 43:7, 9, "I will dwell among the sons of Israel forever," is formulaic and traditional, as is the reference to חֻקּוֹת עוֹלָם תָּמִיד, "a continual ordinance for all time," in 46:14. Cf. חֻקַּת עוֹלָם (Exod 12:14, 17; 28:43; 29:9; Lev 3:17; 7:36; 10:9; 17:7, 29, 31, 34; 23:14, 21, 31, 41; 24:3; Num 10:8; 15:15; 18:23; 19:10, 21) and חָק־עוֹלָם "permanent statute" (Exod 29:28; 30:21; Lev 6:11, 15; 7:34; 10:15; 24:9; Num 18:8, 11, 19; also Jer 5:22) in the Mosaic Torah.

35. According to Alexander ("Ezekiel," 974), a messianic interpretation is excluded by the facts that natural children are envisaged for the prince (46:16) and, even more important, he must make a sin offering for himself (45:22). Cf. the sinlessness of Christ (Heb 4:15).

36. This point is argued convincingly by Stevenson, *Vision of Transformation*, 11–30.

of peace with Israel would be renewed, and he would establish his permanent residence in their midst. It would have been inconceivable for Ezekiel to envision a full restoration of his people without a literal fulfillment of each of these elements. Nevertheless, in view of the considerations cited above, it seems best to interpret chapters 40–48 ideationally.[37] The issue for the prophet is not physical geography, but *spiritual* realities. As in his earlier vision, historical events are described from a theological plane, and the interpreter's focus must remain on the ideational value of that which is envisioned. At the time of Ezekiel's prophetic inauguration, the sight of YHWH enthroned above the cherubim had reassured him of his presence even in Babylon among the exiles (1:1–28a). His visionary ingestion of the scroll spoke of the importance of accepting the divine message and its incorporation into his own experience (1:28b—3:15). The observation of the abominations in the temple and the consequent departure of the divine *kābôd* provide theological justification and rationalization for Nebuchadnezzar's razing of Jerusalem (8:1—11:25). The vision of the revivified dry bones in chapter 37 is not a prophecy of literal individual resurrection, but a declaration of the certainty of the eventual resuscitation of Israel by a new infusion of breath from YHWH.

While more complex and extensive than any of these, Ezek 40–48 should be interpreted along similar lines. The prophet is hereby introduced to the theological realities awaiting his own people. Whereas 37:26–27 had spoken of the establishment of YHWH's permanent residence among his people, following their homecoming, the present vision picks up the theological theme and describes the spiritual reality in concrete terms, employing the familiar cultural idioms of temple, altar, sacrifices, נָשִׂיא, and land. In presenting this theological constitution for the new Israel, YHWH announces the righting of all the old wrongs, and the establishment of permanent, healthy deity-nation-land relationships.

37. The expression is more readily understood and more accurate than Stevenson's "territoriality."

Figure 3: The Sacred Reserve

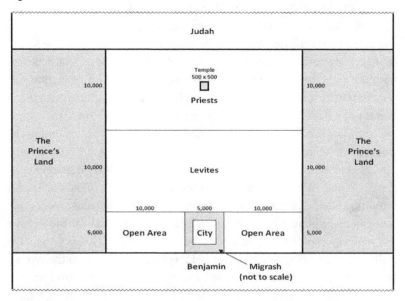

This new reality is demonstrated most dramatically by the sacred reserve sandwiched between the tribes of Benjamin to the south and Judah to the north. The reserve is neither the topographic center of the land nor the mid-point between the tribes—seven tribes are to the north, and five are to the south. However, the east-west layout of the reserve is perfectly proportioned and symmetrical (Fig. 3). At its heart is a square, 25,000 cubits wide and 25,000 cubits deep. The territory on either side, extending to the Jordan and the Mediterranean is under the jurisdiction of the "prince" (נָשִׂיא), the civil representative of YHWH and sponsor of the cultic activity that transpires in the temple. This square is divided horizontally[38] into three rectangles, the northern two measuring 10,000 by 25,000 cubits and the southern tract 5,000 by 25,000 cubits. The northern tract is allocated to the Zadokite priests who officiate in the temple, the sanctuary being located within this area. The middle tract is designated for the Levites, who play a supporting role in the cultic service of the temple. The southern tract is divided symmetrically into three parts, with "the city," a perfect square 4,500 by 4,500 cubits and surrounded by 250 cubit מִגְרָשׁ ("pasture land"). The city is perfectly proportioned with three gates named after

38. From the north-orientation of modern western cartography. To the ancients, with their east orientation, the rectangles would have appeared on a map as vertical lines.

three tribes on each side to give easy access for all the people. As if to highlight the sanctity of the city, though without doing so overtly, the city is called יְהוָה שָׁמָּה, "YHWH is There." Residing in the temple, the glorious aura of YHWH's presence will emanate forth from beyond the sacred residence, pervading the entire reserve, and reaching the tribal territories. Located at the heart of the final allotments, in design and function this reserve transforms a symbol of mere social and civic egalitarianism into a portent of a new spiritual reality. Under the new order, where the people are, there is YHWH. He not only invited them to himself in the temple; he will come to them!

Ezekiel's final vision presents a lofty spiritual ideal: Where God is, there is Zion.[39] Where God is, there is order and the fulfillment of all of his promises. Furthermore, where the presence of God is recognized, there is purity and holiness. Ezekiel hereby lays the foundation for the Pauline spiritualization of the temple. Under the new covenant, God is present literally in Jesus Christ, God incarnate. He replaces the temple as the symbol of the divine determination to dwell among human beings. Furthermore, in the new order even gentiles may be transformed into the living temple of God (1 Cor 3:16–17). Indeed, through the indwelling presence of the Spirit of God, those who believe in Jesus become temples, residences of Deity (1 Cor 6:19).

39. This is preferable to Tuell's, "Wherever the people of the Lord are, there is Zion," in "The Temple Vision of Ezekiel 40–48," 102.

9

Guarding the Glory of YHWH

Ezekiel's Geography of Sacred Space[1]

Introduction

WHEN I BEGAN THE research on this paper I was surprised at how seldom the Old Testament speaks about sacred space. The expression "holy
place" (מְקוֹם הַקֹּדֶשׁ, literally "place of holiness") occurs only twice (Lev
10:17; 12:13); "holy ground" (אַדְמַת־קֹדֶשׁ, literally "ground of holiness")
only once (Exod 3:5), "holy land" (אַדְמַת הַקֹּדֶשׁ) only once;[2] and "holy
city" (עִיר הַקֹּדֶשׁ, literally "city of holiness") only four times.[3] The most
common expression conjoining קֹדֶשׁ with a geographic designation is
הַר־קֹדֶשׁ, "holy mountain," which occurs twenty times.[4] Remarkably,

1. This previously unpublished paper was presented to the Evangelical Theological Society, in Danvers, MA, on November 18, 1999.

2. In Zech 2:16[12] the prophet declares that YHWH will claim Judah as his portion in the "holy land" (אַדְמַת הַקֹּדֶשׁ) and will again choose Jerusalem. Remarkably אֶרֶץ
הַקֹּדֶשׁ, "holy land," never occurs.

3. Isa 48:2; 52:1; Neh 11:1, 18; Dan 9:24 (cf. "the city and the sanctuary in v. 26).
The plural form, "cities of your holiness," occurs in Isa 64:9[10].

4. Isa 11:9 (a place of peace); 27:13 (the place to worship YHWH in Jerusalem);
56:7 (a place of prayer and sacrifice); 57:13 (possessed by those who take refuge in
YHWH); 65:11 (to forsake YHWH is to forget the Holy Mountain); 65:25 (a place
of peace); 66:20 (a place for the nations to bring sacrifices); Jer 31:23 (the abode of
righteousness); Ezek 20:40 (the "high mountain of Israel" where people and offerings

phrases involving "land," like "holy land," are never used.[5] An examination of the context in which these expressions occurs confirms the conclusion of Sara Japhet that what renders an area sacred is the presence of God. In most instances the "holy place" is so called because it YHWH's, his chosen place of residence; in a few instances, as in theophanic descents for purposes of revelation, his presence is only temporary.[6] Ezekiel employs another expression, תְּרוּמַת־הַקֹּדֶשׁ, "sacred reserve," in a spatial sense. Although originally (as in Exod 36:6) the phrase referred to contributions brought by the people for the construction of the sanctuary, in Ezek 45:1–8 and 48:8–22 the exilic prophet uses the expression in a territorial sense. In these passages it refers to the special tract of holy real estate, 25,000 cubits long and 10,000 cubits wide, which the people are to reserve (הֵרִים) for YHWH. Although neither of these two pericopes refers to this tract of land as the residence of YHWH, the final paragraph in the book names the square city on the southern border יְהוָה שָׁמָּה, "YHWH Shammah!" ("YHWH is there"). Curiously this city is designed to accommodate a human population, and is separated by some distance from the temple proper. But more will be said on this below.

Our concern in this paper is Ezekiel's understanding of sacred space. We shall look first at his view of the land of Israel as a sacred land, and then spend most of our time on the temple as sacred space.

---

are received by YHWH); 28:14 ("holy mountain of God"); Dan 9:16 (associated with Jerusalem, YHWH's city); 9:20 ("the holy mountain of my God"); Joel 2:1 (= Zion); 4:17[3:17] (= Zion, where YHWH dwells); Obad 16 (place where the people drank); Zeph 3:11 (place where people are humbled and offerings are received); Zech 8:3 (when YHWH returns to Zion and dwells in the midst of Jerusalem the city will be called "the city of truth" and the mountain of YHWH of hosts will be called "the holy mountain"); Ps 2:6 (= Zion, where YHWH has installed his king); 3:5 (the place from which YHWH hears the prayer of his own); 15:1 (abode of the righteous); 38:2[1] (= city of our God); 43:3 (the dwelling of God and the goal of the pilgrimage); 99:9 (the place to worship YHWH).

5. The antiphonal cry of the seraphim in Isa 6:3 comes the closest: "Holy! Holy! Holy! The fullness of all the earth is his glory!"

6. As in the Sinai theophanies described in Exod 3 and 19. The root קדשׁ is missing in Gen 28, but Jacob is careful to mark the ground where he has been visited by God as a sacred site. For a full discussion see Japhet, "Some Biblical Concepts of Sacred Space," 55–72.

The Land of Israel as Sacred Space

Given Ezekiel's parochial perspective it is not surprising that he never speaks of the earth as a holy orb. Nor does he ever specifically declare the land of Israel to be a holy land. But there are several hints, especially in his salvation oracles, that he perceived the latter as such. First, he uses the language of defilement to describe what the Israelites have done to the land. According to 36:17, with their abominable conduct the people had polluted (טִמֵּא) the land like woman in her menstrual impurity (נִדָּה).[7] In the Old Testament the root טמא is used of two kinds of pollution: ceremonial and moral. Whereas the former resulted from non-moral actions/experiences, not associated with guilt or shame,[8] the latter was incurred by violating the will of the deity. A land could be defiled in two ways: by a pagan foreigner invading it (Ps 79:1), or by the native population violating the will of the divine Sovereign. The latter is obviously the case here. The land that YHWH had graciously given to the family of Israel as their grant (נַחֲלָה) and as their possession (מוֹרָשָׁה) had been defiled with their unrestrained lawlessness (חָמָס, 8:17; 12:19) and bloody crimes (דָּמִים, 7:23; 9:9). By the sixth century the pollution of the land of Israel had reached the saturation point, beyond repentance or sacrifice. The radical removal of the defiling population remained the only way of purgation.[9]

Second, the prophet declares that having been driven from the land, wherever the Israelites went they profaned (חִלֵּל) the reputation (שֵׁם) of YHWH, inasmuch as even though they were the people of YHWH, they had left his land. As described in verses 24–30, this problem will be resolved through a series of "name-sanctifying" actions by YHWH. Inasmuch as the purified people will be indwelt by the Spirit of YHWH, when they return to the land he will return with them and take up residence in it. In any case, the reconstituted land is compared to the garden of Eden, which elsewhere is called "the holy mountain of God" (28:13–16), and to Jerusalem at festival time, when the city is filled with people who have

7. The expression כְּטֻמְאַת הַנִּדָּה, "like the menstrual defilement," occurs elsewhere only in Lev 15:26, where it is used in its normal hygienic sense. Ezekiel uses the figure elsewhere in 7:19–20; 18:6; 22:10.

8. E.g., touching a carcass or experiencing a bodily discharge. Such pollutions were considered contagious, but no harm came to the person affected, other than temporary isolation from the community and alienation from all things sacred during the period of uncleanness. When the period of uncleanness was past, the individual could be restored to a state of purity by participating in ceremonial purification rites (Frymer-Kensky, "Pollution, Purification, and Purgation," 401–4).

9. See ibid., 406–12, for further discussion.

come to bring their sacrifices to YHWH, that is the holy city. But the point is made obliquely, rather than overtly.

Third, in chapter 47 it is scarcely coincidental that the river, whose waters cause the Dead Sea to become fresh, bring life to all creatures, produce fish in abundance for fishermen, and nourish all kinds of trees bearing a constant supply of fruit, and whose leaves have miraculous healing power, has its source in the "house" (47:1), that is the sanctuary (הַמִּקְדָּשׁ, v. 12). Apparently, through the river the holiness that is concentrated in the temple extends to the entire land.

This centrifugal image of territorial sanctification is reinforced by the distribution of the tribal lands, with the sacred reserve (תְּרוּמַת הַקֹּדֶשׁ) at the heart. The manner in which the tribal territories are allotted signals a return to an ancient theocratic ideal.[10] Rather than following traditional tribal or natural topographical boundaries the present plan implicitly criticizes Israel's increasing "feudalism."[11] However, it is not feudalism *per se* that is criticized, but the exploitative nature of Israel's past monarchic feudalism. Ezekiel does not call for the abolition of "feudal" structures; his plan proposes a restoration of the kind of theocratic feudalism that had been intended for the nation from the beginning. YHWH is Israel's true king; the land is his, not an earthly monarch's, to distribute among the tribes as he sees fit. In fact, each tribe is to view its territory as its נַחֲלָה, its special grant, received from the divine overlord as an act of grace to be sure, but also as an honorarium for services to be rendered. The strictly parallel boundaries reflect the order that rules in this reconstituted land.

For all the order that characterizes the tribal allotments, Ezekiel's cartographic scheme rivets the attention on the sacred reserve (45:1–8; 48:8–22). Scholars are not agreed on how to visualize this reserve. The placement and design of the reserve appear to be governed by two considerations, a sense of proportion and a concern to reflect gradations of sanctity as one moves from one part to the next (see Figure 4).[12]

10. For a discussion of the principles governing the territorial allotments see Block, *Ezekiel* 25–48, 720–24.

11. Thus Macholz ("Noch Einmal," 340), who also speaks of a "theological geography" (ibid., 331).

12. For a full discussion see Block, *Ezekiel* 25–48, 725–46.

Figure 4: Ezekiel's Map of the Land of Israel[13]

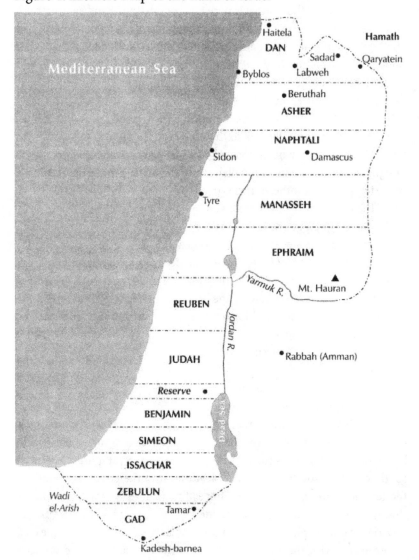

The תְּרוּמָה is sandwiched between the tribes of Benjamin to the south and Judah to the north. Remarkably this is neither the topographic center of the land nor the mid-point between the tribes.[14] Seven tribal

13. Adapted from Block, *Ezekiel 25–48*, 711.

14. However, the image is symmetrical, so far as the descendants of Jacob's actual wives are concerned. The four Leah and Rachel tribes are found on each side.

allotments lie north of the תְּרוּמָה, and five lie to the south. However, the east-west layout of the reserve is perfectly proportioned and symmetrical. At its heart is a square, 25,000 cubits wide and 25,000 cubits deep. The territory on either side, extending to the Jordan and the Mediterranean is under the jurisdiction of the נָשִׂיא, the civil representative of YHWH and sponsor of the cultic activity that transpires in the temple. This square is divided horizontally[15] into three rectangles, the northerly two measuring 10,000 by 25,000 cubits and the southern tract 5,000 by 25,000 cubits. The northern tract is allocated to the Zadokite priests who officiate in the temple, the sanctuary being located within this area. The middle tract is designated for the Levites, who play a supporting role in the cultic service of the temple. The southern tract is divided symmetrically into three parts, with "the city," a perfect square 4,500 by 4,500 cubits and surrounded by 250 cubit מִגְרָשׁ ("pasture land"). The city is perfectly proportioned with three gates named after three tribes on each side to give easy access for all the people. As if to highlight the sanctity of the city, though without doing so overtly, the city is called יְהוָה שָׁמָּה, "YHWH is There." As we have seen, a place is rendered holy by the presence of YHWH. Residing in the temple, the glorious aura of his presence will emanate forth from beyond the sacred residence, pervading the entire reserve. Located at the heart of the tribal allotments, in design and function this תְּרוּמָה transforms a symbol of mere social and civic egalitarianism into a portent of a new spiritual reality. Under the new order, where the people are, there is YHWH. He does not only invite them to himself in the temple; he will come to them!

But this does not mean that all or any of the degrees of sanctity have been dissolved. Although we disagree with Jonathan Smith on the basic layout of the תְּרוּמָה, he is correct in recognizing a central spine on a north-south, or better south-north axis,[16] leading from the city in the south to the temple in the north. As one moves from south to north one passes through a series of spaces that are increasingly sacred: (1) the מִגְרָשׁ, an apparently unoccupied strip of pasture land around the city;[17] (2) the city, whose gates, with their number (twelve), their location (three on each side), and their names (the twelve tribes of Israel), highlight the accessibility of the city to all Israel; (3) the reserve of the Levites, the tribe set

15. From the north-orientation of modern Western cartography. To the ancients, with their east orientation, the rectangles would have appeared on a map as vertical lines.

16. J. Z. Smith, *To Take Place*, 68.

17. In an earlier period the term identified the strip of land surrounding Levitical towns set apart as pastureland for the Levites' livestock (Num 35:4–5).

aside by YHWH for spiritual ministry; (4) the priestly reserve, set aside for the Zadokites, a sub-set of Levites responsible for the temple ritual; (5) and the temple, reserved for God himself. It is to a consideration of this temple that we now turn.

THE TEMPLE COMPOUND AS SACRED SPACE

On the analogy of the call of Moses one might have concluded that the glorious appearance of YHWH to Ezekiel in Babylon might have transformed the spot near the Chebar canal where YHWH appeared into holy ground. The prophet does indeed respond appropriately to the theophany by falling on his face to the ground. However, the absence of any reference to "holy ground" or "sacred space" in this autobiographical account by a prophet of priestly heritage, and who functions as priest among the exiles, is striking. As we have seen, in this book the notion of sacred space is always associated with YHWH's residence in the temple in the land of Israel.[18]

The issue of the sanctity of temple space surfaced early in Ezekiel's prophetic ministry. The prophet's first pronouncements of judgment upon his people are cast in the form of a series of sign-acts (4:1—5:4) followed by a comprehensive interpretation (5:5-17). According to the latter, the coming judgment of Judah and Jerusalem has been precipitated by the nation's rebellion against their divine suzerain expressed generally in the rejection of his revealed will (the laws and ordinances) and specifically in the defilement (טִמֵּא) of his sanctuary (מִקְדָּשׁ) with all their disgusting (שִׁקֻּצִים) and abominable (תּוֹעֵבוֹת) idolatrous actions and objects (5:11). Ezekiel does not elaborate at this point, but in the book's characteristic style, by *resumptive exposition* the topic is picked up and developed in detail in chapter 8.[19]

According to the account in chapter 8, in a vision YHWH transported his prophet to Jerusalem where he brought him into the temple and gave him a tour so that he might observe the desecrations of his people. In four stops he observes successively a provocative pagan image to the north of the altar gate (vv. 3b-6), seventy elders under the supervision of Jaazaniah ben Shaphan burning incense to seventy disgusting images in a dark room (vv. 8-13), women weeping the Tammuz at the north gate of

18. Though 11:16 speaks strangely of YHWH being "a sanctuary in small measure" (מִקְדָּשׁ מְעַט) in the countries of Israel's exile.

19. For an explanation of the concept see Block, *Ezekiel 1-24*, 25-26.

the inner court (vv. 14–15), and twenty-five men turning their backs on YHWH in the temple and prostrating themselves before the sun within the inner court. The violation of sacred space occurs at several levels: (1) in accordance with the abominations committed by Manasseh (2 Kgs 21:7), the introduction of foreign/pagan objects of worship into the temple: the provocative statue at the north gate, the seventy images carved in the wall of the dark room; (2) the performance of pagan rituals in the Tammuz lament and prostration before the sun; (3) the introduction of lay people into the temple compound: the seventy elders and the women; (4) heterodox verbal utterances: "YHWH does not see us; YHWH has forsaken the land" (v. 12; cf. 9:9). Not only does this declaration become a self-fulfilling prophecy; ironically, in the utterance pagans become the vehicle through which the theme of this complex vision is announced (8:1—11:25).[20]

But the desecration of temple space consisted not only in the presence of alien images, prohibited personnel, pagan practices, and heterodox utterances. In the sequence of scenes we witness also the desecration of increasingly holy space: the provocative image is apparently located in the outer court guarding the entrance to the inner court; the abominations of the seventy elders are apparently performed within rooms associated with the gateway leading to the inner court; the women weeping the Tammuz appear to be just inside the inner court; and the men bowing to the sun were positioned within the "sacred spine"[21] between the altar and the porch of the temple proper. YHWH responds by abandoning the temple. But the manner in which the abandonment is portrayed is scarcely coincidental. Ezekiel witnesses the divine כְּבוֹד־יְהוָה ("Glory of YHWH") leaving the temple in four stages, matching the four phases of Ezekiel's tour. However, the course of the tour is reversed. Instead of moving from spheres of lesser to greater sanctity the כְּבוֹד־יְהוָה moves from spheres of greater to lesser sanctity: (1) from above the cherubim in the Holy of Holies to the threshold of the temple (9:3; 10:4); (2) from the threshold to the throne chariot parked at the entrance of the east gate of the temple proper (10:18–19); (3) from the east gate to the midst of the city, and (4) from the midst of the city to the mountain east of the city (11:22–23). And with the departure of YHWH from the temple and the city both lose their sanctity and both lose YHWH as their divine protector. Indeed, YHWH

20. The theme of the desecration of the temple through the violation of sacred space with pagan images and actions is not limited to this context. Cf. 7:20–24 (חָלַל); 23:36–45 (טָמֵא and חָלַל).

21. On which see below.

himself commissions his own agents to desecrate (חִלֵּל) the temple with the corpses of the slain (9:6–7) and personally brings in foreigners, the vilest of nations to profane (חִלֵּל) it (7:20–24). In 24:21 YHWH is more direct: he will desecrate (חִלֵּל) his sanctuary himself. Obviously, with the departure of YHWH the temple becomes a profane structure and Jerusalem is reduced to a city like any other. The sanctity of space depends upon YHWH's personal presence.

Figure 5: Ezekiel's Second Temple Tour

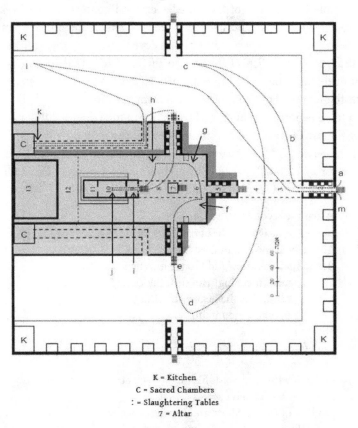

K = Kitchen
C = Sacred Chambers
: = Slaughtering Tables
7 = Altar

But when we think of the geography of sacred space in the book of Ezekiel our intention is drawn naturally to the final vision, whose purpose is to show that when YHWH's relationship with his people and his land is finally normalized all the abuses of the past will be corrected. Cast in the form of a report of a temple tour (Fig. 5), the amount of attention devoted to the temple in the final vision is remarkable; of the 260 verses that make up the last nine chapters more than half are devoted to the design and layout of the temple compound and its appurtenances.[22] The description is interrupted by a portrayal of the reestablishment of the temple as the residence, which provides the basis for its holiness (43:1–9). Much of the remainder involves prescriptions for the cult officials among whose activities securing the sanctity of the temple is primary.[23]

Thanks to the work of Victor (Avigdor) Hurowitz, we now have a fuller understanding of the importance of temple construction accounts in the ancient Near East and are able to interpret Ezekiel's description of the temple in the light of the broader cultural context. While Ezekiel's interest in the temple and its design are at home in the ancient picture, his description displays several striking deviations from analogous extra-biblical accounts.[24] Especially noteworthy are Ezekiel's detailed description of the buildings and other appurtenances (like the altar) associated with the temple. For the most part, ancient accounts of temple building tend to be general in nature, and laudatory in tone, highlighting particularly the use of treasured and rare materials, the high artistic level of the craftsmanship, and the unparalleled beauty, immensity, and sophistication of the construction. The following grandiose description of Esarhaddon's reconstruction of Ešarra, the temple of Aššur, is typical:

When the second year came
I raised to heaven the head of Ešarra, my lord Aššur's dwelling.
Above, heavenward, I raised high its head.
Below, in the underworld I made firm its foundations.
Eḫursaggula, [meaning] House of the Great Mountain
I made beautiful as the heavenly writing.
I piled it up like a mountain.
That temple,
from foundation to top,
I built and completed.
I filled it with luxury astonishing to look at.
Beams of cedars and cypress
produce of Mount Sirara and Mount Lebanon,
whose fragrance is sweet, I spread over it.

22. Ezek 40:1–49; 42:1–26; 42:1–20; 43:10–17; 46:19–24.

23. Ezek 43:18–27; 44:1–31; 45:9–25; 46:1–18.

24. Hurowitz (*I Have Built You an Exalted House*, 247–48) recognizes "an independent Israelite or Judaean tradition of describing buildings" that is continued in post exilic Jewish tradition, most notably the Temple Scroll from Qumran and the rabbinic Mishnaic tractate *Middoth*.

I bound up cypress doors with gold bands and set them in its portals.
The disordered chapels, daises, stands, and drawings,
I restored and improved
and made bright as the sun.
Its lofty head scraped the sky,
below, its roots spread in the subterranean water.
All the furnishings needed for Ešarra
I made anew and planted therein.[25]

The obvious aim of this account is to glorify the builder. No attempt is made to describe the structure to help the reader visualize it.[26] Ezekiel's account presents a striking contrast in four significant respects. First, the prophet envisions a structure already built, presumably by God himself.[27] Second, nowhere does Ezekiel highlight the beauty and magnificence of the building. This is implicit in its design, but comments concerning glory are reserved for YHWH himself (43:1–5). Third, Ezekiel's emphasis throughout is on the horizontal spacial design, which he describes in great detail: the width of walls, the dimensions of structures and spaces, etc.[28] Fourth, although Ezekiel highlights the height of the Temple Mount (40:2), and he recognizes that the temple compound rises in stages above the mount, he makes no comments whatsoever regarding the height of any of the structures. There is no need for us to describe in our own words what Ezekiel envisions. Rather, we shall attempt to highlight the significance of what he sees, noting in particular the aesthetic and functional significance of its design.

25. As translated by Hurowitz, *I Have Built You an Exalted House*, 245. For the Akkadian text see Borger, *Inschriften Asarhaddons*, 5 Ass A, V 27–VI 27. For a discussion of Esarhaddon's temple construction projects in Babylon see Porten, *Images, Power, and Politics*, 41–67.

26. For a Seleucid era description of Esagila, the temple of Marduk, see Unger, *Babylon*, 237–40, 246–52.

27. Contrary to pervasive popular opinion, Ezekiel's plan is not presented as a blueprint for a future temple to be constructed by human hands in Jerusalem. This point is convincingly argued by Stevenson, *Vision of Transformation*, 11–30.

28. Hurowitz (*I Have Built You an Exalted House*, 250) has identified several ancient documents whose descriptions invite the reader to visualize a temple building or its furniture, but none compares with Ezekiel's account.

AESTHETICS AND FUNCTION IN EZEKIEL'S DESIGN

Ezekiel 43:10–11 provides the key to the interpretation of Ezekiel's temple:

> As for you, human, describe the temple (הַבַּיִת) to the family
> of Israel so they may be humiliated for their crimes. Let them
> measure the perfection, and they themselves will be humiliated[29]
> for everything they have done. As for the design of the temple—
> its layout, exits, and entrances, as well as all its regulation and
> laws—make known. Write them down in their sight so they may
> observe all my rulings and all my regulations by executing them.

The key words in this text are תָּבְנִית, "perfection,"[30] צוּרַת הַבַּיִת, "the
design of the house," and תְּכוּנָתוֹ, "its layout." What is involved in these
terms is specified in the following list of terms: the temple's exits and
entrances, as well as all the regulations and laws (מִשְׁפָּטִים and חֻקּוֹת) governing the rituals to be performed within the compound.[31] While little
has been said so far about the temple ritual, this addition recognizes that
knowledge of the lay of sacred space and of the principles of access is insufficient for the maintenance of its holiness. Its sanctity is also affected by
the manner in which cultic activities are performed within its borders.[32]
But the intended effect of Ezekiel's presentation of the temple plan and its
ritual on his audience is striking: the recognition of the perfection, proportion, and order of the entire system will create in them intense shame
for their own iniquitous actions (עֲוֹנוֹת) and shatter all assumptions of
worthiness. This spiritual map of holiness will put them in their place: in
contrast to the perfection of God and his residence they will see that they
are sinners whom God invites to his presence by grace alone.

But what are the features of the design of sacred space that evoke this
response? A discussion of the aesthetics of Ezekiel's temple must take into

29. Reading יְאָם יִכָּלְמוּ, with LXX and Vg. The unconditionality of the foregoing
renders a conditional clause at this point improbable. Cf. Gese, *Verfassungsentwurf*,
40.

30. Appealing to LXX, Syr, and Tg, Zimmerli (*Ezekiel 2*, 410) emends MT's תכנית
to תכנתו, "its layout," assuming either the haplographic omission of waw before the following ואם or the transposition of תו to ות (miswritten as ית). However, this involves an
unnecessary switch from the root תכן to כון (cf. Stevenson, *Vision of Transformation*,
17–19). The present form occurs elsewhere only in 28:12, and Tg and Vg support an
identical rendering here.

31. For the textual problems involved in these verses see Block, *Ezekiel 25–48*,
586–90.

32. The juxtaposing of the verbs שָׁמַר, "to keep, guard," and עָשָׂה, "to do, perform,"
in the last line of verse 11 is deliberate.

consideration two dimensions of his design: its location and vertical design (what little information is given) on the one hand, and its horizontal design on the other.

With regard to the former, we notice that Ezekiel's temple was literally a city on a hill. In the first place, it was located on an extremely high mountain (הַר גָּבֹהַ מְאֹד) in the land of Israel (40:2). The prophet's refusal to name either mountain or city reflects his continuing polemic against official Jerusalem theology, even though it had been discredited fourteen years earlier in 586 BC. At the same time he invites the reader to associate this mountain with the world mountain, from which peace and prosperity emanate forth to all the world,[33] and/or Sinai, where the divine King had first revealed himself to his people (Exod 19).

As if the natural height of land is insufficient to express the lofty nature of the temple, during his tour of the compound Ezekiel observes several series of steps that throw its exaltation into even sharper relief. First, leading up to the outer gateways were seven steps (40:6, 22, 26). Second, once one has entered the outer court eight steps lead up to the gates of the inner court (40:31, 34, 37). These steps probably represented a pavement of eight terraces, though a stairway between the two levels is also possible. Third, once one enters the inner court ten steps lead up to the porch (אֻלָם) of the temple (40:49).[34] Again, these steps may represent a pavement of ten terraces. The difference in elevation increases with each unit of the sacred complex, as one moves from the outside to the center: seven steps to the outer wall, eight from the outer wall to the inner gates, ten from these gates to the temple itself, yielding a total of twenty-five, a number that governs the entire plan. But there is more. The peak of the mountain is actually represented by the altar at the very center of the compound. According to 43:17 this object was also mounted by steps. We may only speculate how many steps there were, but if the altar is six cubits high (about ten feet),[35] ten is a reasonable number.[36] As a whole the scene is impressive. The observer's eyes are drawn ever upward to the top of this Temple Mount, where stands, not only the magnificent and utterly holy residence of God, but also the altar, which represents the link between a holy God and a sinful people. The vertical geography of Ezekiel's temple proclaims not only the glory and transcendence of God, but also his mercy.

33. Cf. Levenson, *Theology of the Program of Restoration*, 7–36.

34. Reading עֶשֶׂר with LXX instead MT's meaningless אֲשֶׁר.

35. See my calculations in *Ezekiel 25–48*, 601–2.

36. For pictorial representations of the altar, see Block, *Ezekiel 25–48*, 598; Milgrom and Block, *Ezekiel's Hope*, 598

The concern for perfection in design of the temple extends to its spatial arrangements as well (see figure 5 above). When we look at the dimensions of the temple compound as a whole and the dimensions of its individual structures we are immediately struck by its remarkable symmetry and proportion. The importance of its dimensions is highlighted by the genre of the account: in a vision Ezekiel is taken on a tour of the compound, in the course of which he observes a man taking measurements of its structures. It is God's way of emphasizing to the prophet and eventually to his audience that nothing about its design is haphazard or coincidental. The shape and size of the entire complex reflect a lofty theological and spiritual ideal; it is a perfect design, in keeping with the perfection of the divine resident.

Moving in from the outside we notice first of all that the compound itself is a perfect square, 500 cubits by 500 cubits (42:15–20). The east-west distance agrees with length computed from the respective dimensions of the internal structures described earlier in chapters 40:1—42:14:

Depth of the eastern exterior gate	50 cubits (40:15)
Distance between exterior and inner gates	100 cubits (40:19)
Depth of the inner east gate	50 cubits (40:33)
Depth of the inner temple court	100 cubits (40:47)
Length of the temple with auxiliary structures	100 cubits (40:48—41:9)
Depth of the restricted area at rear of temple	20 cubits (41:9)
Depth of the בִּנְיָן (inclusive of the walls)	80 cubits (41:12)
Total distance, east to west	500 cubits

In keeping with Israelite tabernacle and temple tradition, the eastern gate is the most important gate. This is the gate through which YHWH alone may enter (43:1–5), though the "prince" (נָשִׂיא) may eat in the gateway before YHWH (44:3). But if one were to enter from this gate what one would observe is a perfectly symmetrical design; what one would see to the north is perfectly mirrored by what one sees to the south. While the views from either the northern or southern gates would have been asymmetrical,[37] the commitment to proportion is reflected also in the de-

37. In the center one would see the altar, but to its left the terraced temple courts, and to the right the temple itself and the auxiliary structures behind it.

sign of the internal structures. The gate structures all measure 50 cubits deep by 25 cubits wide (40:13–15, 33, *et passim*). This same 2:1 depth to width proportion is evident also in the temple building, which, as a whole measures 100 cubits deep by 50 cubits wide (40:48—41:11), and the Great Hall of the temple (הֵיכָל), which is 40 cubits deep and 20 cubits wide (41:2).

Even more important than these perfectly proportioned rectangles is the series of perfect squares in the compound. The entire compound is a perfect square 500 cubits by 500 cubits. The most sacred area of all, the דְּבִיר (*dĕbîr*; Holy of Holies) in the temple is a square 20 cubits deep and 20 cubits wide (41:4). Since this is conceived of as YHWH's throne room, one might have expected it to be located at the center of the 100 cubit square inner court in the center of the compound. Instead, this spot is occupied by the altar, another square structure whose platform measures 14 cubits by 14 cubits (43:17), but whose outer perimeter, inclusive of the bottom gutter and its curb, measures 20 x 20 cubits (about 34 feet).[38] This too must have been intentional, for it matches the size of the Holy of Holies. The fact that the altar, rather than the throne room, is at the center of the compound is highly significant, for this means that when one looks from the outside through the outer and inner gate structures this is what one sees. Although ancient temples were perceived primarily as the residence of the deity, from this design the worshiper is reminded that access to the deity presupposes correctly administered sacrifices. The altar represents the key to communion between worshiper and deity.

If the symmetrical and proportional dimensions of the temple and its surroundings reflect the perfection of YHWH, the design that Ezekiel sees is not primarily about the structures themselves, but the space within those structures. This conclusion is reinforced by the manner in which the respective spaces are demarcated and the way in which access to them is regulated. In fact, it is evident that this compound is intentionally designed to correct/preclude past abuses, when unauthorized persons seem to have entered and left the temple in Jerusalem at will. From 44:6–8 it appears that in the past the Levites who had been assigned guard duty to the temple had not only been lax in protecting the sanctity of sacred space, but had themselves ushered foreigners and uncircumcised individuals into the temple. The problem is illustrated in Ezekiel's first temple vision in chapter 8, referred to earlier. The concern to prevent this from ever happening again is obvious from the design of the compound.

38. Cf. my discussion in *Ezekiel 25–48*, 595–604. The size and location of the altar contrast with the design of the tabernacle, which calls for a smaller portable altar and locates it near the front entrance to the court. For a diagram see Milgrom, *Leviticus*, 135.

In the first instance, the compound itself is compared to an עִיר (40:2). To translate עִיר as "city" is misleading to a modern reader, inasmuch as we tend to think of cities as large urban centers. But the Hebrew word says less about size and population than about form: a "city" is by definition a settlement/compound to which access is controlled by walls and gates, "a walled enclosure."[39]

Second, the nature of the outer wall is striking on several counts. On the one hand, according to 40:5, the outer wall was 6 cubits high and six cubits thick! This was no token barrier. The width in particular seems designed to correct past abuses. On the other hand, entrance through the wall is controlled by three identical gate structures, each patterned after ancient fortifications with three guard rooms on each side of the passage way to be occupied by defensive personnel who would ensure that only authorized persons would enter (40:6–27). Later we will learn that only YHWH may enter the east gate (43:1–5), and that once he has entered it will be permanently shut (44:2).

Third, once inside the wall, worshipers discover that the temple compound is divided into a series of spheres that increase in sanctity as one moves from the outside in. Ordinary worshipers may enter the compound through the gates of the outer walls, but they are barred access to areas where the cultic rituals are actually performed by a second series of gates matching those on the outside wall. The text does not mention walls between these gates, but one may assume such, unless the gates have purely symbolic and ornamental value. In any case, the north and south gates appear to be flanked by buildings/rooms that in effect function as walls.[40] The gate structures are identical to the outer gates in size and design. Only Zadokite priests and supporting casts of Levites may enter through these gates to the inner court.

Fourth, as one moves in toward the temple itself the areas of space increase in sanctity, a fact reflected in a heightening concern to control access (Fig. 6). While Levites performing cultic service may enter the inner court, access to the temple itself was restricted to the Zadokite priests. The defensive features of the temple proper are impressive. In the first instance, to get to the Holy of Holies at the back one needed to pass through two rooms, the front porch (אֻלָם) and the Great Hall (הֵיכָל).

39. So also Levine, "The Temple Scroll," 16. The influence of the present text on the Temple Scroll from Qumran is evident in the designation of that temple as עִיר־הַמִּקְדָּשׁ, "city of the sanctuary" (XL:12), on which see Milgrom, "'Sabbath' and 'Temple City,'" 6–27.

40. See the diagrams in Block, *Ezekiel 25–48*, 508, 541.

But as one proceeds, the passages narrow, from 14 cubits (the entrance to the porch), to 10 cubits (the entrance to the Great Hall), to 6 cubits (the entrance to the Holy of Holies). In the second instance, while only one wall demarks the porch, the sacred space inside the temple is guarded by a double wall with a 4 cubit space between. To a modern reader the thickness of the walls seems disproportionate to the size of the rooms they outline: rooms 20 cubits wide are bounded by walls 6 cubits (ca. 10 feet) and 5 cubits (ca. 8.5 feet) thick respectively! Combined the double wall plus the 4 cubit space between total 15 cubits, three-fourths the width of the rooms they define.

Figure 6: The Ground Plan of the Temple with Its Walls and Doorways

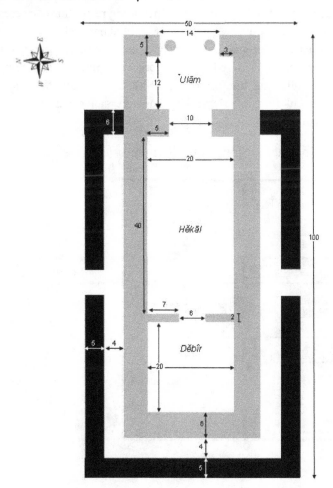

Earlier, when describing the sacred reserve we noted that at its core was a sacred spine of increasing sanctity as one moved from south to north through "the city," through the territory of the Levites, through the territory of the priests to the temple. A bird's eye view of this compound reveals another central spine of sacrality, increasing as one moves horizontally from east to west (Fig. 7).[41] The prophet's description recognizes eleven elements along this central spine: the eastern steps (1) lead up to the eastern outer court gate (2), which opens to inner court (3), which leads to inner court steps (4), which lead up to the inner court gate (5), which opens to the inner court (6), where one encounters the altar (7), which stands before ten vestibule steps (8), leading up to the vestibule (9), which leads to the Great Hall (10), and the Holy of Holies—YHWH's throne room (11). Behind the temple proper one finds the גִּזְרָה, "restricted area" (10) and the בִּנְיָן, "Building" (12). Increasing restrictions on access to the respective areas are reflected in the sequential narrowing of entryways and the placement of guards at strategic points. Accordingly, one may recognize increasingly sacred spheres along this spine accessible respectively to the following: the "prince" (44:1–3), Levitical priests, Zadokites, YHWH. But cult functionaries and lay worshipers alike will enter and exit only through the north and south gates (46:9).

Figure 7: The Sacred Spine of the Temple

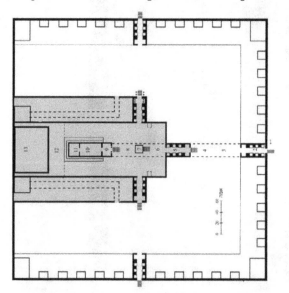

1. Eastern Steps
2. Outer court gate
3. Outer court
4. Inner court steps
5. Inner court gate
6. Inner court
7. Altar
8. Vestibule steps
9. Vestibule
10. Temple hall
11. YHWH's throne room
12. "Restricted space"
13. "The Building"

41. Cf. J. Z. Smith, *To Take Place*, 57–58.

CONCLUSION

There is much more that could be said about Ezekiel's portrayal of sacred space, but I shall conclude with a few observations on the theological significance of the design. Kalinda Stevenson has rightly argued that this vision is driven by *territorial rhetoric.*[42] But the question for the interpreter is, "What is the rhetorical agenda that is being advanced by this vision?" The question may be answered in several ways.

First, to a people in exile, perplexed over YHWH's failure to defend them in their hour of need, Ezekiel's final vision declares that YHWH's eternal promises still stand. When Nebuchadnezzar's armies had approached Jerusalem they had based their (eternal) security on their God's four immutable declarations: YHWH's eternal covenant with his people; YHWH's gift of the land of Canaan as an eternal possession; YHWH's choice of Zion as the place of his residence; and YHWH's promise to David of eternal title to the throne of Israel. While his commitment to the last of these is muted in this vision, YHWH's fidelity to the first three is emphatically proclaimed by Ezekiel's vision of sacred space. To disillusioned exiles this vision announces the renewal of God's covenant with his people, his reunion of the people with their hereditary homeland, and his permanent residence in their midst.

Second, and as a corollary to the preceding, to exiles who wondered what had become of YHWH's promises of divine patronage this vision signals that, contrary to present appearance, he remains the divine King of Israel, and in keeping with his eternal promise he will reestablish his relationship with and his presence in Israel. His kingship had been thrown into question by his departure from the temple, as envisioned in chapters 8–11, and its subsequent destruction at the hands of the Babylonians, the people of Marduk. But even before that event, in a carefully crafted judgment speech in which he traces the history of his people through seven phases the prophet had declared in emphatic terms that one day YHWH would reestablish his kingship over the people (20:33). The return of the Glory of YHWH (כְּבוֹד־יְהוָה) envisioned in 43:1–9 declares the fulfillment of this promise. The sacred precinct that Ezekiel has been touring YHWH identifies as "the place of my throne and the place of the soles of my feet where I will dwell in the midst of the descendants of Israel forever" (v. 3). Israelite political and theological theory had declared for centuries that the nation was a theocracy, but for most of the nation's history this had

42. Stevenson, *Vision of Transformation*, 143–60.

been a lie. But no more! YHWH hereby promises to return, and this time his residence will be permanent. The significance of the vision of YHWH's return to his temple is reinforced by the name given to "the city" of the people in the glorious final declaration of the book: יְהוָה שָׁמָּה, "YHWH is there."

Third, to a people in exile because they had lost sight of the difference between that which is holy and that which is profane (cf. 44:23), and because they had flagrantly violated sacred space, this vision proclaims the holiness of God and all that he touches. The vision declares that the land that had been defiled by the people and the temple that had been desecrated by pagans will be transformed by the presence of YHWH. In accord with the conclusion of Sara Japhet, it is the return of YHWH that renders the city at the top of this mountain holy,[43] and we may add that it is from this mountain that his holiness emanates to the entire land. But the vision also teaches that even though the relationship between YHWH and his people will be restored, the holiness of God precludes casual contact between deity and people. The layout of the temple compound and the design of the temple itself are driven by a concern to protect the people from lethal doses of divine "radiation," on the one hand, and to preserve the distinction between divinity and humanity, on the other. Accordingly, the compound is divided into a series of spheres, with the intensity of holiness increasing as one moves up the central spine from the outer east gate to the Holy of Holies, where YHWH is enthroned. Access to these spheres is strictly regulated and strictly controlled by a complex system of walls and gates and a special order of Levites assigned to guard the entryways.

Fourth, to a people in exile who despaired of ever finding acceptance with YHWH again the design of the temple compound offers hope. YHWH's recommissioning of the Zadokite priests and Levites to represent the people before him and to offer sacrifices on their behalf, and his appointment of the "prince" as patron of the cult declare his concern to receive the people again. However, the centrality of the altar in the overall plan provides a powerful symbol of the purpose of the entire scheme. Stuck in a pagan land, without temple and altar, the people must have wondered if YHWH would ever accept them again. The design of this compound answers that question emphatically, for all who entered at the outer gates could look up through the inner gates and see the priests on the altar presenting the sacrifices of the people as acts of communion with YHWH. Indeed Ezekiel's temple serves as a mediator between heaven and

43. See the comments at the beginning of this essay.

earth, a holy God and a sinful people. On the one hand, it symbolizes YHWH's determination to commune with his people, and on the other, it proclaims the transformation of his people.

Fifth, to people in exile to a large extent because their kings had led them in their apostate ways Ezekiel's vision calls for an end to the old monarchic abuses. On the one hand, the thickness of the walls and the size of the gate houses bar kings from ever encroaching upon sacred space the way they had in the past by building their thresholds and door posts next to YHWH's thresholds and door posts, and by their funerary offerings (43:6–9). On the other hand, the regulations concerning the נָשִׂיא, "the prince," should be seen as a reaction to the high-handed monarchic style of past kings of Israel. Stevenson overstates the case when she suggests that a Davidic king is missing in the human geography of this new Israel.[44] It is difficult to dissociate this figure from the Davidic נָשִׂיא promised in 34:23–24 and 37:22–25, but the preference for the designation נָשִׂיא over מֶלֶךְ reflects the radical transformation of his role and the stringent curtailing of his power. The נָשִׂיא's primary role is not civil, but religious; he is the patron of the cult, who oversees the sacrifices, but does not present them himself. In fact, it is necessary for the priests to offer sacrifices on his behalf. He governs special land allotted to him on either side of the sacred reserve, presumably to pasture the livestock the people bring for their sacrifices, but he has no throne, no palace, no capital city. The closest Ezekiel's vision comes to providing for a capital is "the city" at the end of chapter 48, but with its twelve gates named after the tribes of Israel, this city belongs to the people. If anything, its name, יְהוָה שָׁמָּה, "YHWH is there," celebrates the presence of YHWH, rather than the king.[45]

Finally, to a people in exile in a foreign land, wondering about their future as a people, this vision declares that they remain YHWH's special people. Like the rest of Ezekiel's prophecy, the territorial rhetoric of this vision is narrowly parochial. The design of sacred space has no place for the nations. Far from being construed as a cosmic mountain, linking heaven and earth, the mountain, the city, and the altar envision only a link between YHWH and his people. To be sure, non-Israelites are to be treated the same as native Israelites when the property is distributed (47:22–23), but the text assumes their integration into one of the twelve tribes. Nowhere are the temple doors opened to the nations; nor does

44. Stevenson, *Vision of Transformation*, 151–54, 165.

45. For further discussion of the נָשִׂיא's role see Block, "Bringing Back David," 167–88; reproduced above.

the vision foresee the worshipers of YHWH sharing his grace with the nations. Like the rest of the book of Ezekiel, the territorial rhetoric of the vision concerns Israel, and Israel alone.

Where then does this leave us? In the first place it introduces us non-Israelites to the God whose words never fail. In the second place, even though Ezekiel has none of this in mind, with Paul in Rom 9–11 we rejoice that by his grace God grafts Gentiles into his people, adopting them as his sons and daughters, and making them joint heirs in the promises to the Fathers. And third, this vision prepares for the Messiah/Christ, who in his own person will replace both temple and altar. In the Hebrew Bible the temple is a gracious provision, a magnificent means divinely inspired and divinely provided to link fallen human beings with the holy God. But with the coming of Christ, the temple itself becomes passé as the focal point of divine grace. In Christ, the ultimate sacrifice, heaven comes down and glory fills our souls. To God be the glory!

Bibliography

Ackroyd, P. R. "The "Seventy Year Period." *Journal of Near Eastern Studies* 17 (1958) 23–27.

Ahroni, R. "The Gog Prophecy and the Book of Ezekiel." *Hebrew Annual Review* 1 (1977) 1–27.

Albertz, Rainer. *A History of Israelite Religion in the Old Testament Period*. Vol. I, *From the Beginnings to the End of the Monarchy*. Translated by J. Bowden. Louisville: Westminster John Knox, 1994.

———. *Israel in Exile: The History and Literature of the Sixth Century BCE*. Studies in Biblical Literature. Atlanta: Society of Biblical Literature, 2003.

Albright, William F. "Gog and Magog." *Journal of Biblical Literature* 43 (1924) 381–82.

Alexander, Ralph A. "Ezekiel." In *The Expositor's Bible Commentary*, edited by F. E. Gaebelein, 6.737–996. Grand Rapids: Zondervan, 1986.

Allen, Leslie C. *Ezekiel 20–48*. Word Biblical Commentary 29. Dallas: Word, 1990.

Amiet, Pierre. *Art of the Ancient Near East*. New York: Abrams, 1980.

Andersen, Francis I., and David N. Freedman. *Hosea: A New Translation with Introduction and Commentary*. Anchor Bible 24. Garden City: Doubleday, 1980.

Andersen, Francis I. *The Hebrew Verbless Clause in the Pentateuch*. Journal of Biblical Literature Manuscript Series 14. Nashville: Abingdon, 1970.

Anderson, Bernard W. "The Place of Shechem in the Bible." *Biblical Archaeologist* 20 (1957) 10–19.

Arnold, Bill. T., and H. G. M. Williamson, editors. *The Dictionary of the Old Testament: Historical Books*. Downers Grove, IL: InterVarsity, 2005.

Astour, Michael C. "Ezekiel's Prophecy of Gog and the Cuthean Legend of Naram-Sin." *Journal of Biblical Literature* 95 (1976) 567–79.

Balentine, Samuel E. *The Hidden God: The Hiding of the Face of God in the Old Testament*. Oxford: Oxford University Press, 1983.

Baltzer, D. "Literarkritische und Literarhistorische Anmerkungen zur Heilsprophetie im Ezechiel-Buch." In *Ezekiel and His Book: Textual and Literary Criticism and Their Interrelation*, edited by J. Lust, 166–83. Bibliotheca ephemeridum theologicarum lovaniensium 74. Leuven: Leuven University Press, 1986.

Barnett, R. D. *Ancient Ivories in the Middle East*. Qedem Monographs, 14. Jerusalem: Ahva Press, 1982.

Barthélemy, Dominique, et al., editors. *Critique textuelle de l'Ancien Testament, 1. Josué, Juges, Ruth, Samuel, Rois, Chroniques, Esdras, Néhémie, Esther: Rapport final du Comité pour l'analyse textuelle de l'Ancien Testament hébreu institué par l'Alliance Biblique Universelle*. Orbis biblicus et orientalis 50. Göttingen: Vandenhoeck & Ruprecht, 1982.

———. *Preliminary and Interim Report on the Hebrew Old Testament Text Project*. Vol. 5, *Prophetical Books II: Ezekiel, Daniel, Twelve Minor Prophets*. New York: United Bible Societies, 1980.

Batto, Bernard F. *Slaying the Dragon: Mythmaking in the Biblical Tradition*. Louisville: Westminster John Knox, 1992.

Bea, A. "Jojachin in Keilschrifttexten." *Biblica* 23 (1942) 78–82.

Becker, Joachim. "Erwägungen zur ezechielischen Frage." In *Künder des Wortes: Beiträge zur Theologie der Propheten*, edited by L. Ruppert, et al., 137–50. Würzburg: Echter, 1982.

———. Review of *Josiah and David Redivivus*, by Antti Laato. *Biblica* 71 (1994) 250–55.

———. *Der priesterliche Prophet: Das Buch Ezechiel*. 2 vols. Stuttgarter Kleiner Kommentar, Altes Testament, 12/1–2. Stuttgart: Katholisches Bibelwerk, 1971.

Begg, Christopher. "The Identity of the Princes in Ezekiel 19: Some Reflections." *Ephemerides Theologicae Lovaniensis* 65 (1989) 358–69.

Beitzel, Barry. *The Moody Atlas of the Bible*. Chicago: Moody, 1985.

Berridge, John M. "Jehoiachin." In *Anchor Bible Dictionary*, edited by D. N. Freedman, 3.661–63. Garden City, NY: Doubleday, 1992.

Berry, G. R. "The Date of Ezekiel 38:1—39:20." *Journal of Biblical Literature* 41 (1922): 224–32.

Bertholet, Alfred, and Kurt Galling. *Hesekiel. Handbuch zum Alten Testament*. Tübingen: Mohr (Siebeck), 1936.

Black, J. A. "The New Year Ceremonies in Ancient Babylon: 'Taking Bel by the Hand' and a Cultic Picnic." *Religion* 11 (1981) 39–59.

Blenkinsopp, Joseph. *Ezekiel*. Interpretation. Louisville: John Knox, 1990.

Block, Daniel I. *The Book of Ezekiel Chapters 1–24*. New International Commentary on the Old Testament. Grand Rapids: Eerdmans, 1977.

———. *The Book of Ezekiel Chapters 25–48*. New International Commentary on the Old Testament. Grand Rapids: Eerdmans, 1998.

———. "Bringing Back David: Ezekiel's Messianic Hope." In *YHWH's Anointed: Interpretation of Old Testament Messianic Texts*, edited by P. E. Satterthwaite, et al., 167–88. Grand Rapids: Baker, 1995.

———. "Divine Abandonment: Ezekiel's Adaptation of an Ancient Near Eastern Motif." In *Perspectives on Ezekiel: Theology and Anthropology*, SBL Symposium Series 9, edited by Margaret S. Odell and John T. Strong, 15–42. Atlanta: Scholars Press, 2000. Reprinted in *By the River Chebar: Historical, Literary, and Theological Studies in the Book of Ezekiel*, 73–99. Eugene, OR: Cascade, 2013.

———. "Envisioning the Good News: Ten Hermeneutical Keys to Ezekiel's Final Vision." Paper presented at the annual meeting of the Evangelical Theological Society. Chicago, November 18, 1994.

———. "The Foundations of National Identity: A Study in Ancient Northwest Semitic Perceptions." D.Phil. Dissertation. University of Liverpool, 1982. Ann Arbor, MI: University Microfilms, 1983.

———. *The Gods of the Nations: Studies in Ancient Near Eastern National Theology*. 2nd ed. Evangelical Theological Society Monographs 2. Eugene, OR: Cascade, 2013. Reprint of 2000 edition by Baker, with added translation of "The Prophetic Speech of Marduk."

———. "Gog in Ezekiel's Eschatology." In *"The Reader Must Understand": Eschatology in Bible and Theology*, edited by K. Brower and M. Elliott, 85–116. Downers Grove, IL: InterVarsity, 1997.

———. "Gog and the Pouring Out of the Spirit: Reflections on Ezekiel XXXIX 21–29." *Vetus Testamentum* 37 (1987) 257–61.

————. "Gog in Prophetic Tradition: A New Look at Ezekiel XXXVII 17." *Vetus Testamentum* 42 (1992) 152–72.

————. "Nations." In *International Standard Bible Encyclopedia*. Rev. ed, edited by G. Bromiley, 3.492–96. Grand Rapids: Eerdmans, 1986.

————. "People." In *International Standard Bible Encyclopedia*. Rev. ed, edited by G. Bromiley, 3.759–60. Grand Rapids: Eerdmans, 1986.

————. "The Prophet of the Spirit: The Use of *rwh* in the Book of Ezekiel." *Journal of the Evangelical Theological Society* 32 (1989) 34–41.

————. "Transformation of Royal Ideology in Ezekiel." In *Transforming Visions: Transformations of Text, Tradition, and Theology in Ezekiel*, edited by W. A. Tooman and M. A. Lyons, 208–46. Princeton Theological Monographs 127. Eugene, OR: Pickwick, 2010.

Bloesch, Donald. "'All Israel Will Be Saved': Supersessionism and the Biblical Witness." *Interpretation* 43 (1989) 130–42.

Boadt, Lawrence. "The Function of the Salvation Oracles in Ezekiel 33 to 37." *Hebrew Annual Review* 12 (1990) 1–21.

Bodi, Daniel. *The Book of Ezekiel and the Poem of Erra*. Orbis biblicus et orientalis 104. Freiburg/Göttingen: Universitätsverlag/Vandenhoeck & Ruprecht, 1991.

Boehmer, Julius. "*mlk* und *nś'* bei Ezechiel." *Theologische Studien und Kritiken* 73 (1900) 112–17.

————. "Wer ist Gog von Magog? Ein Beitrag zur Auslegung des Buches Ezechiel." *Zeitschrift Für Wissenschaftliche Theologie* 40 (1897) 321–55.

Borger, Riekele. "An Additional Remark on P. R. Ackroyd, *Journal of Near Eastern Studies* XVII, 23–27." *Journal of Near Eastern Studies* 18 (1959) 74.

————. *Die Inschriften Asarhaddons Königs von Assyrien*. Archiv für Orientforschung Beihefte 9. Graz, Austria: Weidner, 1956.

————. "Gott Marduk und Gott-König Sulgi als Propheten: Zwei prophetische Texte." *Bibliotheca Orientalis* 28 (1971) 3–24.

Born, A. van den. "Études sur quelques toponyms bibliques." *Oudtestamentische Studiën* 10 (1954) 197–201.

————. *Ezechiël*. De Boeken van het Oude Testament. Roermond en Maaseik, Belgium: Romen & Zonen, 1954.

Botha, P. J. "The Socio-Cultural Background of Ezekiel 19." *Old Testament Essays* 12 (1999) 249–65.

Browne, Laurence E. *Ezekiel and Alexander*. London: S.P.C.K., 1952.

Campbell, D. J., and J. L. Townsend, editors. *A Case for Premillennialism: A New Consensus*. Chicago: Moody, 1992.

Caquot, André. "La parole sur Juda dans le testament lyrique de Jacob (Genese 49,8–12)." *Semitica* 26 (1976) 5–32.

————. "Le messianisme d'Ézéchiel." *Semitica* 14 (1964) 13–23.

Carley, Keith W. *The Book of the Prophet Ezekiel*. Cambridge Bible Commentary. Cambridge: Cambridge University Press, 1974.

Cazelles, Henri. "Shiloh, the Customary Laws and the Return of the Ancient Kings." In *Proclamation and Presence*, edited by J. I. Durham and J. R. Porter, 239–51. London: SCM, 1970.

Childs, Brevard. "The Enemy from the North and the Chaos Tradition." *Journal of Biblical Literature* 78 (1959) 187–98.

Clements, Ronald E. *God and Temple*. Philadelphia: Fortress, 1965.

Clifford, R. J. *The Cosmic Mountain in Canaan and the Old Testament.* Harvard Semitic Monographs 4. Cambridge: Harvard University Press, 1972.

Cody, A. *Ezekiel.* Old Testament Message 11. Wilmington, DE: Michael Glazier, 1984.

Cogan, Mordechai, and Haim Tadmor. *II Kings: A New Translation with Introduction and Commentary.* Anchor Bible 11. Garden City: Doubleday, 1988.

———. "Gyges and Ashurbanipal: A Study in Literary Transmission." *Orientalia* 46 (1977) 65–85.

Cohn, N. *The Pursuit of the Millennium.* Rev. ed. New York: Oxford University Press, 1970.

Collins, John J. "The Jewish Apocalypses." *Semeia* 14 (1979) 21–59.

———. "Towards the Morphology of a Genre." *Semeia* 14 (1979) 1–19.

Coogan, Michael David. "Patterns in Jewish Personal Names in the Babylonian Diaspora." *Journal for the Study of Judaism* 4 (1973) 183–91.

———. *West Semitic Personal Names in the Murashu Documents.* Harvard Semitic Monographs 7. Missoula, MT: Scholars, 1976.

Cooke, G. A. *A Critical and Exegetical Commentary on the Book of Ezekiel.* International Critical Commentary. Edinburgh: T. & T. Clark, 1936.

Cooper, Lamar E. *Ezekiel.* New American Commentary. Nashville: Broadman & Holman, 1994.

Crane, Ashley S. *Israel's Restoration: A Textual-Comparative Exploration of Ezekiel 36–39.* Vetus Testamentum Supplements 122. Leiden: Brill, 2008.

Cross, Frank M. *Canaanite Myth and Hebrew Epic: Essays in the History of the Religion of Israel.* Cambridge: Harvard University Press, 1997.

Cuffey, Kenneth H. "Gog." In *Anchor Bible Dictionary,* edited by D. N. Freedman, 2.1056. Garden City, NY: Doubleday, 1992.

Daniel D. Luckenbill. *The Annals of Sennacherib.* 2 vols. Chicago: University of Chicago Press, 1924.

Dalley, Stephanie. *Myths from Mesopotamia: Creation, the Flood, Gilgamesh, and Others.* Rev. ed. Oxford: Oxford University Press, 2009.

Darr, Katheryn Pfisterer. "Ezekiel." In *The New Interpreter's Bible,* edited by L. E. Keck, et al., 6.1073–1607. Nashville: Abingdon, 2001.

———. "The Wall around Paradise: Ezekielian Ideas about the Future." *Vetus Testamentum* 37 (1987) 271–78.

Davidson, A. B. *The Book of the Prophet Ezekiel.* Cambridge: Cambridge University Press, 1900.

Davis, Ellen F. *Swallowing the Scroll: Textuality and the Dynamics of Discourse in Ezekiel's Prophecy.* Journal for the Study of the Old Testament Supplements 78. Sheffield: Almond, 1989.

Diakonoff, I. M. *Predystorija Armjanskogo Naroda: [Protohistory of the Armenian People].* Erevan, Armenia: AN Armjanskoj SSR, 1968.

Driver, G. R. "Linguistic and Textual Problems: Ezekiel." *Biblica* 19 (1938) 175–87.

Duguid, Iain, M. *Ezekiel and the Leaders of Israel.* Vetus Testamentum Supplements 55. Leiden: Brill, 1994.

Ewald, Georg H. A. von. *Commentary on the Prophets of the Old Testament.* Vol. IV, *Hézeqiél, "Yesaya," XL–LXVI, with Translation.* Translated by J. F. Smith. London: Williams and Norgate, 1880.

Fager, Jeffrey A. *Land Tenure and the Biblical Jubilee: Uncovering Hebrew Ethics through the Sociology of Knowledge.* Journal for the Study of the Old Testament Supplement 155. Sheffield, UK: JSOT, 1993.

Feinberg, Charles Lee. *The Prophecy of Ezekiel: The Glory of the Lord.* Chicago: Moody, 1969.

Filson, Floyd V. "The Omission of Ezekiel 12.26–28 and 36.23b–38 in Codex 967." *Journal of Biblical Literature* 62 (1943) 27–32.

Fishbane, Michael. *Biblical Interpretation in Ancient Israel.* Oxford: Clarendon, 1985.

Fohrer, Georg. *Ezechiel.* Handbuch zum Alten Testamentum 13. Tübingen: J. C. B. Mohr, 1955.

Foulkes, F. "Jehoiachin." In *New International Dictionary of Old Testament Theology & Exegesis,* edited by Willem VanGemeren, 4:744–45. Grand Rapids: Zondervan, 1997.

Fowler, Jeaneane D. *Theophoric Personal Names in Ancient Hebrew: A Comparative Study.* Journal for the Study of the Old Testament Supplement 49. Sheffield, UK: JSOT, 1988.

Frese, P. R., and S. J. M. Gray. "Trees." In *The Encyclopedia of Religion,* edited by M. Eliade, 15:26–33. New York: Macmillan, 1987.

Friebel, Kelvin. *Jeremiah's and Ezekiel's Sign-Acts: Rhetorical Nonverbal Communication.* Journal for the Study of the Old Testament Supplement 283. Sheffield, UK: Sheffield Academic Press, 1999.

Fritz, Volkmar. *1 & 2 Kings: A Continental Commentary.* Translated by A. Hagedorn. Continental Commentaries Old Testament. Minneapolis: Fortress, 2003.

Frymer-Kensky, Tikva. "Pollution, Purification, and Purgation in Biblical Israel." In *The Word of YHWH Shall Go Forth: Essays in Honor of David Noel Freedman in Celebration of His Sixtieth Birthday,* edited by C. L. Meyers and M. O'Connor, 399–414. Winona Lake, IN: Eisenbrauns, 1983.

Fuhs, Hans. F. *Ezechiel II.* Neue Echter Bibel. Würzburg, Germany: Echter, 1988.

Galil, Gershon. *Chronology of the Kings of Israel and Judah.* Studies in the History and Culture of the Ancient Near East 9. Leiden: Brill, 1996.

Garfinkel, Yosef. "The Eliakim Na'ar Yokan Seal Impressions: Sixty Years of Confusion in Biblical Archaeological Research." *Biblical Archaeologist* 53 (1990) 74–79.

Garscha, J. *Studien zum Ezechielbuch: Eine redaktionskritische Untersuchung von 1–39.* Europäische Hochschulschriften 23. Bern/Frankfurt: Herbert/Peter Lang, 1974.

Gentry, Peter J. "Rethinking the 'Sure Mercies of David' in Isaiah 55:3." *Westminster Theological Journal* 69 (2007) 279–304.

Gerhards, M. "Die Begnädigung Jojachins—Überlegungen zu 2 Kön.25,27–30 (mit einem Anhang zu den Nennungen Jojachins auf Zuteilungslisten aus Babylon)." *Biblische Notizen* 94 (1998) 64–66.

Gese, Hartmut. *Der Verfassungsentwurf des Ezechiel [Kap. 40–48] traditionsgeschichtlich untersucht.* Beiträge zur historischen Theologie 25. Tübingen: Mohr, 1957.

Ginsburg, H. L., translator. "The Legend of King Keret." In *Ancient Near Eastern Texts Relating to the Old Testament,* edited by J. B. Pritchard, 143–49. 3rd ed. Princeton: Princeton University Press, 1969.

———. "Poems about Baal and Anath." In *Ancient Near Eastern Texts Relating to the Old Testament,* edited by J. B. Pritchard, 129–42. 3rd ed. Princeton: Princeton University Press, 1969.

Glassner, J. *Mesopotamian Chronicles.* Society of Biblical Literature Writings of the Ancient World 19. Atlanta: Society of Biblical Literature, 2004.

Goudoever, J. van. "Ezekiel Sees in Exile a New Temple-City at the Beginning of a Jobel Year." In *Ezekiel and His Book: Textual and Literary Criticism and Their*

Interrelation, edited by J. Lust, 344–49. Bibliotheca ephemeridum theologicarum lovaniensium 74. Leuven: University of Leuven Press, 1986.

Goulder, M. "'Behold My Servant Jehoiachin.'" *Vetus Testamentum* 52 (2002) 175–90.

Gowan, Donald E. *When Man Becomes God: Humanism and Hybris in the Old Testament*. Pittsburgh Theological Monograph Series 6. Pittsburgh, PA: Pickwick, 1975.

Grayson, Albert K., and W. G. Lambert, "Akkadian Prophecies." *Journal of Cuneiform Studies* 18 (1964) 12–14.

Grayson, Albert K. *Babylonian Historical-Literary Texts*. Toronto: University of Toronto Press, 1975.

Greenberg, Moshe. "The Design and Themes of Ezekiel's Program of Restoration," *Interpretation* 38 (1984) 181–208.

———. *Ezekiel 1–20: A New Translation with Introduction and Commentary*. Anchor Bible 22. Garden City, NY: Doubleday, 1983.

Gressmann, Hugo. *Der Messias*. Forschungen zur Religion und Literatur des Alten Testaments 6. Göttingen: Vandenhoeck & Ruprecht, 1929.

Gross, W. "Israel's Hope for the Renewal of the State." *Journal of Northwest Semitic Languages* 14 (1988) 101–33.

Halpern, Baruch. *The Constitution of the Monarchy in Israel*. Harvard Semitic Monographs 25. Chico, CA: Scholars, 1981.

Hals, Ronald M. *Ezekiel*. The Forms of Old Testament Literature 19. Grand Rapids: Eerdmans, 1989.

Hammershaimb, E. "Ezekiel's View of the Monarchy." In *Some Aspects of Old Testament Prophecy from Isaiah to Malachi*, 51–62. Teologiske Skrifter 4. Copenhagen: Rosenkilde Og Bagger, 1966.

Hanson, Paul D. "Apocalypse, Genre." In *The Interpreter's Dictionary of the Bible*. Supplementary Volume, edited by K. Crim, 27–28. Nashville: Abingdon, 1976.

———. *The Dawn of Apocalyptic: The Historical and Sociological Roots of Jewish Apocalyptic Eschatology*. 2nd ed. Philadelphia: Fortress, 1979.

Haran, Menahem. "The Law-Code of Ezekiel XL–XLVI and its Relation to the Priestly School." *Hebrew Union College Annual* 50 (1979) 45–71.

Heinisch, Paul. *Das Buch Ezechiel*. Die Heilige Schrift des Alten Testaments 8. Bonn: Hanstein, 1923.

Hengstenberg, E. W. *Christology of the Old Testament and a Commentary on the Messianic Prophecies*. Translated by R. Keith. 1847. Reprint. Grand Rapids: Kregel, 1970.

Herrmann, J. *Ezechiel übersetzt und erklärt*. Kommentar zum Alten Testament. Leipzig and Erlangen, Deichert, 1924.

Heskett, R. *Messianism within the Scriptural Scroll of Isaiah*. Library of the Hebrew Bible Old Testament Studies 456. New York: T. & T. Clark, 2007.

Hitzig, Ferdinand. *Der Prophet Ezechiel*. Kurzgefasstes exegetisches Handbuch zum Alten Testament 8. Leipzig: Weidmann, 1847.

Hobbs, T. R. *2 Kings*. Word Biblical Commentary. Waco, TX: Word, 1985.

Hölscher, G. Hesekiel: *Der Dichter und das Buch*. Beihefte zur Zeitschrift für die alttestamentliche Wissenschaft 39. Giessen: Töpelmann, 1924.

Hoffmann, Yair. "The Day of the Lord as a Concept and a Term in Prophetic Literature." *Zeitschrift für die Alttestamentliche Wissenschaft* 93 (1981) 45–47.

————. "The Root *QRB* as a Legal Term." *Journal of Northwest Semitic Languages* 10 (1982) 70–73.

Holladay, W. L. *The Root šûbh in the Old Testament with Particular Reference to its Usages in Covenantal Texts.* Leiden: Brill, 1958.

Hossfeld, F. *Untersuchungen zu Komposition und Theologie des Ezekielbuches.* Forschung zur Bibel 20. Würzburg, Germany: Echter, 1977.

Hurowitz, Victor (Avigdor). *I Have Built You an Exalted House: Temple Building in the Bible in the Light of Mesopotamian and Northwest Semitic Writings.* Journal for the Study of the Old Testament Supplement Series 115. Sheffield, UK: JSOT, 1992.

Irwin, William A. *The Problem of Ezekiel: An Inductive Study.* Chicago: University of Chicago, 1943.

Japhet, Sara. "Some Biblical Concepts of Sacred Space." In *Sacred Space: Shrine, City, Land,* edited by B. Z. Kedar and R. J. Z. Werblowsky, 55–72. New York: New York University Press, 1998.

Jastrow, Marcus. *A Dictionary of the Targumim, the Talmud Babli and Yerushalmi, and the Midrashic Literature.* 1971. Reprint. New York: Judaica, 1985.

Jenni, Ernst. "Das Wort עוֹלָם in Alten Testament." *Zeitschrift für die altestamentliche Wissenschaft* 64/65 (1952/1953) 197–221/1–34.

————. "עוֹלָם *'ōlām* Ewigkeit." In *Theologisches Handwörterbuch zum Alten Testament,* edited by E. Jenni and C. Westerman, 2.228–43. Munich: Kaiser, 1976.

Joannès, F., and A. Lemaire, "Trois tablettes unéiformes onomastique ouest-sémitique." *Transeuphratène* 17 (1999) 17–34.

Job, J. B. *Jeremiah's Kings: A Study of the Monarchy in Jeremiah.* Society for Old Testament Studies Monograph Series. Burlington, VT: Ashgate, 2006.

Johnson, A. C., H. S. Gehman, and E. H. Kase. *The John H. Scheide Biblical Papyri: Ezekiel.* Princeton. University Press, 1938.

Joyce, Paul. "King and Messiah in Ezekiel." In *King and Messiah in Israel and the Ancient Near East: Proceedings of the Oxford Old Testament Seminar,* edited by J. Day, 323–37. Journal for the Study of the Old Testament Supplement Series 270. Sheffield, UK: Sheffield Academic, 1998.

Keel, Othmar. *The Symbolism of the Biblical World: Ancient Near Eastern Iconography and the Book of Psalms.* Translated by T. J. Hallett. New York: Seabury, 1978.

Keil, C. F. *Biblical Commentary on the Prophecies of Ezekiel.* Translated by J. Martin (from 1882 German edition). 2 vols. Grand Rapids: Eerdmans, 1950.

Kim, U. Y. "Jehoiachin." In *The New Interpreters Dictionary of the Bible,* edited by Katherine Doob Sakenfeld, 3.205. Nashville: Abingdon, 2008.

Kittel, Gerhard. "ἔσχατος." In *Theological Dictionary of the New Testament,* edited by G. Kittel and G. Friedrich, translated by G. W. Bromiley, 2:697–98. Grand Rapids: Eerdmans, 1964.

Klein, Jacob. "Akitu." In *Anchor Bible Dictionary,* edited by D. N. Freedman, 1.138–39. Garden City, NY: Doubleday, 1992.

Klein, Ralph. *Ezekiel: The Prophet and his Message.* Studies on Personalities of the Old Testament. Columbia: University of South Carolina Press, 1988.

Kohn, Risa Levitt. *A New Heart and a New Soul: Ezekiel, the Exile and the Torah.* JSOT Supplement 358. Sheffield: Sheffield Academic Press, 2002.

Konkel, August. *1 & 2 Kings.* New International Version Application Commentary. Grand Rapids: Zondervan, 2006.

Kraetzschmar, R. *Das Buch Ezechiel.* Göttingen: Vandenhoeck & Ruprecht, 1900.

Bibliography

Laato, Antti. *Josiah and David Redivivus: The Historical Josiah and the Messianic Expectations of Exilic and Postexilic Times.* Coniectanea Biblica Old Testament 33. Stockholm: Almqvist & Wiksell, 1992.

Ladd, G. Eldon. "Apocalyptic." In *International Standard Bible Encyclopedia*, rev. ed, edited by G. Bromiley, 1.151–61. Grand Rapids: Eerdmans, 1979.

Lang, Bernhard. *Kein Aufstand in Jerusalem: Die Politik des Propheten Ezechiel.* Stuttgarter Biblische Beiträge. Stuttgart: Katholisches Bibelwerk, 1981.

———. "Street Theater, Raising the Dead, and the Zoroastrian Connection in Ezekiel's Prophecy." In *Ezekiel and His Book: Textual and Literary Criticism and Their Interrelation*, edited by J. Lust, 297–316. Bibliotheca ephemeridum theologicarum lovaniensium 74. Leuven: Leuven University Press, 1986.

Larsson, G. "When did the Babylonian Captivity Begin?" *Journal of Theological Studies* 18 (1967) 417–23.

Lemke, W. E. "Life in the Present and Hope for the Future." *Interpretation* 38 (1984) 165–80.

Levenson, Jon D. *Sinai and Zion: An Entry into the Jewish Bible.* Minneapolis: Winston, 1987.

———. *Theology of the Program of Restoration of Ezekiel 40–48.* Harvard Semitic Monographs 10. Missoula: Scholars, 1976.

———. "Zion Traditions." In *Anchor Bible Dictionary*, edited by D. N. Freedman, 1.138–39. Garden City, NY: Doubleday, 1992.

Levey, Samson H. *The Messiah: An Aramaic Interpretation. The Messianic Exegesis of the Targum.* Cincinnati: Hebrew Union College Press, 1974.

———. *The Targum of Ezekiel.* Aramaic Bible 13. Wilmington, NC: Glazier, 1987.

———. "The Targum to Ezekiel." *Hebrew Union College Annual* 46 (1975) 139–58.

Levine, Baruch. "The Temple Scroll: Aspects of its Historical Provenance and Literary Character." *Bulletin of the American Schools of Oriental Research* 232 (1978) 5–23.

Lindblom, J. *Prophecy in Ancient Israel.* Philadelphia: Fortress, 1962.

Lipschits, Oded. *The Fall and Rise of Jerusalem: Judah under Babylonian Rule.* Winona Lake, IN: Eisenbrauns, 2005.

———. "'Jehoiakim Slept with his Fathers . . .' (II Kings 24:6)—Did He?" *Journal of Hebrew Scriptures* 4 (2002) 1–33.

Liver, J. "Jehoiachin." In *Encyclopaedia Judaica*, 2nd ed., edited by Fred Skolnik, 11:106–7. Farmington Hills, MI: Gale, 2007.

Longman, Tremper III. *Fictional Akkadian Autobiography.* Winona Lake, IN: Eisenbrauns, 1991.

Luckenbill, Daniel D. "The Black Stone of Esarhaddon." *American Journal of Semitic Literature* 41 (1925) 165–73.

Lundbom, J. R. *Jeremiah 37–52: A New Translation with Introduction and Commentary.* Anchor Bible 21C. New York: Doubleday, 2004.

Lust, Johan. "Exegesis and Theology in the Septuagint of Ezekiel: The Longer 'Pluses' and Ezek 43:1–9." In *VI Congress of the International Organization for Septuagint and Cognate Studies, Jerusalem 1986*, edited by C. E. Cox, 201–32. Septuagint and Cognate Studies 23. Atlanta: Scholars, 1987.

———. "Ezekiel 36–40 in the Oldest Greek Manuscript." *Catholic Biblical Quarterly* 43 (1981) 517–33.

———. "Messianism and Septuagint." In *Congress Volume Salamanca 1983*, edited by J. A. Emerton, 174–91. Vetus Testamentum Supplements 36. Leiden: Brill, 1985.

Lyons, M. A. From Law to Prophecy: Ezekiel's Use of the Holiness Code.

Macholz, G. Ch. "Noch Einmal: Planungen für den Wiederaufbau nach der Katastrophe von 587." *Vetus Testamentum* 19 (1969) 322–52.

Maier, J. *The Temple Scroll: An Introduction, Translation and Commentary.* Translated by R. T. White. Journal for the Study of the Old Testament Supplement 34. Sheffield, UK: JSOT, 1985.

Malamat, A. "A Forerunner of Biblical Prophecy: The Mari Documents." In *Ancient Israelite Religion, Frank M. Cross Volume.* Edited by Patrick D. Miller et al, 33–52. Philadelphia: Fortress, 1987.

Martinez, F. Garcia. "L'interprétation de la Torah d'Ézéchiel dans les mss. de Qumran," *Revue de Qumran* 13 (1988) 441–52.

May, Herbert G. "The Book of Ezekiel." In *The Interpreter's Bible*, edited by G. A. Buttrick et al, 6:39–338. New York and Nashville: Abingdon, 1956.

McCarter, P. K. *II Samuel: A New Translation with Introduction and Commentary.* Anchor Bible 9. New York; Doubleday, 1984.

McConville, J. Gordon. "Priests and Levites in Ezekiel: A Crux in the Interpretation of Israel's History." *Tyndale Bulletin* 34 (1983) 3–31.

Mettinger, T. N. D. "YHWH Zebaoth." In *Dictionary of Deities and Demons in the Bible*, rev. ed., edited by K. van der Toorn, et al., 920–24. Leiden: Brill, 1999.

Metzger, Martin. "Der Weltenbaum in vorderorientalischer Bildtradition." In *Unsere Welt, Gottes Schöpfung: Eberhard Wölfel zum 65. Geburtstag am 16. April 1992*, edited by M. Marquardt and W. Nethöfel, 1–34. Marburg: Elwert, 1992.

———. "Zeder, Weinstock und Weltenbaum." In *Ernten, was man sät: Festschrift für Klaus Koch zu seinem 65. Geburtstag*, edited by D. R. Daniels, U. Glessmer, and M. Rösel, 197–229. Neukirchen-Vluyn: Neukirchener, 1991.

Milgrom, Jacob. *Leviticus: A New Translation with Introduction and Commentary.* Anchor Bible 3. New York: Doubleday, 1991.

———. *Numbers.* JPS Torah Commentary. Philadelphia: Jewish Publication Society, 1990.

———. "'Sabbath' and 'Temple City' in the Temple Scroll." *Bulletin for the American Schools of Oriental Research* 232 (1978) 25–27.

Millard, Alan R. "La prophétie et l'écriture: Isräel, Aram, Assyrie." *Revue de l'Histoire des Religions* 202 (1985): 125–45.

Moeinikes, A. "Messianismus im Alten Testament (vorapokalyptische Zeit)." *Zeitschrift für Religions- und Geistesgeschichte* 40 (1988) 289–306.

Monsengwo-Pasinya, L. "Deux textes messianiques de la Septante: Gen 49,10 et Ez. 21,32." *Biblica* 61 (1980) 356–76.

Moor, J. C. de and Dijkstra, M. "Problematic Passages in the Legend of Aqhatu." *Ugarit Forschungen* 1 (1975) 171–215.

Moran, W. L. "Gen. 49,10 and its Use in Ez. 21,92." *Biblica* 39 (1958) 424–25.

Morris, Leon. *Apocalyptic.* Grand Rapids: Eerdmans, 1972.

Müller, Hans-Peter. *Ursprünge und Strukturen alttestamentlicher Eschatologie.* Beihefte zur Zeitschrift für die Alttestamentliche Wissenschaft 109. Berlin: Töpelmann, 1969.

Murray, D. F., and D. Janzen. "An Ambiguous Ending: Dynastic Punishment in Kings and the Fate of the Davidides in 2 Kings 25.27–30." *Journal for the Study of the Old Testament* 33 (2008) 39–58.

Mykytiuk, Lawrence J. *Identifying Persons in Northwest Semitic Inscriptions of 1200–539 B.C.E.* Society of Biblical Literature Academia Biblica 12. Atlanta: Scholars, 2004.

Myres. J. L. "Gog and the Danger from the North in Ezekiel." *Palestine Exploration Fund Quarterly Statement* 64 (1932) 213–19.

Bibliography

Nelson, Richard D. Richard D. Nelson. *The Double Redaction of the Deuteronomistic History*. Journal for the Study of the Old Testament Supplements 18. Sheffield: JSOT Press, 1981.

Niditch, Susan. "Ezekiel 40–48 in a Visionary Context." *Catholic Biblical Quarterly* 48 (1986) 208–24.

Niehr, H. "נָשִׂיא *nāśîʾ*." In *Theological Dictionary of the Old Testament*, edited by G. J. Botterweck and H. Ringgren, translated by D. E. Green, 10:44–53. Grand Rapids: Eerdmans, 2001.

Nobile, Marcus. "Beziehung zwischen Ez 32,17–32 und der Gog-Perikope [Ez 38–39] im Lichte der Endredaktion." In *Ezekiel and His Book: Textual and Literary Criticism and Their Interrelation*, edited by J. Lust, 255–59. Bibliotheca ephemeridum theologicarum lovaniensium 74. Leuven: Leuven University Press, 1986.

Noth, Martin. *The Deuteronomistic History*. 2nd ed. Translated by J. S. Doull. Journal for the Study of the Old Testament Supplement Series 15. Sheffield, UK: JSOT, 1991.

———. *Die Israelitische Personennamen Im Rahmen der Gemeinsemitischen Namengebung*. 1928. Reprint. Hildesheim: Olms, 1966.

Nougayrol, J. "Textes hépatoscopiques d'époque ancienne conserveé au Museé du Louvre II." *Revue d'assyriologie et d'archéologie orientale* 40 (1946) 56–97.

Odell, Margaret S. "Are You He of Whom I Spoke by My Servants the Prophets?": Ezekiel 38–39 and the Problem of History in the Neobabylonian Context." Ph.D. diss., University of Pittsburgh, 1988.

———. "The City of Hamonah in Ezekiel 39:11–16: The Tumultuous City of Jerusalem." *Catholic Biblical Quarterly* 56 (1994) 479–89.

———. *Ezekiel*. Smyth & Helwys Bible Commentary. Macon, GA: Smyth & Helwys, 2005.

———. "From Egypt to Meshech and Tubal: The Extent of Rebellion against YHWH in Ezekiel 38–39." Paper presented to the annual meeting of the Society of Biblical Literature. Anaheim, CA, November 1989.

Ollenburger, Ben C. *Zion The City of the Great King: A Theological Symbol of the Jerusalem Cult*. Journal for the Study of the Old Testament Supplement Series 41. Sheffield, UK: JSOT, 1987.

Oppenheim, A. Leo, translator. "I. Nebuchadnezzar II (605–562)." In *Ancient Near Eastern Texts Relating to the Old Testament*, 3rd ed., edited by J. B. Pritchard, 307–8. Princeton, Princeton University Press, 1969.

———. "Cyrus." In *Ancient Near Eastern Texts Relating to the Old Testament*, 3rd ed., edited by J. B. Pritchard, 315–16. Princeton, Princeton University Press, 1969.

———. "The Mother of Nabonidus." In *Ancient Near Eastern Texts Relating to the Old Testament*, 3rd ed., edited by J. B. Pritchard, 560–62. Princeton: Princeton University Press, 1969.

Orr, Avigdor. "The Seventy Years of Babylon." *Vetus Testamentum* 6 (1956) 304–6.

Parpola, Simo. "The Assyrian Tree of Life: Tracing the Origins of Jewish Monotheism and Greek Philosophy." *Journal of Near Eastern Studies* 52 (1993) 161–208.

Pearce, L. E. "New Evidence for Judaeans in Babylonia." *Judah and the Judeans in the Persian Period*, edited by O. Lipschits and M. Oeming, 399–411. Winona Lake, IL: Eisenbrauns, 2006.

Petersen, David L. "Eschatology (OT)." In *Anchor Bible Dictionary*, edited by D. N. Freedman, 2.575–79. Garden City, NY: Doubleday, 1992.

———. *Haggai and Zechariah 1–8: A Commentary*. Old testament Library. Louisville: Westminster John Knox, 1984.

Petter, Donna L. *The Book of Ezekiel and Mesopotamian City Laments*. Orbis biblicus orientalis 246. Fribourg: Academic, 2011.

Pili, Filippo. "Posibili casi di metatesi in Genesi 49,10 e Salmo 2,11b–12a." *Augustinianum* 15 (1975) 457–71.

Pope, Marvin H. "Notes on the Rephaim Texts from Ugarit." In *Essays on the Ancient Near East in Memory of Jacob Joel Finkelstein*, edited by M. deJong Ellis, 163–82. Memoirs of the Connecticut Academy of Arts & Sciences 19. Hamden, CT: Archon, 1977.

———. "Review of *Beatific Afterlife in Ancient Israel and in the Ancient Near East*, by K. Spronk." *Ugarit Forschungen* 19 (1987) 452–63.

———. "Seven, Seventh, Seventy." In *The Interpreter's Dictionary of the* Bible, edited by G. A. Buttrick, 4.294–95. New York: Abingdon, 1962.

Porten, Bezalel N. *Images, Power, and Politics: Figurative Aspects of Esarhaddon's Babylonian Policy*. Philadelphia: American Philosophical Society, 1993.

Preuss, Horst Dieter. *Eschatologie im Alten Testament*. Wege der Forschung 480. Darmstadt: Wissenschaftliche Buchgesellschaft, 1978.

Provan, Iain W. *1 & 2 Kings*. Old Testament Guides. Sheffield, UK: Sheffield Academic, 1997.

———. "The Messiah in the Book of Kings." In *The Lord's Anointed: Interpretation of Old Testament Messianic Texts*, edited by P. E. Satterthwaite and R. S. Hess, 67–85. Grand Rapids: Baker, 1995.

Rad, Gerhard von. *Old Testament Theology*. Vol. 2, *The Theology of Israel's Prophetic Traditions*. Translated by D. G. M. Stalker. New York: Harper & Row, 1965.

———. *Studies in Deuteronomy*. Translated by D. Stalker. Chicago: Regnery, 1953.

Rainey, Anson F. "A Rejoinder to the Eliakim Na'ar Yokan Seal Impressions." *Biblical Archaeologist* 54 (1991) 61.

Ribichini, Sergio, and Paolo Xella. "'La valle dei passanti' (Ezechiele 39:11)." *Ugarit Forschungen* 12 (1980) 434–37.

Rofé, Alexander. "Qumranic Paraphrases, The Greek Deuteronomy and the Late History of the Biblical *nāśî*.'" *Textus* 14 (1988) 163–75.

Rooker, Mark. "Evidence from Ezekiel." In *A Case for Dispensationalism: A New Consensus*, edited by D. J. Campbell and J. L. Townsend, 119–34. Chicago: Moody, 1992.

Rose, W. H. *Zemah and Zerubbabel: Messianic Expectations in the Early Postexilic Period*. Journal for the Study of the Old Testament Supplement Series 304. Sheffield, UK: Sheffield, 2000.

Russell, D. S. *The Method and Message of Jewish Apocalyptic*. Old Testament Library. Philadelphia: Westminster, 1964.

Sack, Ronald Herbert. *Amēl-Marduk, 562–560 B.C.: A Study Based on Cuneiform, Old Testament, Greek, Latin and Rabbinical Sources*. Alter Orient und Altes Testament. Sonderreihe 4. Neukirchen-Vluyn: Neukirchener, 1972.

———. "Evil-merodach." In *Anchor Bible Dictionary*, edited by D. N. Freedman, 2.679. Garden City, NY: Doubleday, 1992.

Scalise, Pamela D. J. *From Prophet's Word to Prophetic Book: A Study of Walther Zimmerli's Theory of "Nachinterpretation."* Ph.D. diss., Yale University. Ann Arbor, MI: University Microfilms, 1982.

Schipper, Jeremy. "'Significant Resonances' with Mephibosheth in 2 Kings 25:27–30: A Response to Donald Murray." *Journal of Biblical Literature* 124 (2005) 521–29.

Schultz, Samuel J. "Jehoiachin." In *International Standard Bible Encyclopedia*, rev. ed., edited by G. Bromiley, 2.976. Grand Rapids: Eerdmans, 1982.

Schunck, Klaus-Dietrich. "Die Attribute Des Eschatologischen Messias." *Theologische Literaturzeitung* 111 (1986) 641–52.

———. "Die Eschatologie der Propheten des Alten Testaments und ihre Wandlung in exilisch-nachexilischer Zeit." In *Studies on Prophecy: A Collection of Twelve Papers*, 116–32. Vetus Testamentum Supplements 26. Leiden: Brill, 1974.

Seebass, Horst. "אַחֲרִית *aḥarīth*." In *Theological Dictionary of the Old Testament*, edited by G. J. Botterweck and H. Ringgren, translated by D. E. Green, 1.207–12. Grand Rapids: Eerdmans, 1974.

Seitz, Christopher R. *Theology in Conflict: Reactions to the Exile in the Book of Jeremiah.* Berlin: de Gruyter, 1989.

Simian-Yofre, Horacio. *Die theologische Nachgeschichte der Prophetie Ezechiels: Form- und Traditionskritische Untersuchung zu Ez 6; 35; 36.* Forschung zur Bibel. Würzburg: Echter, 1974.

Skinner, John. "The Book of Ezekiel." In *An Exposition of the Bible*, 4:213–350. Hartford: S. S. Scranton, 1903.

Smend, R. *Der Prophet Ezechiel.* Kurzgefasstes exegetisches Handbuch zum Alten Testament 8. Leipzig: S. Hirzel, 1880.

Smith, Gary V. "Prophet, Prophecy." In *International Standard Bible Encyclopedia.* Rev. ed., edited by G. W. Bromiley, 3.986–1004. Grand Rapids: Eerdmans, 1986.

Smith, Jonathan Z. *To Take Place: Toward Theory in Ritual.* Chicago Studies in the History of Judaism. Chicago: University of Chicago Press, 1987.

Smith, Mark S. "The Baal Cycle." In *Ugaritic Narrative Poetry*, ed. Simon B. Parker, 81–180. SBL Writings from the Ancient World 9. Atlanta: Scholars Press, 1997.

Speiser, E. A., translator. "Etana." In *Ancient Near Eastern Texts Relating to the Old Testament*, edited by J. B. Pritchard, 114–18. 3rd ed. Princeton: Princeton University Press, 1969.

Spronk, Klaus. *Beatific Afterlife in Ancient Israel and in the Ancient Near East.* Alter Orient und Altes Testament. Neukirchen-Vluyn: Neukirchener, 1986.

Stevenson, Kalinda R. *The Vision of Transformation: The Territorial Rhetoric of Ezekiel 40–48* Society of Biblical Literature Dissertation Series 154. Atlanta: Scholars, 1996.

Stoebe, H. J. *Das zweite Buch Samuelis.* Kommentar zum Alten Testament 8B. Gütersloh: Gütersloher, 1994.

Stolper, Matthew W. "Fifth Century Nippur: Texts of the Murašûs and from Their Surroundings." *Journal of Cuneiform Studies* 53 (2001) 83–132.

———. "Murashû, Archive of." In *Anchor Bible Dictionary*, edited by D. N. Freedman, 4.927–28. Garden City, NY: Doubleday, 1992.

———. "A Note on Yahwistic Personal Names in the Murashu Texts." *Bulletin of the American Oriental Society* 222 (1976) 25–28.

Stromberg, J. "The 'Root of Jesse' in Isaiah 11:10: Postexilic Judah, or Postexilic Davidic King?" *Journal of Biblical Literature* 127 (2008) 655–69.

Sweeney, Marvin A. *I & II Kings.* Old Testament Library. Louisville: Westminster John Knox, 2007.

Talmon, Shemaryahu. "הַר *har*." In *Theological Dictionary of the Old Testament*, edited by G. J. Botterweck and H. Ringgren, translated by D. E. Green, 3.427–47. Grand Rapids: Eerdmans, 1974.

Taylor, John B. *Ezekiel: An Introduction and Commentary.* Tyndale Old Testament Commentaries. Downers Grove, IL: InterVarsity, 1969.

Terrien, S. "The Omphalos Myth and Hebrew Religion." *Vetus Testamentum* 20 (1970) 315–38.

Thomas, D. Winton. "Mount Tabor: The Meaning of the Name." *Vetus Testamentum* 1 (1951) 229–30.

Torrey, C. C. *Pseudo-Ezekiel and the Original Prophecy.* Yale Oriental Series, Researches 18. 1930. Reprint. New York: Ktav 1970.

Tuell, Steven S. *The Law of the Temple in Ezekiel 40–48.* Harvard Semitic Monographs 49. Atlanta: Scholars, 1992.

———. "The Temple Vision of Ezekiel 40–48: A Program for Restoration?" *Proceedings Eastern Great Lakes Biblical Society* 2 (1982) 96–103.

Unger, E. *Babylon: Die heilige Stadt nach der Beschreibung der Babylonier.* 2nd ed. Berlin: de Gruyter, 1970.

Van Dyke Parunak, H. *Structural Studies in Ezekiel.* Ph.D. diss., Harvard University. Ann Arbor, MI: University Microfilms, 1983.

Vawter, Bruce, and Leslie J. Hoppe. *A New Heart: A Commentary on the Book of Ezekiel.* International Theological Commentary. Grand Rapids: Eerdmans, 1991.

Wallace, Howard N. "Tree of Knowledge and Tree of Life." In *Anchor Bible Dictionary,* edited by D. N. Freedman, 6:656–60. Garden City, NY: Doubleday, 1992.

Walton, John H. *Ancient Near Eastern Thought and the Old Testament: Introducing the Conceptual World of the Hebrew Bible.* Grand Rapids: Baker, 2006.

Weidner, E. F. "Jojachin, König von Juda, in babylonischen Keilschrifttexten." In *Mélanges syriens offerts à Monsieur René Dussaud,* 925–96. 2 vols. Bibliothèque archéologique et historique 30. Paris: Geuthner, 1939.

Weinfeld, Moshe. *Deuteronomy and the Deuteronomic School.* Winona Lake, IN: Eisenbrauns, 1992.

Weippert, Manfred. "Heiliger Krieg in Israel und Assyrien." *Zeitschrift für die altestamentliche Wissenschaft* 84 (1972): 460–93.

Wevers, J. *Ezekiel.* New Century Bible. Grand Rapids: Eerdmans, 1969.

Whitcomb, John C. "Christ's Atonement and Animal Sacrifices in Israel." *Grace Theological Journal* 6 (1985) 201–17.

Whitley, C. F. "The Term Seventy Years Captivity." *Vetus Testamentum* 4 (1954) 60–72.

Wilson, John A., translator. "Lists of Asiatic countries under the Egyptian Empire." In *Ancient Near Eastern Texts Relating to the Old Testament,* 3rd ed., edited by J. B. Pritchard, 242–43. Princeton, Princeton University Press, 1969.

Winter, Uwe. "Der Lebensbaum in der altorientalischen Bildsymbolik." In *". . . Bäume braucht man doch!" Das Symbol des Baumes zwischen Hoffnung und Zerstörung,* edited by H. Schweizer, 57–88. Sigmaringen, Germany: Thorbecke, 1986.

Wiseman, D. J. "Jehoiachin." In *Illustrated Bible Dictionary, Part 2: Goliath-Papyri,* edited by J. D. Douglas, 2:737–38. Leicester, UK: InterVarsity, 1980.

———. *Nebuchadrezzar and Babylon: The Schweich Lectures.* Oxford: Oxford University Press, 1985.

Wolff, H. W. *A Commentary on the Book of the Prophet Hosea.* Hermeneia. Philadelphia: Fortress, 1974.

———. *Joel and Amos: A Commentary on the Books of the Prophets Joel and Amos.* Hermneneia. Philadelphia: Fortress, 1977.

Woude, A. S. van der. "Panim Angesicht." In *Theologisches Handwörterbuch zum Alten Testament,* edited by E. Jenni and C. Westerman, 2.457–58. Munich: Kaiser, 1976.

Wright, J. "A Tale of Three Cities: Urban Gates, Squares, and Power in Iron Age II, Neo-Babylonian and Achaemenid Israel." Paper presented at the annual meeting of the Society of Biblical Literature. New Orleans, November 1990.

Yadin, Yigael, editor. *The Temple Scroll.* 2 vols. Jerusalem: Israel Exploration Society, 1983.

Yamauchi, Edwin. *Foes from the Northern Frontier.* Grand Rapids: Baker, 1982.

Yee, G. A. "Anatomy of Biblical Parody: The Dirge Form in 2 Samuel 1 and Isaiah 14." *Catholic Biblical Quarterly* 50 (1988) 565–86.

Zadok, Ran. *The Jews in Babylonia During the Chaldean and Achaemenian Periods: According to the Babylonian Sources.* Studies in the History of the Jewish People and the Land of Israel 3. Haifa: University of Haifa, 1979.

———. "Notes on Syro-Palestinian History, Toponomy and Anthroponymy." *Ugarit-Forschungen* 28 (1996) 721–49.

Zimmerli, Walther. *A Commentary on the Book of the Prophet Ezekiel: Chapters 1–24.* Translated by R. E. Clements. Hermeneia. Philadelphia: Fortress, 1979.

———. *A Commentary on the Book of the Prophet Ezekiel: Chapters 25–48.* Translated by J. D. Martin. Hermeneia. Philadelphia: Fortress, 1983.

Index of Modern Authors

Index of Selected Subjects

Index of Scripture References and Ancient Sources

2 Samuel (*cont.*)

5:7	2
5:9	2
7	25, 27, 32, 33, 35, 61, 66, 67, 70, 77, 87, 88, 91
7:1–16	30
7:5	35, 81, 87, 113, 141
7:7	35
7:8	35, 80, 81, 87
7:13	73, 81, 87, 98
7:15	98
7:16	73, 81, 86, 87
7:18	40
7:19–29	35
7:19	33, 67, 87
7:20	87
7:21	87
7:23–27	36
7:24–29	81
7:24	87, 98
7:25	87, 98
7:26	81, 87, 98
7:27	87
7:28	87
7:29	87, 98
9:9–13	71
22:28	33, 67
23:5	98

1 Kings

2:4	88, 98
5:12[4:32]	22, 54
5:13[4:33]	22, 54
5:22–28[8–14]	22, 54
7:2	22, 54
8:12–21	98
8:12–13	98
8:25	40, 98
9:5	98
9:9	112
10:15	55
11–12	35, 79
11:1–8	12

11:14	79
11:34	36, 48, 82
13:24–28	18
14:10	112
14:14	79
15:26	14, 49
15:34	14, 49
17:13	132
20:35–36	18
21:21	112
22:53	49
24:2	132

2 Kings

	47, 71
8:18	15, 49
8:27	15, 49
9:7	132
13:2	15, 49
14:9	22, 54
14:24	15, 49
15:1	52
15:9	15, 49
15:18	15, 49
15:24	15, 49
15:28	15, 49
17:2	15, 49
17:13	81, 132, 133, 136
17:23	132, 133, 136
17:25–26	18
20:16–18	viii
21:2	15, 49
21:4–15	11
21:7	182
21:10	132
21:12	112
21:18–25	11
21:20	15, 49
22:16	112
22:19	15, 31, 63
22:20	112
23:1–25	viii
23:25	15, 31, 63
23:30–33	50

Esther

1:1	49
2:6	49
3:7	51

Job

1:8	81
2:3	81
5:11	67
13:24	148
34:29	148
42:7–8	81

Psalms

2:6	176
3:5	176
7:2[1]	17
8	42
10:9	17
13:2[1]	148
15:1	176
17:12	17
18:28[27]	33, 67
22:13[12]	17
22:21[20]	17
22:25[24]	148
27:9	148
29:5	22, 54
30:8[7]	148
38:2[1]	176
43:3	176
44:25[24]	148
46:10–11[9–10]	5
48	98, 170
48:1–3[1–2]	2
48:3[2]	1
58:8–9[7–8]	114
68:16–19[15–18]	98
69:18[17]	148
75:8[7]	33, 67
76:4[3]	5
78:68–73	32, 66
78:68–71	98
78:68–69	2
78:70–72	5, 35, 81
79:1	177
80:9–20[8–19]	26
87	98
88:15[14]	148
89:2–5[1–4]	30
89:3–4[2–3]	35
89:4–5[3–4]	88, 98
89:19–29[18–28]	35
89:20–38[19–37]	30
89:28–29[27–28]	73, 81
89:29–38[28–37]	88
89:29–30[28–29]	98
89:33–36[32–35]	81
89:34–38[33–37]	83
89:34–37[33–36]	73
89:37–38[36–37]	98
89:39–52[38–51]	30
92:13	22, 54
99:9	176
102:3[2]	148
104:16	22, 54
104:29	148
105:6	81
105:10	97
105:11	55
105:42	81
110:2	24, 59
113:1	81
114	114
132:10–18	32, 66
132:10–12	30, 98
132:11–12	5
132:13–16	2, 98
132:13	88
132:17–18	5
132:17	75
134:1	81
135:1	81
138:6	33, 67
143:7	148
147:6	67

Daniel

CPSIA information can be obtained
at www.ICGtesting.com
Printed in the USA
LVHW111015010321
680252LV00005B/35